CORPORATE STRATEGIES FOR SOUTHEAST ASIA AFTER THE CRISIS

Corporate Strategies for Southeast Asia after the Crisis

A Comparison of Multinational Firms from Japan and Europe

Edited by

Jochen Legewie
Deputy Director
German Institute for Japanese Studies, Tōkyō

and

Hendrik Meyer-Ohle
Assistant Professor
National University of Singapore

First published 2000 by
PALGRAVE
Houndmills, Basingstoke, Hampshire RG21 6XS and
175 Fifth Avenue, New York, N. Y. 10010
Companies and representatives throughout the world

PALGRAVE is the new global academic imprint of
St. Martin's Press LLC Scholarly and Reference Division and
Palgrave Publishers Ltd (formerly Macmillan Press Ltd).

ISBN 0–333–91784–7 hardback

This book is printed on paper suitable for recycling and made from fully managed and sustained forest sources.

A catalogue record for this book is available from the British Library.

Library of Congress Cataloging-in-Publication Data

Corporate strategies for Southeast Asia after the crisis: a comparison of multinational firms from Japan and Europe / edited by Jochen Legewie and Hendrick Meyer-Ohle; foreword by Irmela Hijiya-Kirschnereit.
    p. cm.
Includes bibliographical references and index.
ISBN 0–333–91784–7 (cloth)

    1. International business enterprises—Asia, Southeastern—Management.
2. International business enterprises—Asia, Southeastern—Finance.
3. Corporations, Japanese—Asia, Southeastern—Case studies.
4. Corporations, European—Asia, Southeastern—Case studies.
5. Financial crises—Asia, Southeastern.   I. Legewie, Jochen.
II. Meyer-Ohle, Hendrick, 1965–

HD2901.C67 2000
388.8′8859—dc21   00–040447

10 9 8 7 6 5 4 3 2 1
09 08 07 06 05 04 03 02 01 00

Printed in Great Britain by
Antony Rowe Ltd
Chippenham, Wiltshire

Contents

v

List of Tables

List of Figures

Foreword

It seems that after the 'Asian miracle' and the 'Asian crisis' we have now reached a new stage – time to take a fresh look at the state of economic affairs in Asia. This book, an initiative by the German Institute for Japanese Studies (DIJ, Deutsches Institut für Japanstudien) in Tōkyō, does just that. It brings together experts dealing with the economic transformations in Southeast Asia and the strategic responses by Japanese and European firms.

The DIJ is one of Germany's foreign research institutes and is concerned with academic research on contemporary Japan. Founded in 1988 through a decision by the Federal Ministry of Research and Technology – the present Federal Ministry for Education and Research – the Institute is funded by the Federal Government but maintains its independence in matters of research. The DIJ is thus a manifestation of a new awareness in Germany of the need to obtain a better understanding of East Asia and Japan in particular. To this end, the DIJ conducts research in the fields of the humanities, the social sciences, and the economy of modern Japan. As a research institute located in Tōkyō, the DIJ benefits from close contacts with Japanese institutions and scholars, while also capitalizing on its growing worldwide networks in Japan-related research.

In its endeavour to identify issues of special relevance from a European perspective, the DIJ launched a multidisciplinary research project in 1997 dealing with *Japan in Asia*. Given the geopolitical developments in the 1990s, Japan's locus in the global context and the re-definition of its relations with Asia are of considerable interest. This is all the more so as the question of *Japan in Asia*, equally acute in the political, social, economic and cultural spheres, always implies changes in Japan's relationship to Europe or the 'West'.

In the closely interrelated areas of politics and economics, we concentrate on the process of political and economic integration in Asia and Japan's role within it. From the perspective of political science, the domestic debate concerning Japan's future role in Asia and the influence of business and interest groups on Japanese foreign policy decision-making is being scrutinized. Economic relations between Japan and Asia in general, and on current changes in Japanese business networks within the Asian region in particular, are also a focus within this framework.

In June 1999, the DIJ organized an international conference in Tōkyō titled 'Economic Crisis and Transformation in Southeast Asia: Strategic Responses by Japanese and European Firms' comparing the behaviour of European and Japanese multinational companies. Given the timeliness of the topic, and the fact that the European–Japan comparison appeared to be a new perspective in the face of the more common US–Japan comparison, the conference met with considerable attention both in Japan and abroad. In the fall of 1999, the results of the Tōkyō conference were presented at several seminars in Germany, including presentations in Cologne, Hamburg and Berlin. With one exception all contributions in this volume are based on presentations at the Tōkyō conference.

The DIJ gratefully acknowledges cooperation with the Friedrich-Ebert Foundation, Nihon University, the EU Japan Centre for Industrial Cooperation, and the Fujitsu Research Institute. The Japan Foundation and the German Embassy also generously supported the conference.

As is well-known, a conference is one thing, but the publication of a book based on conference presentations is quite another. I want to thank all the contributors from Japan, Southeast Asia and Europe for their willingness to form their papers into book chapters and their cooperation with the editors. Last, but not least, we owe special thanks to Dr Jochen Legewie and Dr Hendrik Meyer-Ohle, both from the Economics section of the DIJ, who not only organized the conference but also oversaw the speedy and efficient transformation of the papers into this book.

IRMELA HIJIYA-KIRSCHNEREIT
Director, German Institute for Japanese Studies (DIJ)
Tōkyō

Preface

In the year 2000 many observers had declared the Asian financial and economic crisis over. The crisis started with the devaluation of the Thai baht in July 1997 and soon spread to engulf the entire region. Three years later the crisis seems to have brought about less the end of the Asian economic miracle than an opportunity for a necessary house-cleaning and a reorientation of strategies. In 1999, all Southeast Asian countries achieved positive growth rates.

The articles in this book take a micro-economic point of view, rather than the more common macro-economic approach, to understanding the causes and effects of the Asian crisis. Our emphasis on corporate behaviour and strategies mirrors the confidence that multinational companies have displayed in the region's production base and growing markets. Over the last three years firms from Europe and Japan have stabilized the economies of Southeast Asia. They remained in the region, restructured their operations, and reshaped their strategies in order to strengthen their presence and achieve long-term profitability.

Multinational firms will continue to be a driving force in the Southeast Asian economy of the future. This book examines the activities of Japanese and European Multinational Corporations (MNCs) in Southeast Asia since 1997 and also evaluates their prospects for the future. At the same time, the analysis bears in mind the character of national differences that might impact firm behaviour. By comparing differences and similarities in the areas of production, marketing and corporate finance, the authors provide a framework that covers the issues that constitute a corporate strategy. The approach is applicable to both an understanding of the strategic changes of MNCs in Southeast Asia and the strategic behaviour of crisis-stricken MNCs in developing countries more generally.

By multinational companies (MNCs) we mean companies engaged in the border-crossing production and marketing of goods and services; thus operating on a multinational scale. The use of the term multinational does not differentiate between multinational and international, global, or transnational companies. As for the Europe–Japan focus, the comparison of Japanese and European firms reflects a deliberate attempt to correct an overemphasis on US–Japanese comparisons. It also draws on the institutional strengths that the editors, who both worked at the German Institute for Japanese Studies (DIJ) – a European institute based in Japan, brought to the project.

The project's regional focus on Southeast Asia, and its core countries of Singapore, Malaysia, Thailand, Indonesia and the Philippines, makes sense for at least three reasons. First, more than any other region in the world the countries of Southeast Asia may be called a 'level playing field' for international actors. Since the colonial era, European companies have been active in the region; Japanese companies see Southeast Asia as their 'home ground' due to its geographical proximity. Second, the core ASEAN countries are at a distinctively different development stage from other crisis-hit countries like Korea and Hong Kong or Taiwan. Singapore merits inclusion because it is heavily integrated into the regional strategies of MNCs for Southeast Asia. The concerns of the core ASEAN countries also differ from those of China. Third, ASEAN is the only institution that groups the countries of Southeast Asia apart from the rest of Asia. Thus, micro-economic analysis of the region, including questions about the behaviour of MNCs, can test whether ASEAN as a regional grouping really matters for corporate strategies.

Many people have contributed to the completion of this book. First, we thank our contributors for taking on the difficult task of collecting empirical data and analysing developments at an early stage of the Asian crisis. Many contributors were at first reluctant to join the project, but all of them have found different solutions for overcoming obstacles to offer what are, in the end, very sound analyses. The research here owes its success to the cooperation of many representatives from European and Japanese companies and economic institutions. We thank them for their readiness to make time in their busy schedules and to freely share ideas with us.

We also thank those who assisted in the task of turning the research project into a book. In particular, Katsuhiko Hirasawa who not only cooperated on one article but also provided us with valuable help in other areas deserves special mention. Darryl Flaherty and Peter von Staden aided in the important task of proof-reading. Our colleagues at the DIJ, Jörg Raupach, Hanns Günther Hilpert and René Haak, reviewed parts of this book. Of course the responsibility for any mistakes that may remain lies with the editors. Finally, we thank Stephen Rutt and Zelah Pengilley for a fast and efficient publishing process.

January 2000   JOCHEN LEGEWIE and HENDRIK MEYER-OHLE
Tōkyō and Singapore

List of Abbreviations and Acronyms

ADB	Asian Development Bank
AFTA	ASEAN Free Trade Area
APEC	Asia-Pacific Economic Cooperation
ASEAN	Association of Southeast Asian Nations
BIS	Bank for International Settlements
BIBF	Bangkok International Banking Facility
BKPM	Investment Coordinating Board (Indonesia)
BOI	Board of Investment (Thailand, Philippines)
CAFTA	Canada–US Free Trade Agreement
EAM	East Asian Miracle
EC	European Community
EDB	Economic Development Board (Singapore)
EEC	European Economic Community
EU	European Union
FDI	foreign direct investment
FY	fiscal year
GDP	gross domestic product
GTC	General Trading Company
HPAEs	High-Performing Asian Economies
HQ	headquarters
IMF	International Monetary Fund
M&A	mergers and acquisitions
MIDA	Malaysian Industrial Development Authority
MITI	Ministry of International Trade and Industry (Japan)
MNC	multinational company, multinational corporation
MOF	Ministry of Finance (Japan)
NAFTA	North America Free Trade Agreement
NICs	Newly Industrializing Countries
NIEs	Newly Industrializing Economies
OECD	Organisation for Economic Co-operation and Development
R&D	research and development
SES	Stock Exchange of Singapore
SIMEX	Singapore International Monetary Exchange
SME	small- and medium-sized enterprise

UK	United Kingdom
UNCTAD	United Nations Conference on Trade and Development
US	United States
USA	United States of America
WTO	World Trade Organization

Notes on the Contributors

Keri Davies is Senior Lecturer in the Department of Marketing, University of Stirling, Scotland.

Steen Hemmingsen works as a financial advisor for several companies and is Examiner in Finance and Business Economics at Copenhagen Business School, Denmark.

Katsuhiko Hirasawa is Professor of Management at the Faculty of Commerce of Nihon University, Tōkyō, Japan.

Etsuko Katsu is Associate Professor for International Finance at the School of Political Science and Economics of Meiji University, Tōkyō, Japan.

Jochen Legewie is Deputy Director and Head of the Economics Section at the German Institute for Japanese Studies, Tōkyō, Japan.

Arie Y. Lewin is Professor of Business Administration and Sociology at the Fuqua School of Business, Duke University, USA.

Hendrik Meyer-Ohle worked for the German Institute for Japanese Studies from 1995 to 1999 and is currently Assistant Professor in the Department of Japanese Studies, National University of Singapore.

Corrado Molteni is Associate Professor at Milan State University and Head of Research at ISESAO (Institute of Economic and Social Studies for East Asia), Universita Comerciale Luigi Bocconi, Milano, Italy.

Tomoaki Sakano is Professor of Management at the School of Commerce, Waseda University, Tōkyō, Japan.

Annette A. Singh is a research analyst at the Centre of Management of Innovation and Technopreneurship (CMIT), Singapore.

Dennis S. Tachiki is a Senior Research Fellow at the Fujitsu Research Institute, Tōkyō, Japan.

Poh Kam Wong is Associate Professor at the Business School of the National University of Singapore and director of the Centre for Management of Innovation and Technopreneurship (CMIT).

Naoko Yamada is a PhD candidate at the Graduate School of Commerce, Waseda University, Tōkyō, Japan.

Tōru Yanagihara is Special Advisor for Research at the Asian Development Bank Institute, Tōkyō, Japan.

Stephen Young is Professor of International Business in the Department of Marketing, University of Strathclyde, Scotland.

Hideki Yoshihara is Professor of International Business at the Research Institute for Economics and Business Administration of Kobe University, Japan.

Part I

Multinational Companies in Southeast Asia and in the Global Economy

1 The Multinational Corporation: The Managerial Challenges of Globalization and Localization

Stephen Young

INTRODUCTION

The aim of this chapter is to provide an overview of the business environment facing multinational corporations (MNCs) at global, regional and local levels, and to assess their strategic responses, highlighting changes over time. From this overview, the chapter focuses upon the challenges confronting the MNC at corporate and subsidiary level at the dawn of the new millennium. By taking this holistic approach, the objective is to contribute an understanding of both the global environmental and strategic contexts, within which the responses of Japanese and European firms in Southeast Asia can be better understood and interpreted.

In commencing this chapter, however, it is important to recognize the significance of the topics being discussed in this volume. International business researchers have been active for around 40 years. During this period there has been enormous growth in international business in all its modalities, but principally in the form of international production by multinational corporations. By the early 1990s, MNCs' international production had surpassed international trade as the main mechanism for servicing international markets; while trade itself was increasingly conducted within and between MNCs. And the characteristics, behaviour and boundaries of the firm have changed dramatically over time. The upshot is that research has struggled to keep pace with and fully understand the dynamics of international business. In general, moreover, the research emphasis among international business scholars has tended to be on foreign direct investment

(FDI) flows, and on the one-off decisions, say, to enter particular markets rather than on the dynamics of strategy. Conversely, business strategy researchers have in the main paid less attention to the inter-national/global dimensions. At the same time, insufficient attention has been given to the firm-level behaviour of MNCs and their new agendas, which requires qualitative and case-based research – a curi-ous omission given the strong tradition of qualitative research in the area of the internationalization of small- and medium-sized enter-prises. Some of the specific areas of importance for research, from this author's perspective, include the following (see also Caves 1998):

- longitudinal research, tracking MNCs over time (for past work in this tradition, see Curhan, Davidson and Suri 1977);
- comparisons of the strategies of MNCs from different source coun-tries and into different host nations;
- globalization and global strategies: definitions, extent, character-istics, implications;
- globalization versus regionalization versus localization by the dif-ferent value-adding activities of the firm;
- factors in the location of value-adding activities between countries, and new location factors, for example the significance of spatial clusters of agglomerative activity (Dunning 1998); and
- headquarters/subsidiary relationships – an under-researched area despite the strong interest in the subsidiary *per se* in the recent past.

These topics represent a corporate-focused segment of the required avenues of research within the broad field of international business. Missing, for example, is the whole issue of linkages between MNCs and country economic development, a critical area at a time when development theory has largely lost its way. They are, furthermore, empirical questions in the main; although conceptual work that models the dynamics of MNCs and their new agendas is equally important (Buckley and Casson 1998).

The studies within this volume utilize qualitative research meth-odologies and fit clearly within the above research agenda, and thus represent a major contribution. The emphasis on European and Japanese firms and Southeast Asia is also welcome when so much prior research has, understandably, been USA-focused. The difficult-ies should not, of course, be forgotten, particularly the diversity among 'European' enterprises and among Southeast Asian economies. Research at a time of crisis is also problematic, not only obtaining the cooperation of MNCs (companies are naturally reluctant to highlight problems and especially failures) but isolating the effects of a particular event (the financial crisis in Asia) as well. By providing the bigger picture on the business environment and the characteristics and evolution of MNC strategies, this chapter illustrates the global choices and challenges facing corporations as they tackle the Asian contagion.

THE EVOLUTION OF THE MNC

The early work of Perlmutter (1969; see also Chakravarthy and Perlmutter 1985) was a classic in its predictions concerning the evolution of the MNC. Management culture and mentality was considered to evolve from ethnocentrism or polycentrism to geocentrism, with a regiocentric mentality as an intermediate state. In a geocentric corporation 'the firm's subsidiaries are neither satellites nor independent city states, but parts of a whole ... each part making its unique contribution with a unique competence' (1969, p. 13).

The evolution of MNC strategy post-Second World War mirrors this perspective. Early MNCs were forced to develop local operations in national markets across the world in order to circumvent barriers to trade and investment, and to meet the specific customer requirements of these markets. This led to the dominant type of polycentric multidomestic MNC, mainly of American origin as the principal player at the time. This stage was characterized by a duplication of the value chain across countries, and local autonomy. The creation of the EEC in 1958 and its enlargement, and prospects in regional markets elsewhere in the world, led to a process of restructuring of activities across nations with specialization of plants and activities. This regiocentric phase favoured the new MNCs – Japanese and later Korean and other Asian MNCs – which could plan component production, assembly, R&D and marketing in a rational way to take advantage of opening regional markets.

The third and current phase is much more complex and challenging from a management perspective, since it encompasses two separate, albeit interrelated, processes (Table 1.1). First, multilateral trade and investment liberalization expands the integration process from a regional to a global domain, while technological developments offer opportunities to extend globalization beyond the production sphere to other value-chain activities. Second, however, the emergence of the knowledge economy has caused many MNCs to rethink their competitive

Table 1.1   Characteristics of MNC evolution

Strategic Thrust	Prevailing Orientation
1. Multi-domestic	Polycentric
2. Regional coordination/integration • Product specialization • Vertical integration of production	Regiocentric
3. Global coordination/integration and disintegration • Redefinition of corporate mission and core competencies • Coordination of all value-adding activities • Global supply chain management • Internal supply vs external supply vs collaboration • Globalization and localization	Geocentric

strategies with major implications for all aspects of business. Added to these evolutionary processes, globalization has increased competition enormously and set off a wave of mergers, acquisitions and alliances across national frontiers.

While there is no general agreement on the meanings of terms such as global company or global strategy, a number of the broadly accepted concepts stem from Porter (1986), Prahalad and Doz (1987), and Bartlett and Ghoshal (1989). A global strategy is one which involves a geographically coordinated and/or integrated approach to operating internationally. In refining this notion, however, scholars have emphasized the differential nature of industry characteristics affecting value-chain activities (for example R&D compared with sales and marketing), leading to a continuum with varying degrees of globalization and localization. Others (for example Enright 1999) have high-lighted a growing localization of competitive advantage at the same time as economic activity is becoming increasingly globalized. The former process is linked to agglomeration economies and the exist-ence of regional clusters, and is evidenced in the fact that many of the same firms are located in the same nation, region and even city (Storper 1992); by this view, clustering constrains globalization.

The globalization debate has extended to a questioning of the actual extent of the phenomenon. There are integrated global companies in industries such as microelectronics and consumer electronics, office machinery, household appliances, instruments, pharmaceuticals and financial services (UNCTAD 1994). But the most common feature within these and other companies is the emergence of global commodity chains in which MNCs outsource to low-cost developing areas in Asia and elsewhere, using their own subsidiaries or local supply networks.

The debate also concerns the extent to which MNCs are genuinely geocentric (Bartlett and Ghoshal (1989) use the term 'transnational corporations' to describe a similar type of enterprise), as opposed to being home-based multinationals with a distinct home-nation centre of gravity for their management and critical activities (compare the views of Porter 1990 with Rugman 1993). The reality is that while many MNCs may have a global strategic vision, their activity focus is primarily national and regional (see also Dicken 1998, chapter 6). The concept of regional centres of power was presented in Ohmae's (1985) *Triad Power*, with USA enterprises concentrating upon and dominating in North and South American markets, European corporations in Europe, Middle East and Africa, and Japanese firms focusing upon the Asian region. Regionalism is partly associated with 'psychic distance', which encompasses physical and cultural distance; and partly with economic integration, where initiatives have primarily stemmed from the regional level. For many products and processes, economies of scale may be optimized at the regional level; and, with possibilities for exploiting regional 'taste' differences, policies of corporate regional integration have been pursued more vigorously historically than those of globalization and global integration.

Regionalization strategies are particularly important for this volume, where the EU is the most strongly integrated regional bloc. From the early years of its formation, US MNCs treated the six original EEC members as one market, and commenced production specialization and vertical production integration following the expansion of the EC to include the UK and other members in 1973. Further expansions, plus the Single Market programme and most recently the launch of the euro, have provided further stimuli to both economic and corporate integration.

The evidence of the EU's history indicates advantages for latecomer MNCs. European companies were disadvantaged by their national market fragmentation and commitment, creating problems of rationalization. While taking a pan-European perspective, American corporations faced a series of reorganization moves in production as enlargements proceeded; while product development and marketing activities were nationally or subregionally oriented (according to zones of language and cultural similarity – Usunier 1993). The latecomer Japanese and other Asian MNCs were able to take a more genuinely pan-European approach (as well as perspective), although again their production networks may prove suboptimal as the EU expands east-wards. Initial motivations were, however, related to overcoming trade friction, and NICs such as Korea may have been induced into pre-mature FDI in the EU because of fears of 'fortress Europe'.

Historically the activities of continental European MNCs have been strongly European-focused, with the USA a more recent target (for recent work on Germany, see Barrell and Pain 1999). UK corpora-tions, by contrast, reoriented their activities from the 1970s onwards from the Commonwealth to North America, usually through acquisi-tions (often very large-scale and involving the purchases of brands); continental Europe has been problematic for UK MNCs because of barriers to takeovers in some countries. For both groups, Asia has been of much less interest, a fact that has been of major concern to the European Commission (Jacquemin and Pench 1997).

Inside North America, the 1989 Canada–USA Free Trade Agree-ment (CAFTA) and the 1994 North America Free Trade Agreement (NAFTA) have lowered trade and investment barriers, leading to integration of international production decisions, especially in the automotive and consumer electronic industries (Eden and Monteils 2000). Much US FDI in Canada had been established to overcome tariff barriers and was characterized by small-scale and 'miniature replica' status. There were, therefore, fears for the future of this US investment following CAFTA. While there were closures, many Canadian subsidiaries were also integrated into a continental North American production system (Blank and Krajewski 1995). The export processing zones along the Mexican border (*maquiladoras*) have been incorporated into the production networks of US MNCs for many years. Preliminary evidence post-NAFTA indicates investment diver-sion from other developing countries into Mexico, with a further pattern of relocations within Mexico towards the border cities (Hanson 1998).

Within this 'global, but regionalized world system of the 21st cen-tury' (Mirza 1999), a specific manifestation has been the rise of East Asia. From the early 1980s, MNCs' activities grew rapidly in East Asia, with Singapore, Hong Kong, South Korea and Taiwan being the principal targets initially. The nature of MNCs' operations varied con-siderably – as between FDI, licensing and subcontracting – according to the economic development strategy pursued in the particular country. According to Mirza (1999), the East Asian production system of a typical US MNC has evolved from the 1970s when outward processing using low-cost, unskilled labour was the norm. By the 1990s, the exportation of fully processed goods using increasingly skilled labour had become common, with evidence of a developmental cycle as products were exported to third-country markets, then to local markets, and thereafter to international markets including the USA; the latest phase has seen an increasing emphasis on sales to the region and the utilization of a regional division of labour.

Japanese MNC activity in East Asia has been interpreted within the context of the 'flying geese' paradigm of economic development (Ozawa 1997), in which five stages have been identified:

1. Import substitution via technology absorption;
2. Domestic rivalry and export growth;
3. Outward FDI (related to trade conflict, appreciation of the yen and rising labour costs at home);
4. Import expansion; and
5. Technological self-reliance.

Most Japanese industries are considered to be in either phases 3 or 4. Labour-intensive light industries are in phase 4, with Japan assembling or subcontracting standardized products (for example electric fans, washing machines) in China and Vietnam; intermediately standardized goods (for example colour TVs, air-conditioners, microwave ovens) in ASEAN, and relatively sophisticated goods (for example personal computers and integrated circuits) in Taiwan and South Korea. Automobiles, automotive parts and high-end electronic goods are in Phase 3 but moving rapidly to Phase 4 (see Legewie 1999), leading to fears of the 'hollowing-out' effect of outward FDI. According to Ozawa (1997, p. 391), 'Japan has used up all of its catching-up opportunities given by the "lead-geese countries" ...' and now needs to create new technologies on its own and join the ranks of the technological lead geese itself. However, it lags behind the USA in new industrial technologies such as the internet, as well as in many service sector businesses (*Financial Times* 13 July 1999).

The additional feature of the East Asia region which is worth mentioning is the emergence of MNCs based in the new industrialized economies of South Korea, Taiwan and Singapore. The latter include large industrial groups (including state-owned enterprises) from South Korea, Singapore and elsewhere; multi-sector diversified conglomerates from Hong Kong, Malaysia and Singapore; and small- and medium-sized MNCs from Taiwan and other countries (Mirza 1999). Such enterprises will have an increasing role to play in integrating the economies of East Asia.

INFLUENCES ON THE GLOBALIZATION AND REGIONALIZATION OF BUSINESS

To set these regional developments within a wider corporate context, Figure 1.1 summarizes a range of the major drivers in the globalization and regionalization of business activity. Foreign direct investment, like its domestic counterpart, is principally influenced by market and growth factors; hence rates of economic growth worldwide have a major effect on MNCs' activities. In respect to corporate integration at global and regional levels, however, the principal additional drivers have been innovations in information and communication technologies and the liberalization of cross-border transactions – chiefly investment liberalization in the 1990s and services liberalization into the 2000s (Brewer and Young 1998). Such drivers promote globalization, but others stimulate regionalization and, indeed, localization (for example national clusters and national innovation systems). In respect to regionalization, NAFTA may be followed up by a Free Trade Area of the Americas by 2005 and, even more speculatively, by a transatlantic free trade area.

Within Europe, regionalization will be promoted by the likely extension of the EU eastwards. (Countries in the first round of negotiations are Poland, Hungary, the Czech Republic, Slovenia and Estonia (plus Cyprus).) It is interesting that democratization in central and eastern Europe has drawn a number of low-labour-cost countries within the boundaries of the region, and thus facilitated possibilities for labour-intensive assembly which might otherwise have gone offshore to South America or Asia. By comparison with North America and Europe, East Asian integration has been hampered by protectionist tariff and non-tariff barriers leading to a fragmentation of production. Full exploitation of the integration potential of the region depends upon the implementation of the AFTA (ASEAN Free Trade Agreement) and APEC (Asia-Pacific Economic Cooperation forum) initiatives. Success in these economic integration efforts should provide major opportunities for latecomer European MNCs.

11

Figure 1.1 Drivers of the globalization and regionalization of business

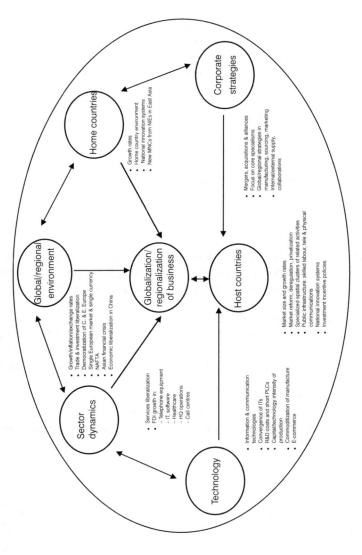

When seen from the 'big picture' perspective of Figure 1.1, multinational corporations are confronted by a continuing stream of global shocks and geopolitical developments which offer both opportunities and threats to their worldwide operations and competitive positions. The economic crisis in Southeast Asia is indeed one of a number of shocks within Asia itself, where the successful conclusion of China's negotiations to join the World Trade Organization, for example, will have major implications for production and marketing in the region.

MANAGERIAL CHALLENGES: THE CORPORATE LEVEL*

What then are the challenges for the MNC manager posed by the events and patterns reviewed above? Figure 1.2 highlights a number of these, distinguishing between the corporate and subsidiary levels of the multinational corporation.

Managing Growth, Reorganization and Rationalization

It is very evident that the world economy is experiencing a period of enormous corporate 'shake-up' and 'shake-out', much of it global in nature and driven by global imperatives. It is apparent in:

- the increasing role of mergers and acquisitions as forms of FDI (over the period 1985–95, 55–60 per cent of FDI flows were accounted for by mergers and acquisitions (UNCTAD 1997), most were concentrated in the Triad and in knowledge and information-intensive sectors);
- the dismemberment or break-up of corporations, with corporate sell-offs, spin-outs and divestments; and
- redefinitions of corporate missions and a focus on core competencies.

---

* This section on Managerial Challenges is derived from information collected as part of a large study in which the author was involved in 1998 and 1999 on inward investment benefits in Scotland, and other work. In addition, the author was an EU-Fulbright Scholar-in-Residence at Georgetown University, Washington DC in autumn 1998; some of the material in this chapter draws on a study undertaken with T. L. Brewer during this period relating to Multilateral Trade and Investment Rules and Corporate Decision-making, involving personal interviews with companies, US government departments and Congressional staff, and national and international organizations.

Figure 1.2   Corporate and subsidiary challenges

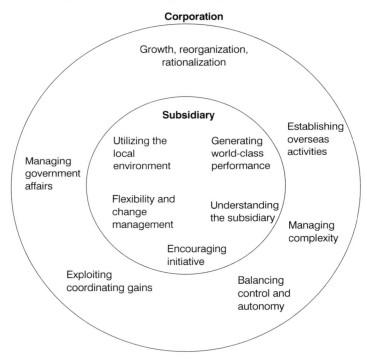

These processes have been less apparent in Japan to date. In many Western countries, stockmarket pressures lead to short planning and performance horizons and, therefore, rapid response to globalization. Structural rigidities and the prevailing social and economic paradigm mean a delayed response in Japan, but a response is likely to occur sooner rather than later (*Financial Times* 13 July 1999).

For the MNC, the changes highlighted above produce enormous costs and uncertainties. Although writers (Eisenhardt and Brown 1999) call for 'patching' (that is, a constant process of interactive change) rather than 'reorganization', the truth is that most change to date has been crisis-driven and hence large-scale and traumatic. A number of implications can be drawn. In the first place, caution in globalization strategies is suggested, particularly where large-scale investments are involved; and, therefore, new forms of knowledge investment (for example technology alliances) may be preferable to traditional investment forms, as may other types of arrangement such as subcontracting which provide greater flexibility. Second, planning for change becomes critically important. This is especially true in companies that have not yet faced up to hard decisions on rationalization and divestment. Third, rationalization has adverse effects on corporate culture, and also harmful impacts on relations between and among subsidiaries around the world, insofar as there are both gainers and losers. Open communications with employees are very important in these circumstances, if defensive and negative attitudes are not to prevail. Finally, the particular challenge for MNCs concerns the management of reorganization in many different countries with very different political, social, legal and economic situations. Country attitudes to MNCs could become increasingly negative.

Establishing Overseas Activities

While this is perhaps a somewhat controversial viewpoint, it seems likely that a number of countries/companies (especially developing country MNCs) have been induced into premature multinational activity. This is evident, for example, in the expansion of Chinese enterprises abroad (Young, Hood and Lu 1998). The State Council of China in the early 1990s determined that the large state-owned trading enterprises should pursue a strategy of 'business diversification, industrialization and internationalization' with the goal of creating 'first-class transnational conglomerates' with 'global perspectives'. Little was said about the need to possess transferable competitive advantages, and factors like prestige and 'copy-cat' behaviour (linked to the experience of Japanese and Korean GTCs) have been paramount for a number of firms. The conclusion reached was that in future this phase of Chinese FDI will prove to have been premature and anomalous. Generalizing from this, care needs to be taken in responding to home-government signals with respect to outward investment.

In a similar vein, writers in Korea speak of 'immature internationalization' when analysing Korean FDI in the west. Historically, tariff barriers have been a significant factor in overseas investment decisions, but it is also essential to ensure that the company has firm-specific attributes that will sustain profitable production behind the tariff wall – the existence of low-cost labour, which provided an advantage at home, is not transferable abroad. More than this, however, it is necessary to consider the time-scales during which the manufacture will be protected by tariff barriers and the implications for flexibility of operation.

There is also evidence of companies lacking experience and cultural understanding (even at the simplest level in terms of language capabilities), and perhaps having unrealistic expectations regarding public sector support, levels of productivity in the short run, training costs and so on. This is a further challenge for East Asian companies making their first investments into western countries and undoubtedly a problem in the reverse direction too.

Additionally, it is important to recognize that the criteria for making investments may be changing. Flexibility and the ease of relocation may now be more important. Is it legitimate to make the distinction between market-seeking investment and efficiency (cost)-seeking investment (Dunning 1993) in the same way as in the past? What possibilities exist for integrating activities within a geographical network or cluster of related activities and specialized support services; and does that constrain the transfer of assets across national boundaries? There are also suggestions that the presence of other foreign investors in a country is becoming more significant as a 'signalling-effect' (Dunning 1998).

Managing Complexity

It is evident that adaptability in a range of areas of business is increasingly necessary to successfully manage the MNC of today. Adaptability and flexibility to handle complexity seems particularly important in a number of areas:

- Flexible boundaries of the firm. The desire for flexibility discourages vertical integration, hence the trend to outsourcing, subcontracting of production, R&D contracting and joint-ventures and so on. Examples exist within MNCs in which all mobile projects are evaluated in terms of comparisons between internal supply, external supply and partnerships or joint ventures. This has gone beyond the situation in earlier days when the emphasis was overwhelmingly on internal supply, with a tendency towards bidding for projects between locations.
- Flexibility in attitudes to countries and markets. Constant review is necessary of the potential in particular countries and regions. For example, Mexico, eastern Europe and China would be obvious choices for companies looking for volume manufacture of

commodity items at low cost. But this broad-brush approach – which is necessary for companies when the range of choices of countries has grown so enormously with the liberalization of markets – may miss the *market* as opposed to *cost* opportunities which exist in these areas. A recent article by Prahalad and Lieberthal (1998) focused on the huge emerging markets in China, India and Brazil noting that: 'In order to compete effectively, MNCs will have to reconfigure their resource base, rethink their cost structures, redesign their product development process and challenge their assumptions about the cultural mix of top managers.'

- Organizational flexibility. The discussion about hierarchies versus heterarchies is a very active one in the academic literature (Hedlund 1993). Buckley and Casson (1998, p. 34) have suggested that 'the efficient managerial processing of information normally requires a hierarchical structure of some kind'. But they also suggest that 'an increased demand [and requirement] for flexibility is best accommodated by flattening the organization whilst maintaining the basic elements of hierarchy'. Observing many MNCs, there is evidence of significant organizational experimentation. However, matrix structures are still commonly in evidence, with all the complexities which go with them. Conversely, moves to a flat structure cannot be undertaken successfully without a long-term commitment. Recruitment of personnel who are independent and self-starters but can also work as part of a team is critical. It takes a lengthy period for employees to adjust to this culture, and undoubtedly there is a potential conflict between a desire for control for efficiency reasons and autonomy for creativity.

Balancing Control and Autonomy

Although this topic is equally significant from a subsidiary level perspective, one area of contention relevant to the present discussion is the role of corporate headquarters. A recent Conference Board study (*Financial Times* 2 March 1999) on this topic highlighted certain common characteristics of headquarters in well-managed companies in the USA, Europe and Asia. First, the head office was small – 2 per cent or less of total group headcount (American companies were most likely to have large head offices). Second, all had reorganized their headquarters significantly in the 1990s. Certain functions had been strengthened, particularly business development, procurement and the exchange of knowledge and best practices. However, one unresolved contentious issue is the two-way pull between centralizing and decentralizing tendencies. On the one hand is a group of forces calling for greater strategic decisions from the centre; on the other is the need to stick close to the customer. It is suggested that the latter pull plus the use of information technology points to a more lateral, team-based organization ('heterarchical' in the terms used above); but managers find this hard to accept, having been used to strong central authority and defined corporate goals.

Exploiting Coordination Gains

Many MNCs still have quite a way to go to capitalize upon the potential coordination gains from globalization. It is partly a function of history and the way in which companies have evolved, but there are still many possibilities in the areas of R&D programmes, procurement programmes, and marketing programmes. There is a need to break down defensive attitudes between different national operations and overcome the 'not-invented-here' syndrome. Of course some of these fears may be genuine ones concerning the possible switch of activities to offshore locations. There may be a view for example, that if production has gone, will R&D follow? An important issue in this respect seems to be the movement of foreign nationals within the MNC and their promotion to senior positions, especially at headquarters. Informal networks thus develop which may be as important as formal mechanisms in encouraging information-sharing and the coordination of activities.

Managing Government Affairs

The topics of political risk analysis and external environmental analysis were significant ones in the 1970s and 1980s, understandable at a time when government attitudes to MNCs were antagonistic, and controls over FDI and MNC behaviour were widespread. In an era of much greater liberalization, fears of the adverse effects of national government intervention have receded to a considerable extent. What are emerging, however, are 'global' agenda items which affect the corporate group as a whole, and which are much more difficult to manage and influence because of their long-term nature. These include the role of the World Trade Organization, the implementation of its rules and its future agenda; the development of regional integration agreements in different parts of the world; environmental regulations; the

Foreign Corrupt Practices Act; global electronic commerce and the issue of privacy; and sustainable development.

The present research of Brewer and Young in the United States indicates that companies are still taking a multi-domestic (sometimes very ethnocentric) approach to their government affairs strategies. They have not understood that a global response is required in this area as in other areas of business (see footnote to p. 12). For global agenda decisions, a coordinated effort across multiple domains and dimensions may be called for. Where government affairs activities are decentralized, leadership may be passed to the executives closest geographically to the centre of power and decision-making. Of course, local/regional issues are important too, and the need to balance the global and the local is as important in government affairs as in other areas of business.

MANAGERIAL CHALLENGES: THE SUBSIDIARY LEVEL

In recent years there has been considerable interest in the management of MNC subsidiaries. This was stimulated initially by interest in and concern over their contribution to host economies, and this is still a major focus in the literature (Young, Hood and Peters 1994; Birkinshaw and Hood 1998a, b; Taggart 1999). The perspective taken here is a slightly different one and concerns the challenges facing corporations as they view their networks of subsidiaries around the globe.

Generating World-class Performance

The management of poorly performing subsidiaries is a challenge for the multinational parent. It appears to be easy to allow subsidiaries to go their own way (especially when control systems from HQ are weak) and then find that they are making losses and otherwise performing unsatisfactorily. Yet when faced with the challenge of turnaround or closure, a remarkable recovery ensues. The conclusion is the very obvious one of balancing the global and the local – maintaining control without stifling initiative. A variety of practices seem to be used to stimulate performance (Dunning 2000) including knowledge-management systems for tracking productive practices that are transferable; league tables that chart the performance of R&D centres, manufacturing plants or marketing operations in key industries; competitions between problem-solving teams at local, regional and worldwide levels; and internal or external benchmarking.

Internal benchmarking is probably the most common practice although it is far from universal. It represents a way of ensuring that subsidiaries understand the realities of intra-firm global competition, but care is required in its implementation so that creativity is not stifled.

Performance measures are also important in helping to raise standards across the group, although cultural factors may limit the worldwide applicability of these. In one company example, economic value added is used as the performance measure in all operations outside East Asia. In this MNC's joint venture in the latter area, by comparison, the performance measures employed are market share, growth, customer satisfaction and employee satisfaction, reflecting differences in Western and Asian capitalist systems.

Understanding the Subsidiary

Research has suggested that MNCs may have little knowledge of, or respect for, entrepreneurial initiatives launched by their foreign subsidiaries. Thus Birkinshaw and Ridderstråle (1999) identified three facets of the so-called 'corporate immune system' (that is, the corporate forces resisting initiatives), namely, ethocentrism, suspicion of the unknown reflected in skepticism about subsidiary capabilities, and resistance to change. Taken together, they represented a formidable barrier to subsidiary initiative.

Encouraging Initiative

Despite the above, there is growing evidence of successful initiatives in creative subsidiaries (Birkinshaw 1996; Pearce 1999), reflecting the obvious point that competencies and capabilities are not unique to the home country and the home corporation. The importance of the home country base is attributed to Porter's (1990) 'diamond' of competitive advantage, but this model ignores the impact on the capabilities of the MNC of global scope. Even in affiliates that are basically production plants, more could be done to exploit subsidiary capabilities for the benefit of the group as a whole. Illustrations might include giving responsibilities for process improvement, encouraging ideas for new manufacturing techniques, and allowing customer contact. There are examples of MNCs' production plants with customers a few kilometres away but absolutely no contacts.

The implication is that an atmosphere should be promoted which encourages individual initiative, with the support of the parent.

Numerous cases exist, by contrast, where subsidiaries have to 'go underground' with off-budget R&D projects to begin development work because this is not sanctioned by their parents.

Flexibility and Inducing Role Change

This is less of an issue in more autonomous subsidiaries because, being responsible for their own bottom line, they have to constantly look for new business opportunities. While it is inevitable that the roles of manufacturing plants are relatively routine and highly constrained, there are ways of inducing role and culture change. In one company analysed, a new managing director with a marketing background totally changed the culture of the subsidiary: bringing in sales and marketing completely altered the way employees had to look at the business. It is helpful if parent corporations are not too rigid in terms of, say, allocation of market franchises. In another sample company, a sales engineer (and a formal member of the marketing team) was given responsibility for a country market because of his networks there. Flexibility may extend to granting a particular subsidiary responsibility for government sales in its own national market (even when this is not formally part of its market franchise), because it can exploit 'buy-local' preferences.

Adapting to and Utilizing the Local Environment

There is no question that host countries still see MNC subsidiaries as in some senses 'local' companies, amenable to local policy initiatives. Similarly, local workers and local management have a strong allegiance to the local community. They may bring more commitment to the subsidiary in the widest sense than foreign managers on tours of duty ever do. Use of local managers (still less common in Japanese subsidiaries) brings the added bonus of cost reduction, since expatriate personnel are very expensive. Mention was made earlier of matrix management systems: these may be a barrier to local commitment since some reporting lines will be external to the subsidiary itself.

There are a number of other implications for the management of subsidiaries. At the very simplest level, involvement in the local community and in local business networks will pay dividends when the company is looking for financial support for its next project. At the next level, assisting local suppliers, initially, to reach the necessary quality standards, and then perhaps to internationalize with the subsidiary, can be beneficial for the group as a whole. More fundamentally, links to universities may generate benefits at very limited cost, for example sponsorship of a lectureship or a PhD student. Of course this requires organizational flexibility in the MNC, coordination mechanisms and, most importantly, a learning and open culture.

From an economic development perspective, there is considerable emphasis at the host-country level on cluster-based strategies aimed at generating agglomeration economies from being part of a geographical network or cluster of related activities and specialized support services. Authors such as Enright (1999) are rightly skeptical of many of these initiatives because the preconditions do not exist within the country; but in some nations, subsidiaries are attracted by the presence of clusters of related activities. In any event, it is important to participate – it may be only to pour cold water on the schemes being proposed; or to get benefits from talking to other managers; or to set up education and training programmes to assure an appropriate supply of skills.

CONCLUDING REMARKS

The world economy is in the midst of an enormous period of change that offers great potential in the different regions and countries of the world albeit with considerable risks. Many MNCs are still dominated by home country nationals. Their technology is driven by home country research labs, and their subsidiaries are production replicas of the parent with a remit to produce at high volume and low cost, with decisions made elsewhere. Into the 21st century, MNCs in this classic, hierarchical, ethnocentric mould face a risky future, at a time when flexibility and rapidity of response are so important. More than this, such strategies fail to exploit the capabilities particular to each region of the the world. This volume shows how two groups of MNCs – from Japan and Europe – are responding to these challenges in one highly dynamic but crisis-ridden region of the world – Southeast Asia.

References

Barrell, R. and N. Pain (1999) *Innovation, Investment and the Diffusion of Technology in Europe. German Direct Investment and Economic Growth in Postwar Europe*, Cambridge: Cambridge University Press.

Bartlett, C. A. and S. Ghoshal (1989) *Managing Across Borders: The Transnational Solution*, Boston, Mass.: Harvard Business School Press.

Birkinshaw, J. (1996) 'How Multinational Subsidiary Mandates are Gained and Lost', *Journal of International Business Studies*, vol. 27(3), pp. 467–95.

Birkinshaw, J. and J. Ridderstråle (1999) 'Fighting the Corporate Immune System: A Process Study of Subsidiary Initiatives in Multinational Corporations', *International Business Review*, vol. 8(2), pp. 149–80.

Birkinshaw, J. and N. Hood (1998a) 'Multinational Subsidiary Evolution: Capability and Charter Changes in Foreign-Owned Subsidiary Companies', *Academy of Management Journal*, vol. 23(4), pp. 773–95.

Birkinshaw, J. and N. Hood (eds) (1998b) *Multinational Corporate Evolution and Subsidiary Development*, London: Macmillan.

Blank, S. and S. Krajewski with H. S. Yu (1995) 'US Firms and North America: Redefining Structure and Strategy', *North American Outlook*, vol. 5(2).

Brewer, T. L. and S. Young (1998) *The Multilateral Investment System and Multinational Enterprises*, Oxford: Oxford University Press.

Buckley, P. J. and M. C. Casson (1998) 'Models of the Multinational Enterprise', *Journal of International Business Studies*, vol. 29(1), pp. 21–44.

Caves, R. E. (1998) 'Research on International Business: Problems and Prospects', *Journal of International Business Studies*, vol. 29(1), pp. 5–19.

Chakravarthy, B. S. and H. V. Perlmutter (1985) 'Strategic Planning for a Global Business', *Columbia Journal of World Business*, vol. 20, pp. 3–10.

Curhan, J. P., W. H. Davidson and R. Suri (1977) *Tracing the Multinationals: A Sourcebook on US-based Enterprises*, Cambridge, Mass.: Ballinger.

Dicken, P. (1998) *Global Shift*, London: Paul Chapman Publishing.

Dunning, J. H. (1998) 'Location and the Multinational Enterprise: A Neglected Factor', *Journal of International Business Studies*, vol. 29(1), pp. 45–66.

Dunning, J. H. (1993) *Multinational Enterprises and the Global Economy*, Wokingham: Addison-Wesley.

Dunning, J. H. (ed.) (2000) *Regions, Globalization and the Knowledge-Based Economy*, Oxford: Oxford University Press.

Eden, L. and A. Monteils (2000) 'Regional Integration and the Location Decisions of Multinational Enterprises: A North American Perspective', in J. H. Dunning (ed.), *Regions, Globalization and the Knowledge-Based Economy*, Oxford University Press.

Eisenhardt, K. M. and S. L. Brown (1999) 'Patching: Restructuring Business Portfolios in Dynamic Markets', *Harvard Business Review*, May–June, pp. 72–82.

Enright, M. (1999) 'The Globalization of Competition and the Localization of Competitive Advantage: Policies Towards Regional Clustering', in N. Hood and Young, S. (eds), *The Globalization of Multinational Enterprise Activity and Economic Development*, London: Macmillan, pp. 303–31.

Hanson, G. (1998) 'North American Economic Integration and International Location', *Oxford Review of Economic Policy*, vol. 14, pp. 30–44.

Hedlund, G. (1993) 'Assumptions of Hierarchy and Heterarchy: An Application to the Multinational Corporation', in S. Ghoshal and E. Westney (eds), *Organization Theory and the Multinational Corporation*, London: Macmillan, pp. 211–36.

Jacquemin, A. and L. R. Pench (1997) *Europe Competing in the Global Economy*, Cheltenham: Edward Elgar.

Legewie, J. (1999) 'Driving Regional Integration: Japanese Firms and the Development of the ASEAN Automobile Industry', *DIJ-Working Paper* 99/1, Tōkyō: German Institute for Japanese Studies.

Mirza, H. (1999) 'The Globalization of Business and East Asian Developing Country Multinationals', in N. Hood and S. Young (eds), *The Globalization of Multinational Enterprise Activity and Economic Development*, London: Macmillan, pp. 202–24.

Ohmae, K. (1985) *Triad Power: The Coming Shape of Global Corporations*, New York: The Free Press.

Ozawa, T. (1997) 'Japan', in J. H. Dunning (ed.), *Governments, Globalization and International Business*, Oxford: Oxford University Press, pp. 377–406.

Pearce, R. (1999) 'The Evolution of Technology in Multinational Enterprises: The Role of Creative Subsidiaries', *International Business Review*, vol. 8(2), pp. 128–48.

Perlmutter, H. (1969) 'The Tortuous Evolution of the Multinational Corporation', *Columbia Journal of World Business*, vol. 4, pp. 9–18.

Porter, M. E. (1986) 'Changing Patterns of International Competition', *California Management Review*, vol. 2, pp. 9–40.

Porter, M. (1990) *The Competitive Advantage of Nations*, New York: The Free Press.

Prahalad, C. K. and K. Lieberthal (1998) 'The End of Corporate Imperialism', *Harvard Business Review*, July–August, pp. 69–79.

Prahalad, C. K. and Y. Doz (1987) *The Multinational Mission: Balancing Local Demands and Global Vision*, New York: The Free Press.

Rugman, A. (ed.) (1993) *Management International Review*, vol. 33(2) (Special Edition on Michael Porter's Diamond of Competitive Advantage).

Storper, M. (1992) 'The Limits to Globalization: Technology Districts and International Trade', *Economic Geography*, vol. 68, pp. 60–96.

Taggart, J. H. (ed.) (1999) *International Business Review*, vol. 8(2) (Special Issue on Subsidiary Strategy).

UNCTAD (United Nations Conference on Trade and Development) (1994) *World Investment Report 1994: Transnational Corporations, Employment and the Workplace*, New York: United Nations.

UNCTAD (United Nations Conference on Trade and Development) (1997) *World Investment Report 1997: Transnational Corporations, Markets, Structure and Competition Policies*, New York: United Nations.

Usunier, J.-C. (1993) *International Marketing: A Cultural Approach*, London: Prentice-Hall.

Young, S., N. Hood and Tong Lu (1998) 'International Development by Chinese Enterprises: Key Issues for the Future', *Long Range Planning*, vol. 31(6), pp. 886–93.

Young, S., N. Hood and E. Peters (1994) 'Multinational Enterprises and Regional Economic Development', *Regional Studies*, vol. 28(7), pp. 657–77.

2 Asian Economies at the Crossroads: Crisis, Transformation, Adaptation

Tōru Yanagihara

The East Asian economic crisis will prove to be an epoch-making event in the history of the economies directly affected, with possible indirect effects on others in Asia. Two years after the onset of the crisis there is some convergence, and yet some sharpening of differences of opinion at the same time in the diagnosis and prognosis of the ongoing East Asian economic dislocation. Convergence is observed in the assigning of faults both to domestic and international factors. The remaining divergences centre around the question as to which side, domestic or international, should be the focus of systemic reform and also around the nature and pace of these needed structural reforms in the crisis-affected economies.

East Asian economies now face the serious challenge of reviving the momentum of their economic development. They had a record of rapid and sustained growth throughout the middle of the 1990s but it is doubtful that this growth trend will be re-achieved easily in the future. The purpose of this chapter is to examine some key issues in the process of crisis – transformation – adaptation in the economies of Southeast Asia from the perspective of long-term development, briefly touching upon the role of MNCs in the new situations and prospects of East Asian economies.

MIRACLE OR MIRAGE?

The crisis that erupted in Thailand in July 1997 and which spread to the rest of East Asia has turned out to be a sobering experience for those of us who were carried away with what appeared as a never-ending saga of the East Asian Miracle. After three decades of sustained growth and the resulting euphoria, a massive and violent reality check hit the region with vengeance causing panic and near total loss of sense of direction. By early 1999, however, the panic was over and the region's economies were on a recovery course. Are the economies back on to the miracle mode? Or are these just technical and temporary rebounds that will not necessarily lead to a road to sustained recovery? Before looking deeper into this question, we need to revisit the miracle phase of the East Asian economic history and ask what went right and what went wrong.

THE PERIOD OF THE ECONOMIC MIRACLE

The World Bank's *East Asian Miracle*

The World Bank report *The East Asian Miracle* (EAM) is essentially about what went right in East Asia, covering both Northeast Asia and Southeast Asia over the period from the 1960s through the 1980s. The message of success comes out very clearly in the overall assessment of the high-growth mechanisms in the high-performing Asian economies (HPAEs) based on the common analytical framework of a 'functional approach to growth' (World Bank 1993, p. 88). The primary emphasis is placed on 'policy fundamentals' comprising a stable macroeconomy, effective and secure financial systems, and limiting price distortions, among others. These policy orientations are stipulated to effect 'market-based competitive discipline' on firms through competition in domestic and export markets. Such competitive discipline in turn is understood to help enhance growth functions in accumulation and allocation of financial, physical and human capital as well as in the increase in productivity. The bottom line message is clear and loud: market competition under undistorted incentives generated high growth in East Asia (*ibid.*, p. 325).

The World Bank report does offer an account of other policy approaches adopted by East Asian economies under the heading of 'selective interventions'. They comprise export push, financial repression, directed credit and selective promotion. Among the approaches in this category, the report accords its full endorsement to export push, or preferences and incentives for export-oriented activities, by calling them 'a successful mix of fundamentals and interventions' and also 'the HPAEs' most broad based and successful application of selective interventions' (*ibid.*, p. 358).

Among the HPAEs, the report differentiates between the nature of the export-push strategy of Northeast Asia and that of Southeast Asia. In Northeast Asia there were efforts to promote specific exporting industries and also to simultaneously institute the promotion of exports and the protection of domestic markets. In contrast, export-push strategies in Southeast Asia 'relied less on highly specific incentives and more on gradual reductions in import protection, coupled with institutional support of exporters and a duty-free regime for inputs into exports' (*ibid.*, pp. 359–60). This distinction between Northeast Asia and Southeast Asia is attributed to the presence of a bureaucratic capacity to design and manage 'contest-based competitive discipline' in the operation of preferences and incentives for exporters. The report claims that 'contest-based incentive structures required high government institutional capability', which Southeast Asian economies lacked, unlike their Northeast Asian counterparts (*ibid.*, p. 359).

The report's verdict is much less sanguine regarding other forms of selective intervention, especially concerning their effectiveness in Southeast Asia. In fact, the distinction between Northeast Asia and Southeast Asia regarding government institutional capability to operate contests is given further emphasis, and the report draws a clear dividing line between Northeast Asia and Southeast Asia on the workability of interventionist policies in the financial sector and selective industrial promotion. What Southeast Asia is credited for is not the success in selective interventions, but their pragmatism and flexibility in abandoning them in timely recognition of an eventual adverse impact on macroeconomic stability and export performance (*ibid.*, p. 147).

Was the World Bank report totally negligent of the apparent or latent underlying causes of the crisis of the late 1990s? This is not a mere academic question since we need to examine and ascertain what part of the miracle legacy can be carried over to the post-crisis period. This question will be taken up in the next section, after confirming the role of FDI during the miracle period.

The Role of FDI during the Miracle Period

Sustained growth is realized through successive identification and generation of investment opportunities and their realization as investment projects with high returns. Thus the sustained process of economic growth is typically characterized by phases of development defined by leading industries and leading actors. In the case of Southeast Asian economies, investment opportunities traditionally were of the nature of exploiting both renewable and exhaustible natural resources. FDI played an important role in large-scale mining, energy development and plantation-type projects throughout the region. Investment opportunities in manufacturing and service sectors were generated either in relation to development, production, distribution, processing and exporting of primary products, or in response to higher household incomes and consumer demands. In the 1960s and 1970s, many of the Southeast Asian governments attempted to promote industrialization through the protection of domestic markets from competition from imports. This protection-cum-promotion policy generated a new type of FDI flow in urban-based, consumer-oriented activities in industry and services. In the 1970s, there emerged yet another distinctive type of FDI in Southeast Asia, that is, the hiving out of some semiconductor manufacturing processes to Malaysia by a number of major US electronics concerns. This was a dominant type of FDI among the first-tier NIEs in Northeast Asia and also proved to be the harbinger of what was to come to Southeast Asia during the following decade (for this and the two following paragraphs see Yanagihara 1993).

The first half of the 1980s turned out to be a period of structural adjustment in the wake of much higher levels of international interest rates and overall declines in international commodity prices. These two factors combined implied drastically reduced debt-servicing capacities, which in turn necessitated contractions in fiscal and monetary management. All these factors came together to produce stagnation in domestic demand and a slowdown in growth. As a result, the Philippines and Indonesia faced serious difficulties in tiding over a period of foreign exchange shortfall, the former resorting to debt-rescheduling and the latter to a series of exceptional financing arrangements. The only way out of the stagnation was the promotion of non-traditional exports. Policy changes were instituted as part of the structural adjustment programme to make export-oriented activities more attractive through the devaluation of the exchange rate and the liberalization of trade and FDI regulations related to export-oriented activities.

These policy changes, as well as the exogenous developments in the appreciation of Japanese, Taiwanese and Korean currencies following the Plaza Accord of 1985, cooperated to generate large volumes of FDI flows in labour-intensive manufacturing operations from these

Northeast Asian economies to the ASEAN 3, that is, Thailand, Malaysia and Indonesia. (The Philippines were still suffering from the after-effects of their political turmoil and failed to benefit from the FDI boom at this juncture.) These investments and their direct and indirect spillover effects restored the ASEAN 3 to a high-investment, high-growth path during the second half of the 1980s. This investment boom set the stage for the overheating of the economy leading up to the eventual crisis.

From the late 1980s through the mid-1990s, the ASEAN 3 underwent a long spell of high growth fuelled by continued inflows of FDI and subsequently by an explosive increase in inflows of portfolio investment and bank lending from overseas. The availability of ample financial resources resulted in rapid increases in domestic credit to private sectors, which in turn led to large increases in investments. Productive investments resulted in overcapacity in many lines of manufacturing, and speculative investments resulted in bubbles and eventual busts in the prices of real property and in stock markets. These developments produced rising percentages of bad loans on the balance sheets of financial institutions, causing concern about their debt-servicing capacity.

It is instructive in this connection that the share prices of financial institutions in Thailand peaked in early 1994 and started a precipitous fall in mid-1996, one year before the eventual onset of the currency crisis. In Thailand, the crisis was most probably triggered by the collapse of export growth in 1996, coming as it did on top of the persistence of current-account deficits in the order of 8 per cent of GDP from 1995 onwards. Underlying such deterioration in macroeconomic performance was the interplay of large inflows of financial capital, inadequate macroeconomic management (that is, the maintenance of a pegging to the US dollar), and the lack of discipline in the domestic financial and corporate sectors. The combination of these factors created a precarious situation that, as we know, led to economic trouble (World Bank 1998b, pp. 73–4).

We should not be bewildered by the mirage of this financial bubble and collapse. There certainly were excesses in both real and speculative investments fuelled by large doses of readily available credits; it is also true that many large-scale investment decisions were influenced by political considerations. It should be remembered, however, that on the whole private investments were sound in Southeast Asian economies until they became carried away with the credit boom fuelled by the foreign capital bonanza. In particular, FDI has made positive overall contributions to the long-term growth of Southeast Asian economies. Their role constitutes one important element of what went right during the miracle period of those economies over the past three decades. Let us now consider what the roles of FDI are in the current phase of recovery and in the long-term prospects for sustained development. Both of these questions should be formulated in terms of investment opportunities and their realizations. The crisis has created new conditions for current and future investment opportunities in the economy and for the capacities and constraints of various actors in realizing them.

CRISIS, TRANSFORMATION, ADAPTATION

The East Asian crisis will prove to be an epoch-making event in the economic history of Southeast Asia. The World Bank's new publication, *East Asia: The Road to Recovery*, presents the following summary assessment:

> The end of the 20th century for East Asia is changing the way business is conducted, the way resources are allocated, and the very economic and, in some cases, political governance of countries.
> (World Bank 1998a, p. 2)

The crisis represents a breakdown of old routines and relationships, thus opening up new opportunities for new actors and new modes of business operations. Transformation is underway, in no small measure led by foreign corporate actors, in the form of the establishment of new patterns of behaviour and rules of engagement and also in the reconfiguration of industrial organization (for example, mergers and acquisitions or strategic alliances). Pressure is mounting and it is a swim-or-sink situation for existing firms. Adaptation to the post-crisis situation will be inescapable even if the ongoing recovery might provide some breathing space for distressed firms and financial institutions. Financial restructuring and reorientation of business activities will be the unavoidable first step for many of the region's business entities.

The Nature of the Crisis

As briefly touched upon above, the crisis needs to be understood as an outcome of the interaction between internal and external financial conditions. During the 1990s, domestic financial markets were liberalized and opened up in many East Asian economies as there emerged tidal waves of capital inflows in search of high returns in the short term. The massive inflows of financial capital, largely channeled through financial intermediaries, accelerated the already rapid pace of credit expansion and compounded the lurking problem of excessive and speculative investments, thus making domestic financial sectors more vulnerable to the ensuing dramatic end to the economic boom.

This two-sided view is presented in two recent publications of the World Bank (World Bank 1998a and 1998b) which convey essentially the same message with regard to the cause and nature of the East Asian crisis. The first of these reports, *East Asia: The Road to Recovery*, represents the most systematic diagnosis and prognosis of the East Asian crisis presented by the World Bank to date. First, the report points to inherent weaknesses that developed in the financial sectors of many East Asian economies in the process of rapid and sustained economic growth:

> Despite the progress of East Asian financial systems, they developed without bond markets, lacked adequate prudential supervision, and in some countries permitted a large role for government. These weaknesses led to serious misallocation of resources, over-exposure to risky sectors, and poor institutional development. Until recently, they were covered up by high growth, high savings, and strong fiscal positions. (World Bank 1998a, p. 34)

These weaknesses, as the report sees them, were compounded by the speed of financial sector developments and of international financial integration, increasing the vulnerability of financial sectors. The report states:

> The reinforcing effects of high and rising investment levels, large private capital inflows and asset booms, combined with underlying weaknesses in financial systems, led to the buildup of a number of vulnerabilities, including increased banking fragility, increased exposure to risky sectors, and increased borrowing short in foreign currency and lending long in domestic currency. (*Ibid.*, p. 39)

These developments, and particularly the high ratio of short-term external debt to foreign currency reserves, 'rendered these countries much more vulnerable to a potential run on their currencies, which could arise from a loss of investor confidence' (*ibid.*, p. 41). Based on these steps of reasoning the report provides the following summary judgement:

> The underlying process of vulnerabilities may have occurred even without the inflows of private capital. However, the expansion of international integration, and easy access to private capital flows became catalysts which increased the magnitude of vulnerability.
>
> (*Ibid.*, p. 41)

The initial response to the outbreak of the East Asian crisis was led by the International Monetary Fund (IMF). The IMF published a preliminary self-assessment of its programmes in Indonesia, Korea and Thailand (IMF 1999), spelling out the basic strategy that the IMF adopted in response to the crisis. The programmes incorporated a three-pronged approach consisting of structural reforms, macro-economic adjustment and financing packages. The central focus of macroeconomic adjustment was placed on the tightening of monetary policy with a view to countering downward pressure on the exchange rate and thus containing its excessive depreciation. In this document and subsequent pronouncements, the IMF has maintained that monetary tightening was the correct policy action in bringing about stability to currency markets in crisis-affected economies. The IMF also maintains that comprehensive structural reforms were needed because the weaknesses in financial systems and in governance were seen to be at the root of the crisis and addressing them was essential in order to restore confidence and stop private capital outflows (IMF 1999, pp. 31–2).

There are criticisms regarding the appropriateness of the approaches adopted by the IMF. Let us first review the representative criticisms of the macroeconomic management, and secondly turn to issues involving structural reforms. With regard to the exceptional severity and duration of the East Asian crisis, some analysts find the main cause of the severe recession in the policy responses initially adopted by the crisis-affected countries under the agreement with the IMF (Yoshitomi and Ohno 1999). They argue that the IMF failed to devise a new set of policy prescriptions suited for the new type of crisis (capital-account crisis) and continued to apply the old prescriptions prepared for the traditional type (current-account crisis). The solutions that were implemented consisted of macroeconomic austerity, high interest rates, the rapid restructuring of the financial sector, and prompt implementation of prudential regulation. Yoshitomi and Ohno claim that 'the Asian crisis has been further aggravated and prolonged by the very policies that were supposed to end it' (*ibid.*, p. 16). The key mechanism that generated the aggravation and prolongation of the crisis was credit contraction. Yoshitomi and Ohno argue: 'in a state of financial turmoil, the [prescribed] measures contributed to the acceleration of financial disintermediation and credit contraction' (*ibid.*, p. 17). According to their analysis old cures killed patients suffering from new diseases.

A similar, albeit not as forceful, sentiment is found in the World Bank's *Global Economic Prospects 1998/99*, which complements the emphasis on credit contraction made by Yoshitomi and Ohno. According to the report's analysis, the condition of systemic bankruptcy in the corporate sector is likely to have produced a 'credit crunch' – reduced willingness to provide credit on the part of banks – in crisis-affected East Asian economies. This factor appears to have been partly responsible for the precipitous decline in domestic demands, and investment expenditures in particular, on top of the overall dampening effects of the pervasive uncertainties (World Bank 1998b, pp. 75–9). The World Bank report also offers the following overall assessment on the effectiveness of the initial policy responses to the crisis:

> In contrast with the crises in Mexico and Argentina in 1994–95, one of the great surprises in East Asia was how little immediate effect the initial policy responses appeared to have had in reducing pressure on currencies or stabilizing investor confidence. To the contrary, much or even most of the deprecation in currencies occurred after these measures were taken. (*Ibid.*, p. 82)

The report pays particular attention to monetary policy and offers a systematic examination as to whether the adoption of a high interest rate in an attempt to defend the currency was advisable. The summary statement is worth quoting in full:

> Overall, the still early state of research into the behavior of interest rates and exchange rates during crises may not allow firm conclusions. There is, however, more evidence about the adverse impact of high interest rates on real economic activity, confirming the importance of undertaking monetary policy in a flexible and nuanced way that gives due consideration to the policy dilemmas

that arise, such as in East Asia, where the financial system is fragile, corporations are highly leveraged, and shortfalls in aggregate demand are large. (*Ibid.*, pp. 90–1)

The World Bank report also examines the advisability of introducing structural reforms simultaneously with the implementation of crisis management, posing questions regarding the fundamental centrality of such reforms in the policy conditionality attached to the financial rescue programmes arranged by the IMF. The main thrust of the structural reforms comprises financial and corporate restructuring, financial regulation and supervision, and corporate governance. In some cases, reforms also covered domestic and international trade liberalization, fiscal subsidies and privatization. The report points to the possibility that structural reforms may complicate the immediate crisis management task during financial crises and in particular cautions against the possibility of exacerbating the credit difficulties facing viable firms (World Bank 1999, pp. 91–3).

Beyond the Crisis

The process of economic transformation and adaptation in post-crisis Southeast Asia may be conceptually divided into three components, that is restructuring, structural reform, and structural adaptation. So far, most of the attention and action has been directed to the design and implementation of restructuring operations. Restructuring signifies the task of debt workout and operational reorientation at the level of individual firms and financial institutions, and also the reconfiguration of relative positions of the various types of actors in industrial and financial sectors. In the financial sector, the main task of restructuring is to resolve the bad assets in weak financial institutions and to strengthen the capital base of the viable institutions. In the industrial sector, corporate restructuring is needed to get rid of excessive financial burdens and excessive productive capacities so that firms are able to resume viable strategies in business operation and in financing. On the whole, there has been more substantive progress in restructuring in the financial sector than in the industrial sector partly due to the need to develop legal and institutional frameworks for bankruptcy and foreclosure procedures to facilitate corporate restructuring (World Bank 1998a, chapter 4).

Structural reforms signify, in general terms, changes in rules and norms governing economic behaviour, relations and management, and comprise the competitive environment, financial and corporate governance, and the role of government. This encompasses the whole range of issues in financial and corporate sectors. Central among them are the design and implementation of banking regulation and supervision, the system of corporate governance, and the broader governance issues of corruption and cronyism. In these areas progress is bound to be slow. Although financial restructuring and legal reforms are introducing increased awareness and new standards that should lead to new modes of corporate governance in the future, the process will take a long time to be completed.

There are two aspects of particular significance to Southeast Asia. One concerns the nature of the business group, typically conglomerates, and the other is that of family control. In reality these two characteristics are merged in many big businesses in Southeast Asia in the form of family-controlled conglomerates (see Khan 1999). From a historical perspective this feature may be viewed as one aspect of one of the stages in the development of these conglomerates; there are obvious reasons for family businesses to be dominant in the early stage of development. Policy-oriented discourse on structural reform sometimes appears to be negligent of historical conditions, when reality should be viewed as such in a more concrete and specific context. The central question now is, to what extent is this group structure, or conglomerate structure, either a positive or a negative factor for the next stage of corporate and industrial development, and also to what extent and in what way is a family-control structure either positive or negative.

If we adopt a stage of development approach in a broad manner, we may see Northeast Asia, including Hong Kong and Singapore for this purpose, moving one step ahead of Southeast Asia. We may see a model there. Korea has maintained a very large family-based conglomerate structure throughout all the phases of industrial development over the past four decades. Presently that structure is about to be drastically modified, but if we take the Korean lesson in a positive light we might be able to hypothesize that there is a positive role for family-based conglomerates for yet another phase of development in Southeast Asia. Also, it is important to note that family businesses have apparently behaved well in Hong Kong and Singapore. So it may not be corporate governance as such which lay at the root of the East Asian crisis (Khan 1999, pp. 25–6). At least, it could not be adequately addressed separately from relevant aspects of policy and institutional environments. One important part of policy environments is the competitive environment, that is, to what extent competition is either encouraged or restrained. One ultimately important factor in overall institutional environments is how governments are themselves governed in the political process.

Proponents of structural reforms emphasize the critical importance of financial and corporate governance as fundamental determinants of overall economic efficiency and thus of long-term growth performance. The key to right investment and financing decisions is found, according to them, in the manner decision-makers are held accountable, to whom and by what mechanism. Some claim that the main weakness of East Asian economies, and the main cause of the Asian crisis, was the failure of financial and corporate governance (see IMF 1999). There is some truth in this view to the extent that there was obvious overinvestment and misallocation of funds. But then again, it is unlikely that the revival of the economy would entail a broad and swift change in rules and norms as currently proposed by the IMF and World-Bank programmes. It is true that the dominance of family-owned businesses is being eroded in the process of financial restructuring, but their position will remain highly significant for the foreseeable future. Overall, we notice a shift from relation-based to arm's-length modes of economic transactions, but the process will be gradual and far from uniform.

Under the ongoing implementation of restructuring and structural reform, all firms are faced with the continuing task of structural adaptation. This implies changes in behaviour, relations and management in order to utilize existing productive capacities and relationships to the fullest extent possible under the new financial and market constraints. One important focus of structural adaptation arises in the wake of corporate restructuring as firms strengthen their focus on core competence. They will need to establish a system of generating new investment opportunities, not through unrelated diversification as was prevalent in the past, but through the process of innovation, product development, vertical integration and diversification based on economies of scope.

East Asian economies now face the serious challenge of reviving the lost momentum of economic development. The crisis has produced new and more productive opportunities for MNCs to utilize their technical, managerial and financial resources and thus contribute to the reconstruction of the East Asian economies. They will play a unique and important role in the interactive process of changes in the institutional framework of the economy (structural reform) and behavioural patterns (structural adaptation) in this epoch-making period of post-crisis transformation.

CONCLUDING REMARKS

In conclusion, it will be appropriate to mention some of the important features in the new roles of multinational corporations (MNCs). Economists typically rely on readily available statistics in trying to capture the activities of MNCs. In doing so they make an error of identifying MNC activities with foreign direct investments. This is a serious error. Many important relations are formed as various types of non-equity relationships such as contract manufacturing, technology licensing, and marketing and franchising arrangements. It is important to know what is happening in those types of MNC activities, but even from that limited information base of readily available statistics, some new features are clearly visible. One of the most conspicuous is the increase of mergers and acquisitions (M&A) in Southeast Asia. This new development seems to be driven by European as well as North American corporations, while Japanese firms do not seem to be act-ively involved. Instead, Japanese firms have been typically pouring in funds for capital replenishment of distressed subsidiaries. This con-trast between MNCs from Europe and their Japanese counterparts clearly emerges from statistics. It appears that Japanese MNCs have been typically more defensive in their approach, trying to maintain as much as possible of existing capacities, to avoid drastic operational restructuring, and to tide over the hardship brought about by the col-lapse in local demand. In contrast, European and North American MNCs have been acting more proactively and strategically, expanding their presence in Southeast Asia.

In the aspect of policy environments, there have taken place a series of decisions aimed at liberalizing the constraints hitherto placed on foreign direct investors. But the commitment does not seem to be unconditional, in the sense that there are certain elements of nation-alism still in place, as manifested in the fact that some of the measures are time-bound. This applies to individual countries as well as to ASEAN schemes of investment promotion. Southeast Asian counties are not embracing liberal economic principles as such; they seem to remain more pragmatic players in judging the levels of incentives needed to attract foreign corporate players.

There remain two important questions. One is how MNCs view the Southeast Asian investment environment. In particular, what new roles is the government promotion of industrial and technological upgrading expected to play from the perspective of MNCs? Governments are not always in tune with the new logic of technological and managerial development. Are there important perception and communication gaps between MNCs and governments that call for immediate attention?

Secondly, there is a question at a somewhat abstract level. One of the most abused concepts in the discourse of the East Asian crisis has been the term 'confidence'. It is argued that the crisis occurred because there was a loss of confidence and that the central task for recovery, therefore, is the restoration of confidence. Maybe this is tautologically true, and yet, unless the determinants of confidence are articulated, this argument is mostly useless. It may very well be that what matters would differ across various categories of investors and that the discourse on investor confidence has been dominated by the concerns of financial investors, bankers and portfolio managers. It is presumed that the key factors in the confidence in economies could be different for real investors, meaning real sector corporations, from those that are high on the list used by financial investors. It is hoped that further investigation will be able to articulate and elaborate on the key determinants of confidence from the perspective of real investors.

References

Arndt, H. W. and H. Hill (eds) (1999) *Southeast Asia's Economic Crisis: Origins, Lessons, and the Way Forward*, New York: St Martin's Press; Singapore: Institute of Southeast Asian Studies.

Asian Development Bank (1997) *Emerging Asia: Challenges and Changes*, Manila: ADB.

Asian Development Bank (1999) *Asian Development Outlook 1999*, Manila: ADB.

International Monetary Fund (1999) *IMF-Supported Programs in Indonesia, Korea and Thailand: A Preliminary Assessment*, Washington DC: IMF.

Jomo K. S. (ed.) (1998) *Tigers in Trouble: Financial Governance, Liberalisation and Crises in East Asia*, London: Zed Books.

Khan, H. A. (1999) 'Corporate Governance of Family Businesses in Asia: What's Right and What's Wrong?' Asian Development Bank Institute Working Paper no. 3, August 1999, Tōkyō: Asian Development Bank Institute.

Montes, M. F. (1998) *The Currency Crisis in Southeast Asia*, Singapore: Institute of Southeast Asian Studies.

World Bank (1993) *The East Asian Miracle*, Washington DC: World Bank.

World Bank (1998a) *East Asia: The Road to Recovery*, Washington DC: World Bank.

World Bank (1998b) *Global Economic Prospects and the Developing Countries 1998/99: Beyond Financial Crisis*, Washington DC: World Bank.

Yanagihara, T. (1993) 'Asia-Pacific Economic Zone: Its Emergence and Evolution', *Journal of International Economic Studies*, vol. 7, pp. 1–17.

Yoshitomi, M. and K. Ohno (1999) 'Capital-Account Crisis and Credit Contraction', Asian Development Bank Institute Working Paper no. 2, May 1999, Tōkyō: Asian Development Bank Institute.

3 The Role of Foreign MNCs in the Technological Development of Singaporean Industries

Poh Kam Wong and Annette A. Singh

INTRODUCTION

Foreign multinational corporations (MNCs) have played a major role in stimulating the technological development of the manufacturing industries in Southeast Asia in general and Singapore in particular. Contrary to concerns that MNCs are footloose, and ever ready to leave their host countries in search of lower cost locations rather than investing in technological upgrading, the experience of Singapore has shown that substantial technological development has been achieved thanks to MNCs. However, the host country's factor endowments and economic development policies obviously influence the contributions of MNCs to technological development. In addition, different MNCs exhibit different strategic behaviour with respect to technology investments in their host countries; in particular, MNCs from the USA and Europe display technology-management approaches significantly different from Japanese MNCs.

This chapter provides an overview of the role of MNCs in the technological development of host developing countries, and briefly examines how Singapore has emerged as a major technological hub in Southeast Asia by leveraging MNC investments. It then highlights the different behaviour of US, European and Japanese MNCs in Singapore in terms of their stimulation of technological development. The chapter concludes by examining likely future developments in the aftermath of the Asian financial crisis.

40

THE ROLES OF FOREIGN MNCS IN STIMULATING TECHNOLOGICAL DEVELOPMENT IN HOST COUNTRIES

Over the last few decades much research has been done on the effects – positive and negative – of foreign MNC activity on the host country. There are continuing concerns that FDI by MNCs may destroy local capabilities; that MNCs are too footloose to build a strong technological base in the host economy; that MNCs contribute too little to the corporate tax base due to the significant tax incentives they enjoy and due to their transfer pricing practices; and that they cause significant capital outflows in later years through profit repatriation. Even so, the empirical literature increasingly points to net positive contributions of FDI in most countries. As a consequence many countries have opened their borders to MNC operations (see for example Dunning and Narula 1996; Blomström and Kokko 1998).

A major reason for the growing support of MNCs is the increasing recognition of their role in stimulating technological development in host countries. While earlier literature examines the contribution of MNCs primarily from the perspective of technology transfer, more recent studies have adopted a broader perspective that investigates the various indirect means by which they can stimulate local technological development. In particular, local industry in the host economy can benefit not only from the direct transfer of product and process technologies and managerial and marketing skills from the parent headquarters to the local subsidiary operations, but also from various indirect processes that induce technological development such as spillovers between suppliers and buyers, imitative responses of local competitors, and collaboration with the host country's public research institutions. We briefly review these various processes below.

Technology Transfer from the Parent Headquarters to the Local Subsidiary

MNCs contribute to the technological development of their host country most importantly through direct technology transfer from the parent company's headquarters to the local subsidiary operation. According to the internalization theory of FDI, foreign MNCs can successfully compete in another country only if they have some advantage that overcomes the handicap of operating in an unfamiliar environment. Domestic firms have an edge over their foreign competitors with their broader knowledge of local markets, consumers and business practices. MNCs generally bring advantages stemming from new product and/or process technologies and management and operational know-how unavailable in the host country (Kagami 1998).

The transfer of new technologies to the local subsidiary needs to be accompanied by technical learning for the local staff employed by the MNC. Transfer of technical and managerial skills takes place on-the-job as workers are given access to knowledge bases in the parent headquarters or in associate companies within the group (Thomsen 1999). The level of learning ranges from basic technological competencies to advanced capabilities and is complemented by other forms of training, for example seminars or formal study. In some cases MNCs set up training centres in the host country, as Toyota did in Thailand (Blomström and Kokko 1998; Kagami 1998).

Linkages between Local Firms and MNCs

Backward and forward linkages between local firms and MNCs are another source of learning for the host country, although there is more evidence of the former than the latter. Local supporting industries learn new technologies and methods through their transactions with the MNCs, and the MNCs have the incentive to assist in their suppliers' development so that they can obtain cost-effective, high-quality inputs. Thus, they may provide training, technical and managerial advice, as well as assistance in establishing production facilities and finding other customers for their supplier firm (Thomsen 1999).

Even without direct assistance supplier firms can be induced to invest in new technologies through their relationships with buyers (Wong 1991, 1992). Suppliers are often reluctant to adopt innovations that are only rarely used in the local context because of uncertainty over costs and benefits. As local companies come into contact with MNCs, they learn more about these innovations, and their uncertainty is dispelled (Blomström and Kokko 1998). A stable supplier–customer relationship with MNCs also encourages domestic firms to invest in technological upgrading; the security of having a long-term customer reduces the risk of making such investments (Wong 1992).

This inducement of technological development relies on the foreign company having a share of local content in its products. If it imports all its inputs from its home country, or from a third country, it will operate in isolation from the rest of the host economy. However, there is evidence that the local content share in MNCs' products – and therefore the development of linkages between them and domestic firms – increases over time (Blomström and Kokko 1998).

R&D Investment to Tap Local Science and Technology Resources

MNC can also take advantage of local science and technology resources in the host country by investing in R&D activities that utilize these resources, by conducting joint R&D with local R&D institutions and local firms for example. Alternatively, they may engage in greenfield investment in R&D centres that either serve their local manufacturing operations, or, in some cases, serve as autonomous regional centres that report to corporate R&D directly.

The scope for this kind of mechanism that induces technological development appears to be growing as the R&D activities of MNCs are increasingly internationalized (Kumar 1998a). However, the location of such internationalized R&D activities remains highly concentrated in a small number of developing countries, primarily the advanced newly industrialized countries which have resources and have developed a sufficiently advanced technological infrastructure, or have a significant pool of advanced highly-trained engineers and scientists.

Technological Diffusion through Competitive Pressure, Personnel Movement and Imitative Learning

MNCs can induce technological diffusion by their mere presence in the local market; the mere presence of a technologically advanced competitor compels local firms to take action to retain market share (Chuang and Lin 1999). Such actions include using existing technology more efficiently and investing in new, more advanced technologies. This rationale for upgrading and increasing efficiency in local companies can be more effective than the traditional profit incentive. Rosenberg (1976) notes that 'threats of deterioration or actual deterioration from some previous state are more powerful attention focussing devices than are vague possibilities for improvements' (cited in Blomström and Kokko 1998).

Competencies existing in the foreign company can be transferred throughout the rest of the host economy through imitative learning and labour mobility. Imitative learning takes place as local firms copy products produced and processes used by the MNCs, which in turn stimulates technological development in local firms as they invest in new technologies to use more advanced processes or produce more sophisticated products.

Technology diffusion also occurs as experienced workers move from MNCs to existing local firms or to new start-ups. Having acquired knowledge of high technology during their employment in a MNC, they take these competencies with them to their new company. In this way, technology is diffused throughout the economy.

FACTORS INFLUENCING THE EXTENT AND SPEED OF TECHNOLOGICAL DEVELOPMENT INDUCED BY MNCs

MNC Characteristics and Policies

To a certain extent, the contribution that the MNC makes to the technological development of its host country depends on the company's own policies and characteristics. These include the degree to which the company fosters networks with local supplier industries, conducts R&D locally, and trains local personnel.

The market-orientation of MNCs, that is, whether they produce for export or for the local market, is thought to influence the propensity for technology transfer. Even so, the direction of its impact is uncertain. On the one hand, MNC operations producing goods for export may generate less technology transfer than those producing for the local market. This occurs for two reasons. Firstly, goods destined for export must meet the standards for quality and price prevailing in the international market; MNCs may thus prefer to use foreign suppliers rather than local firms who do not have the technology or capabilities to produce high-quality inputs in the quantities needed. Secondly, when goods are made for export there is less of an incentive to accommodate the preferences of the local consumers (Kagami 1998; Thomsen 1999). On the other hand, export-oriented operations may exhibit a greater propensity to adopt new technologies in order to stay competitive internationally, whereas domestic-market-oriented operations may be shielded from foreign competition and hence be less subject to competitive pressure to upgrade.

One factor often thought to affect the degree to which local firms benefit from spillovers from MNCs is the degree of foreign ownership of the affiliate, and the perception that local sharing of ownership enhances the spillover effect has led to arguments for restrictions of the foreign ownership of MNC affiliates. However, such arguments find little support from recent empirical studies (see for example Blomström and Sjöholm 1999).

Host-Country Characteristics and Policies

Characteristics of the host country also affect the extent and speed with which MNCs induce technological development. To begin with, general factors such as political and social stability, and the state of infrastructure and local supporting industries affect the willingness of the MNC to locate in the country and to subsequently upgrade the technological intensity of its operations. The level of skills present in the local labour force and supporting industries must be sufficiently developed to be able to absorb the new competencies being passed on by MNCs, otherwise they will not benefit from them (Dunning and Narula 1996). Similarly, the infrastructure must be able to transmit the knowledge from MNCs throughout the host economy. An OECD report on FDI in Southeast Asia found that the limited capacity of local workers to learn the new technologies was one reason for the limited level of technology transfer to the ASEAN 4 countries (Malaysia, Thailand, Indonesia and the Philippines) (Thomsen 1999).

Learning capacity and strategic intents affect a local firm's ability to benefit from MNCs. Those companies that invest in learning about technology and have a greater ability to absorb such learning will obviously benefit more from technological diffusion. Those with lower learning capacities or less receptivity to new technologies will benefit less. Building capacity for learning is extremely important for host countries seeking to become less reliant on MNCs for technological progress over time. Rather, the domestic firms will progress from 'absorption to adaptation, continuous updating and eventually [to] innovation' (Kumar 1998a, p. 42).

The central role for the government with regard to technology transfer from foreign direct investment is to develop a general climate that is conducive to investment. This includes a stable political, economic and social environment; which in turn means developing human capital, fostering local supporting industries, and building infrastructure including roads, airports, seaports, rail facilities and telecommunications (Dunning and Narula 1996). Protection of intellectual property is becoming an important policy consideration as the host countries seek to attract MNC activities involving higher technological intensities such as R&D and software development.

The development of domestic technological capabilities is especially important, because in addition to attracting MNCs it increases the country's absorptive capacity and long-term gain from the technology transfer (Kumar 1998a). Indigenous skills must be developed and accumulated so that the new technologies can be adapted to the needs of the host country, and then further updated to avoid obsolescence. This requires that the government implements proactive manpower development programmes, as well as invests in universities and public R&D institutions.

Creating an environment attractive to R&D investment is also important. Chuang and Lin (1999) found that spillovers from FDI and other forms of technology transfer are substitutes for indigenous R&D activity. However, countries cannot indefinitely rely on technology transfer and avoid furthering their own R&D capabilities, particularly as MNCs are reluctant to share technologies on the higher level of the technology spectrum.

In addition to policies directly designed to influence technology transfer behaviour from MNCs, broader policies also have an effect. These include: immigration policies (particularly with regard to the employment of foreigners), import duties on inputs used by MNCs (such as raw materials and capital goods), foreign ownership regulations, the complexity of bureaucratic procedures, and tax incentives (van Hoesel 1996; Thomsen 1999). Some governments attempt to force technology transfer by imposing restrictions on MNCs, such as limiting foreign ownership and employment, instituting compulsory licensing, and setting a minimum proportion of local content (Thomsen 1999). The advantages of these measures in terms of knowledge transfer must be weighed against the cost of discouraging potential investors.

SINGAPORE'S DEVELOPMENT AS A TECHNOLOGICAL HUB IN SOUTHEAST ASIA

Over the last thirty years, Singapore has emerged as the most technologically advanced hub in Southeast Asia for MNCs. It has done this by adopting an active state role in attracting and leveraging FDI by multinational corporations (Wong *et al.* 1997). The strategy includes offering tax incentives to attract the desired FDI, proactive investment in infrastructure, and manpower development. These measures make Singapore an attractive investment location, and, more generally, Singapore provides a business-friendly environment with political stability, a sound macroeconomic policy, a clean efficient government, and the rule of law. Starting as an offshore production platform for labour-intensive manufacturing activities in the 1960s and early 1970s, Singapore quickly upgraded to skill-intensive manufacturing activities in the late 1970s and 1980s. It shifted into R&D-intensive manufacturing activities in the second half of the 1990s. By the late 1990s, Singapore became a major base for regional operating headquarters (OHQs), lead manufacturing plants, world product charter centres, process technology transfer stations, international procurement offices (IPOs), international logistics centres, and regional marketing, training and technical support centres for global MNCs. It has also increasingly positioned itself as a major regional R&D hub and a regional venture capital hub.

In addition to achieving significant technological progress through successive rounds of more technologically advanced FDI over the years, the government of Singapore also sought to induce technological development in the rest of the economy. It did so by leveraging the MNCs through policies that encouraged backward linkages with suppliers, competitive pressure on local firms to upgrade, and R&D collaboration between MNCs and local firms and public R&D institutions (Wong 1995). Mobility of personnel from MNCs to local firms also contributed significantly to the development of technological capabilities of local firms.

While significant technological improvements have also been experienced in other Southeast Asian countries, they are at distinctly lower levels than in Singapore where MNCs are more R&D-intensive. This is true whether measured by R&D expenditure, scientific manpower, sale of new/improved products or number of patents held. For example, R&D by MNCs in Singapore exceeds that of MNCs in Malaysia (Table 3.1), and Malaysian MNCs in turn exhibit higher levels of technological activity than MNCs in Thailand, Philippines and Indonesia, where MNC manufacturing activities still remain largely labour-intensive.

As the cost of operations in Singapore has risen and the government has changed its focus to the encouragement of higher level operations, there has been a significant redistribution of manufacturing activities away from Singapore since the late 1980s. These activities have been relocated to Malaysia, China and Indonesia (particularly the Riau Islands), and increasingly to the Philippines and Thailand (see Thomsen 1999). One advantage of Southeast Asia as a location for MNC manufacturing activities is the existence of 'economies of

Table 3.1   Technological indicators of MNCs in Singapore
versus Malaysia, 1996

	Singapore	Malaysia
% of firms with R&D/sales > 3%	37.7	29.9
% of firms with S&T degree holders/employees > 5%	58.5	38.2
% of firms with sales derived from new/improved products introduced in last 3 years > 25%	65.4	54.6
% of firms with 1 or more patent	17.0	6.5

Note: S&T = science and technology.
Source: Wong (2000a).

heterogeneity' – a wide range of resource endowments found in close proximity in the countries around the region (Wong 1999a). This has enhanced its attractiveness as a regional platform for manufacturing, especially given new approaches such as just-in-time inventories, which makes proximity all the more desirable (Kumar 1998b).

DIFFERENCES AMONG US, EUROPEAN AND JAPANESE MNCs IN INDUCING TECHNOLOGICAL DEVELOPMENT IN SINGAPORE

Earlier empirical studies by the author suggest that MNCs from the USA, Europe and Japan are found to have significant differences in the way they induce technological development in Singapore (Wong 1992, 1999b, 2000a, 2000b). On the whole, the differences are greatest between American and Japanese firms, with European firms lying somewhere in between. Such differences exist even after controlling for differences in industrial composition between MNCs from the three regions.

Perhaps the most striking difference between MNCs from the USA/Europe and Japan in the area of technology management is the degree of linkage to the host economy. This linkage is measured by the extent to which MNCs utilize suppliers from their home countries rather than turning to local suppliers. On the whole, Japanese firms exhibited a much higher propensity to rely on Japanese suppliers over indigenous suppliers. Even where Japanese firms source locally, the suppliers tend to be Japanese firms that have co-located in Singapore to supply the MNC (Wong 1999b).

Another interesting difference is the pattern of process technology transfer by Japanese operations versus firms from the USA (Wong 1999b). On the whole, Japanese firms tend to emphasize transferring process technologies from the parent plant in Japan, while American firms tend to encourage their local subsidiary operations to develop their process capabilities locally. Thus, Japanese firms typically launch new product manufacturing in parent plants in Japan, and only after the process is relatively stable do they consider transferring it to an overseas manufacturing facility in Singapore. A relatively larger number of Japanese expatriate managers and engineers are typically deployed to Singapore to manage the technology transfer process, with the objective of ensuring that the local operation is able to replicate the operational process from, and to achieve comparable productivity with, the parent plant operation. In contrast, many US firms maintain pilot production facilities in the USA and rely on their manufacturing operations in Singapore to launch volume manufacturing of new products. The Singaporean plants are typically asked to develop the manufacturing process while the parent headquarters concentrates on product development. Local managers and engineers are typically sent to the US headquarters to work with the product development team to ensure smooth product–process development coordination. One consequence of this difference in process technology transfer behaviour is that while many US MNCs have established their lead manufacturing plants in Singapore, few Japanese companies have.

A third major difference can be observed in the area of R&D activities. On the whole, US operations in Singapore are perceived as engendering the highest level of technology transfer from the headquarter to the host country. Japanese firms are rated the lowest, with European firms in between (Wong 2000b). American MNCs also give their local R&D departments the highest levels of autonomy and the most challenging R&D work. Japanese MNCs are rated as giving their local R&D departments the lowest levels of autonomy and the least challenging R&D work. Again, the European MNCs ranked somewhere in between (Table 3.2). The R&D staff members of MNCs in Singapore perceive American companies most favourably. These personnel give the US MNCs high marks for career satisfaction, motivation, a positive R&D work environment, and organizational effectiveness. Japanese firms were perceived the least favorably (Table 3.3).

Lastly, the pattern of diversification from manufacturing to non-manufacturing activities also appears to vary among MNCs from the different regions. On the whole, American firms exhibit a higher

Table 3.2   Perceived characteristics of R&D operations in Singapore, 1996

	MNCs from:		
	USA	*Europe*	*Japan*
Autonomy of local R&D	3.43	3.17	2.54
Technology transfer from HQ	3.29	3.22	2.85
Challenging R&D work	2.94	2.48	2.54

Source: Wong (2000b).

Table 3.3   Perception of R&D staff in Singapore

	MNCs from:		
	USA	*Europe*	Japan
Career satisfaction	2.98	2.80	2.42
Work environment for R&D	3.19	2.97	2.59
Motivational factors	3.48	3.16	2.76
Organizational effectiveness	2.87	2.68	2.32

Source: Wong (2000b).

propensity to diversify into a wider range of non-manufacturing activities over the years. These range from regional marketing and technical support to international procurement offices, regional logistics hubs, regional training hubs, and regional software/data processing centres and regional operational headquarters functions. Consequently, many US firms are transferring new services know-how and providing a more diverse source of new learning for their local subsidiary operations in Singapore.

What factors contribute to such diverse styles of technology management by US, European and Japanese firms? One possible factor could be the difference in market orientation. Are the goods made for export, or to be sold in the host domestic (or nearby regional) markets? If they are produced for export, are they destined for third countries or for their home markets? Japanese firms tend to be more oriented to producing for the domestic market. Where they do engage in export manufacturing, the exports tend to be more oriented towards home markets rather than for export to the rest of the world (Wong

Table 3.4   Return on sales (%) of electronics MNCs in Singapore

	1992/3	1993/4	1994/5	1996/7	1997/8
American	7.5	9.4	9.8	12.7	14.9
European	1.3	3.3	3.9	2.0	2.6
Japanese	1.7	2.0	2.3	2.2	1.0

Source: Wong (1999b).

1999b). Such home and host-market orientations may have induced a strong reliance on a nationally based (Japanese) supplier network, and may have led to some shielding from global competition.

Another contributing factor may be the differences in management style. On the whole, Japanese firms in Singapore exhibit a higher degree of control from the parent headquarters, while American firms tend to give their local manufacturing operations more autonomy. Japanese firms also tend to use more expatriate staff, where US firms tend to localize their management. While quite a few US manufacturing MNC operations have local nationals serving as chief executive officers, hardly any Japanese manufacturing firms have. The strong control from the parent headquarters may have contributed to less emphasis on the development of local process capabilities and local R&D autonomy.

Comprehensive data are not available on the relative profitability of American, European and Japanese MNCs in Singapore. However, information on the performance of the largest MNCs in Singapore in the electronics industry over the last five years suggests that American firms substantially outperformed the Japanese firms, with European firms in between (Table 3.4). While the causes for such differences in financial performance may be varied and complex, it is possible that the differences in the management of technology may be a contributing factor.

IMPLICATIONS OF THE ASIAN FINANCIAL CRISIS

One of the effects of the recent Asian financial crisis was a noticeable drop in direct foreign investment in manufacturing in Southeast Asia as a whole. However, Singapore appears to have been an interesting exception: despite retrenchment in the electronics sector (particularly the hard-disk-drive industry), manufacturing FDI remained strong through 1997–99; indeed, Singapore saw an accelerated development in direct foreign investment in the chemical and life-sciences industries.

We expect manufacturing direct foreign investment in the Southeast Asian region as a whole to recover strongly in the year 2000, despite increasing competition from other countries and regions such as China, Ireland, Eastern Europe and Mexico. In particular, we expect a number of global manufacturing trends, which developed prior to the Asian financial crisis, to be further accelerated in the region after the crisis. In particular, we expect the global trend of manufacturing outsourcing and competition on fast production ramp-up to continue (Wong *et al.* 1997). This will spur the growth of local contract manufacturers and the expansion of supplier networks in Southeast Asia. The trend of redistributing manufacturing activities from advanced newly-industrialized economies (NIEs) like Taiwan and Singapore to the emerging NIEs like Malaysia and Thailand in Southeast Asia and China will also be accelerated as these economies continue to liberalize to attract MNCs, and domestic demand resumes its growth.

Such developments are likely to strengthen the Southeast Asian 'economies of heterogeneity' that benefit MNC manufacturing investments. While Singapore will continue to lose various existing lower value-added manufacturing activities to the region, it is likely to retain its role as a regional hub for the most advanced manufacturing activities by global MNCs. The importance of Singapore as a regional logistics and supply-chain management hub for MNCs is also likely to grow, as it consolidates its role as the most advanced transport and communications hub in Southeast Asia.

We believe that the scope for technology development through direct foreign investment by MNCs in Southeast Asia in general and Singapore in particular will be further expanded as we move into the next millennium. Despite recent setbacks in the WTO negotiations, we believe that there will be increasing migration of FDI from labour- and capital-intensive manufacturing to knowledge-intensive industries. Singapore's pivotal regional role for MNCs is likely to be strengthened, not diminished. Its economy is increasingly positioned to attract FDI into newer knowledge-based activities like e-commerce, software publishing, biotechnology and life-sciences R&D, venture capital, and other supporting services for high-tech start-ups. This positioning benefits from government infrastructure initiatives and new policy incentives. Such new developments may provide the opportunity for high-tech start-ups and knowledge-based SMEs from advanced countries to grow in Asia through Singapore. Unlike the giant MNCs that came to Singapore in the 1970s, 1980s and 1990s, the age of the internet may herald in a new generation of smaller, yet even more global, companies. The challenge for Japanese and European companies would be whether they can be as nimble and globally minded as the US firms to leverage Southeast Asia to compete in the new knowledge-based industries of the twenty-first century.

References

Blomström, M. and A. Kokko (1998) 'Multinational Corporations and Spillovers', *Journal of Economic Surveys*, vol. 12(3), pp. 247–77.

Blomström, M. and F. Sjöholm (1999) 'Technology Transfer and Spillovers: Does Local Participation with Multinationals Matter?' *European Economic Review*, vol. 43(4–6), pp. 915–23.

Chuang, Y. C. and C. M. Lin (1999) 'Foreign Direct Investment, R&D and Spillover Efficiency: Evidence from Taiwan's Manufacturing Firms', *Journal of Development Studies*, vol. 35 (4), pp. 117–37.

Dunning, J. H. and R. Narula (1996) 'The Investment Development Path Revisited: Some Emerging Issues', in J. H. Dunning and R. Narula (eds), *Foreign Direct Investment and Governments: Catalysts for Economic Restructuring*, New York: Routledge.

Kagami, M. (1998) 'New Strategies for Asian Technological Development: Problems Facing Technology Transfer and Backward Linkage', in M. Kagami, J. Humphery and M. Piore (eds), *Learning, Liberalization and Economic Adjustment*, Tōkyō: Institute of Developing Economies, pp. 1–32.

Kumar, N. (1998a) 'Technology Generation and Transfers in the World Economy: Recent Trends and Prospects for Developing Countries', in N. Kumar (ed.), *Globalization, Foreign Direct Investment and Technology Transfer: Impacts on and Prospects for Developing Countries*, London and New York: Routledge, pp. 11–42.

Kumar, N. (1998b) 'Foreign Direct Investments and Technology Transfers in an era of Globalization and Prospects for Developing Countries: A Policy Postscript', in N. Kumar (ed.), *Globalization, Foreign Direct Investment and Technology Transfer: Impacts on and Prospects for Developing Countries*, London and New York: Routledge, pp. 197–215.

OECD (1995) *Foreign Direct Investment: OECD Countries and Dynamic Economies of Asia and Latin America*, Paris: OECD Publications.

OECD (1998) *Foreign Direct Investment and Economic Development: Lessons from Six Emerging Economies*, Paris: OECD Publications.

OECD (1999) *OECD Proceedings: Foreign Direct Investment and Recovery in Southeast Asia*, Paris: OECD Publications.

Teece, D. J. (1977) 'Technology Transfer by Multinational Firms: The Resource Cost of International Technology Transfer', *Economic Journal*, vol. 87 (346), pp. 242–61.

Thomsen, S. (1999) 'Southeast Asia: The Role of FDI Policies in Development', OECD Working Papers on International Investment 1999/1, Paris: OECD Publications.

van Hoesel, R. (1996) 'Taiwan: Foreign Direct Investment and the Transformation of the Economy', in J. H. Dunning and R. Narula (eds) *Foreign Direct Investment and Governments: Catalysts for Economic Restructuring*, New York: Routledge, pp. 280–315.

Wong, P. K. (1991) *Technological Development through Subcontracting Linkages*, Tōkyō: Asian Productivity Organization.

Wong. P. K. (1992) 'Technological Development through Subcontracting Linkages: Evidence from Singapore', *Scandinavian International Business Review*, vol. 1(3), pp. 28–40.

Wong, P. K. (1995) 'Technology Transfer and Development Inducement by Foreign MNCs: The Experience of Singapore', Paper presented at the International Conference on Industrial Strategy for Global Competitiveness of Korean Firms, Seoul, Korea, 10 January, 1995.

Wong, P. K. *et al.* (1997) *Development of Internationally Competitive Indigenous Manufacturing Firms in Singapore*. Tōkyō: Foundation for Advanced Studies of International Development (FASID).

Wong, P. K. (1999a) *Competitive Dynamics of the Hard Disk Drive Industry in Singapore*, San Diego: Information Storage Industry Center Research Report.

Wong, P. K. (1999b) 'Globalization of US, European and Japan Production Networks and the Growth of Singapore's Electronics Industry', manuscript submitted to *International Journal of Technology Management*.

Wong, P. K. (2000a) 'Technology Acquisition Pattern of Firms in Different Stages of Industrial Development: A Comparative Analysis of Singapore and Malaysia', Singapore: NUS–CMIT Working Paper.

Wong, P. K. (2000b) 'R&D Management Strategies of American, European and Japanese Firms in Singapore: Differences and their Determinants', NUS-CMIT Working Paper.

Part II
Production

4 Options for Strategic Change: Screwdriver Factories or Integrated Production Systems?

Hideki Yoshihara

INTRODUCTION

The economic crisis in Southeast Asia started in July 1997 when the floating of the Thai baht sparked a currency crisis that soon spread to other Asian countries. The evolving economic crisis may have brought to an end the high growth period in Southeast Asia that lasted for decades or, it may only mean a temporary setback leading to economic renewal. In either case, this economic crisis forces Japanese and European firms both to review their investment strategies in the region and to formulate new strategies for the future. They well may need a new conceptual framework for their decision-making process.

In formulating a production strategy for Southeast Asia, managers must first analyse the current conditions and develop an economic forecast for the region. This requires an understanding of the development of Southeast Asian production. This chapter provides a conceptual framework for dealing with strategic responses to the economic crisis in Southeast Asia by Japanese and European firms in the area of production. The framework intends to be useful both to practicing managers and academic researchers. To encompass the variables regarding production in this area, the conceptual framework must be comprehensive; it consists of the following topics:

- prospects for the Southeast Asian economy;
- development of production;
- new opportunities for manufacturing investment;
- local content issues;
- R&D;
- transfer of production systems;

57

- ownership policy; and
- linkages between Southeast Asia and other parts of the world.

Although the analysis draws mainly on examples and facts from Japanese cases, the conceptual framework presented here is applicable to both Japanese and European firms.

PROSPECTS FOR THE SOUTHEAST ASIAN ECONOMY

Present Economic Crisis

In formulating a production strategy for Southeast Asia, managers of Japanese and European firms should develop an outlook for the economy. Will the present economic crisis end soon or last a long time? Will Southeast Asian countries return to the high economic growth that they experienced in the past? Will their future economic growth rate be lower than in the past? Future action by companies will inevitably depend on the answers to these questions.

The damage caused by the economic crisis varies by country. The crisis hit Indonesia the worst and it will take many years for it to recover. On the other hand, the economy of Singapore was not badly affected and already shows signs of strong growth once again. The effects of the crisis also differ by industry. Thus a macro forecast of future economic conditions by country should be complemented by a micro forecast by industry.

Any formulation of a production strategy for the region needs to begin with an accurate prediction of the future exchange rates for the currencies of the Southeast Asian countries. The economic crisis started as a currency crisis; a sharp currency-devaluation occurred in many countries, the effects of which differ depending on the production strategy of Asian subsidiaries. On the one hand, export-oriented subsidiaries enjoy the advantages of a lower currency value, but at the same time currency devaluation raises the prices of imports. For Asian subsidiaries that use many imported materials and parts in their production, the benefits of a lower currency disappear. Due to the crisis, demand for manufactured goods in the Asian market decreased, so that subsidiaries enjoy the benefits of a lower currency value only when they export to non-Asian countries. The present economic crisis has similarly strong negative effects for foreign subsidiaries whose products are sold in their local markets where they are located. These companies face difficulties on both the production side and the market side. Higher prices for imports raise production costs while the economic slump lowers demand for products.

Countries and Regions

Our attention focuses on the strategic responses of Japanese and European firms to the economic crisis in Southeast Asia. However, it is necessary to have a wider focus in mind that includes other Asian countries and regions such as Korea, Hong Kong and China. We often talk about the Asian economy or production in Asia treating Asia as one region, but in reality Asia is composed of many countries and economies like Hong Kong or Indonesia which are at strikingly different stages of economic development.

In terms of economic development and per capita GDP, Asian countries, with the exclusion of Japan, fall into four groups (see Table 4.1). The advanced economies of Singapore and Hong Kong make up the first group, in which the per capita GDP of both economies exceeds that of many countries in the EU. Taiwan and Korea, the other two newly-industrializing economies (NIEs), form the second group. Malaysia, Thailand, Indonesia and the Philippines belong to the

Table 4.1 Per capita gross domestic product (US$) of selected Asian countries, 1980, 1990, 1996 and 1998

	1980	*1990*	*1996*	*1998*
Japan	9 146	24 273	36 553	30 120
Singapore	4 682	13 784	30 897	26 710
Hong Kong	5 624	13 111	24 490	24 892
Taiwan	2 325	7 870	12 731	11 958
Korea	1 643	5 917	10 548	6 908
Malaysia	1 785	2 415	4 627	3 199
Thailand	693	1 527	3 175	1 895
Indonesia	491	590	1 140	1 074*
Philippines	675	714	1 162	1 118*
China	302	342	670	770
Vietnam	n.a.	97	317	303
Myanmar	174	573	2 653	3 686*
Laos	n.a.	207	376	338*

Notes: *=1997; figures for Myanmar are based on official exchange rates.
Source: Keizai Kikakuchō (1997); ASEAN Centre (1998).

third group. The emerging economies of China, Vietnam, Myanmar, Cambodia and Laos constitute the fourth group. To complicate the matter, China itself is composed of regions at different stages of economic development with coastal regions being clearly more advanced than inland regions. Differences in the levels of economic development suggest a variety of options for production strategies in the region.

Employment strategies based on the nature of production reflect one approach to the different levels of economic development in the region. Japanese and European firms in labour-intensive industries like textiles and consumer electronics focus their interest on the third group, or countries of the fourth group including China and Vietnam, in order to secure low-wage labour. Even taking into account different levels of productivity, these workers cost less than one-tenth of their Japanese and European counterparts.

When Japanese and European firms need human resources of a higher level, such as engineers, technicians, managers and skilled workers, production strategy might suggest a turn towards the countries of the first and second group. In Singapore, for example, scientists and engineers with skills considered equal to Japanese or European personnel seek employment. As one can see in the case of strategies towards labour, the analysis of Southeast Asian countries should be placed within the framework of a greater Asia that incorporates the differing economies of the neighbouring countries and regions.

Location for Production and/or Sales

Asia was long considered an important place for production mainly because of its abundant low-wage workforce. Markets in Asia for manufactured goods, however, were not well-developed; although Asia always had a large population, overall consumption levels remained low since per capita income was low. The number of middle-class people with substantial buying power was limited in most countries. Thus, manufacturers in Asia exported many products to other areas such as North America, Europe and Japan.

As Asian economies developed, the situation gradually changed until per capita GDP in some Asian countries became equal to or even surpassed that of some advanced European countries in the last decade. During this period, the number of middle-class people in many of the Southeast Asian countries increased. In the 1990s, Asian buying power strengthened and Asia became an important market in itself with the result that many companies could sell most of their products in local markets or in the markets of surrounding Asian countries. Trade liberalization progressed both in Southeast Asia and in other parts of Asia, and foreign manufacturing subsidiaries increased the local content of their products. In addition, trade in intermediate goods such as parts and materials increased among manufacturing firms in Asia. In this way Asia became an important market for both consumer and industrial goods. Thus, Asia will keep its position as an important place for production while it becomes equally important as a market.

China

China is not a Southeast Asian country but it exercises an important influence on the economy of Southeast Asia both as a competitor and a market for Asian products. There are two contrasting views of the future of China. Optimists assert that China will keep its position as the fastest growing country in the world and become the second largest economic power behind the USA. They see China developing as an open, market-oriented economy that will continue to attract investment from Japanese, European and other multinational firms seeking business opportunities in China. Pessimists predict that China will face serious economic, social and political difficulties in the future. Any attempts towards an open, market-oriented economy will widen the economic inequality among people and also among regions, and the restructuring of state-owned companies will increase unemployment. As a result, the economic, social and political systems of China might become highly unstable and possibly devolve into several semi-independent political and economic entities. This would make it difficult for China to continue its high economic growth and thus poses a warning sign to managers. Whether the optimists or the pessimists turn out to be right, the political and economic changes in China will continue to influence the economic fate of Southeast Asian countries.

DEVELOPMENT OF PRODUCTION IN ASIA

Asian countries have attracted strong manufacturing investment from foreign firms, including Japanese and European companies, since the

1960s. Over time, the production of these overseas subsidiaries in Southeast Asia and other parts of Asia has changed in many ways (Yoshihara 1997).

First, the scale of production increased dramatically. In the past the majority of factories were small, and since they suffered diseconomies of scale their production costs were relatively high. These subsidiaries were competitive only in local markets that usually benefited from heavy government protection. Gradually, companies expanded overseas production facilities and often the size of subsidiary factories exceeded that of the parent plant. Such subsidiaries increasingly enjoy scale economies and are becoming competitive in international markets.

Second, parent companies upgraded the manufacturing technologies of their subsidiaries. Until the first half of the 1980s, parent companies kept high technology at home and left low technology to their Asian subsidiaries; home-country plants produced new products that embodied high technology while Asian plants manufactured mature products with standardized technology. A similar kind of division occurred in production technology. Factories of parent firms had the newest production equipment such as robots and computer-controlled machines, whilst the production technology in the Asian factories was simpler, depending more on manual work, thus reflecting the different comparative advantages. This division of labour has become less clear over time. Now, many Japanese and Western factories in Southeast Asia operate at the same technological level as their home parent firms.

The third change occurred in the area of production integration. Screwdriver-type plants were typical in Asia in the past, both for Japanese and Western companies. Usually the parent firms supplied them with semi-finished parts (knock-down production), and Asian subsidiaries simply assembled products. Now, factories that manufacture parts and components in-house have increased.

Fourth, subsidiaries shifted their market orientation to exports as they gained competitiveness on an international level. Furthermore, the change from local market orientation to export orientation has been encouraged by a change in host-government policies (Masuyama, Vandenbrink and Chia 1997). Until 1980, governments generally promoted an import-substitution industrialization policy, after which Asian governments gradually changed their policies towards export promotion and foreign firms have responded to this policy change.

NEW OPPORTUNITIES FOR INVESTMENT

As industries develop in Southeast Asia, new opportunities will open up for manufacturing investment in the region. One of these opportunities is investment in the production of parts and materials and thus in the area of supporting industries. Manufacturing subsidiaries in Asia produce finished goods, both consumer and industrial goods. Subsidiaries in Asian countries manufacture cars, colour televisions, videocassette recorders, personal computers, and many other types of modern high-technology equipment. The production processes is mainly characterized by participation in the final processes of assembly or fabrication, but Asian countries still depend on outside sources for materials and parts. Although foreign manufacturing subsidiaries have increased their production integration, they still depend on their parent companies and other outside sources for intermediate goods.

The governments of most Asian nations encourage investment that increases the local production of parts and materials in order to reduce imports. In the process, governments hope to achieve a more balanced industrial structure. In the case of Japanese industries, small- and medium-sized companies in Japan mainly manufacture parts and materials, and host governments in Asian countries welcome investment by those firms. Investment by such companies, particularly suppliers for the electronic and automobile industries, rose dramatically in the 1990s. Even more important than the positive stance of host governments appears to be the rising need for capable local suppliers that has arisen from the shift to more integrated production systems and the need to foster international competitiveness.

Concretely, one can point to investment in production equipment and software as another new opportunity for foreign manufacturing investment. Production conditions differ all over Asia, so the equipment and software for production used at the parent company often fails to fit conditions in Asian subsidiaries. This point is of special concern for European companies. Local adaptation is necessary and will gradually develop into local production.

LOCAL CONTENT ISSUES

Local content issues have political and economic dimensions. In the past the local content problems in Asia were more political than economic; host governments, for example, demanded that foreign subsidiaries use locally secured materials and parts. However, local products generally meant low quality, high prices and, often, unreliable delivery. Local suppliers were unaccustomed to cooperation in cost-reduction and quality-improvement measures. To meet local content requirements, foreign firms often had to sacrifice economic interests for political interests.

During the 1990s, the situation changed; foreign firms increased the use of locally purchased materials and parts. They did so for reasons of cost-cutting, rather than for politics. The Asian manufacturing subsidiaries of Japanese firms have continuously decreased the volume of materials and parts they import from Japan; although Japanese parts and materials are usually of higher quality, they have become too expensive for foreign subsidiaries seeking to profit in the international market. Now, even without demands from host governments, local subsidiaries themselves energetically increase the local content of their products. European firms have also experienced this kind of change.

There are basically three methods subsidiaries use to increase the local content of their products. The first is to purchase from local suppliers among the rising number of local firms that manufacture parts, materials and machines. Such supporting industries have developed in Taiwan and Korea but also in Southeast Asian countries such as Singapore and Malaysia (mainly in electronics) or Thailand (mainly in the automobile industry). In the development of local suppliers, technology and management guidance by foreign firms has played an important role. As local firms often lack sufficient technological capabilities and management resources they cannot meet the severe cost, quality and service demands of foreign customers. Foreign firms send their managers and engineers to the factories of local suppliers and provide advice on matters of technology and management. There are also many cases in which managers of local suppliers are sent to parent firms in Europe and Japan for training.

The second method for raising the local content is to purchase from the subsidiaries of foreign firms. Recently, foreign subsidiaries whose products are of an intermediate nature have been increasing; such foreign firms are often medium- and small-sized companies from Japan, but also increasingly from Europe, the USA and other more developed Asian countries. In general, the rapid development and maturing of industry in Southeast Asia has attracted a rising share of investment by foreign manufacturers of intermediate goods.

Third, some subsidiaries themselves have started to manufacture parts and materials through in-house production. Under this strategy, foreign firms might establish new subsidiaries, with the potential benefit that the parent company can avoid the difficulty of managing a diversified firm. Also, the subsidiary can often make use of incentives provided by host governments such as pioneer status or tax incentives.

RESEARCH AND DEVELOPMENT IN ASIA

Foreign investment in Asia has now entered a new stage of development that includes local R&D investment (Itagaki 1997; Sakakibara 1995; Yoshihara 1997). It is important to consider why foreign firms conduct R&D in Asia. Local R&D is required to meet the needs of local customers; products developed for home-country customers in Japan and Europe sometimes do not necessarily satisfy the needs of local customers of consumer and industrial goods. Differences revolve around price, function, size, colour and form, and in many cases a local response is the most effective way to modify products. Local adaptation through local R&D also seems to be necessary in the area of production equipment, since equipment used at parent factories is often ill-suited to Asian subsidiaries (see next section).

A quick response to changes in local markets also demands local R&D. Market conditions are almost constantly changing in Asia, through population growth, urbanization, industrialization and economic growth. When R&D is done at the parent firm, it takes more time to accommodate the changes in the local market, particularly when information on changes in customer needs must be transmitted from the Asian subsidiaries to the parent firm.

Physical closeness of R&D with production is a third reason why foreign firms continue to expand overseas R&D. The number of cases is increasing in which products are only produced in foreign subsidiaries, to which parent firms have shifted production of low-price, mature products. Effective production requires frequent exchange of information and close interaction between the section that organizes production and the section that supervises R&D. Difficulties that researchers and developers at parent firms may have in understanding changes in local markets may be compounded by attention to the specific production conditions in foreign plants.

Local R&D is also important in attracting talented local employees. University graduates want to work in firms that do innovative work, and producing goods designed at parent firms in Japan or Europe does not satisfy their needs for innovation. Such employees are looking for work that consists of more than repetitive production; unless engaged in a challenging career, they may gradually lose motivation and even leave the company.

R&D in Asia is also promoted from the standpoint of an international division of R&D between parent firms and foreign subsidiaries. There are lots of tasks to be dealt with in the R&D organization of parent firms and many have to be achieved within tight limits. This situation may be solved by simultaneously conducting R&D at foreign subsidiaries. In addition, local R&D effectively cuts costs by increasing the local content of products used by foreign subsidiaries; as mentioned above, materials and parts imported from parent countries are inclined to be expensive. R&D organizations of parent companies tend to develop products with materials and parts secured in their home-country markets, and to achieve low-cost production it is necessary to reduce the use of these expensive inputs. One way to do so is to use locally designed products that use more local materials and parts.

Foreign subsidiaries conducting local R&D are challenging traditional theories of multinational enterprises. One such theory, the product-cycle theory, emphasizes the actions of parent companies in developing new products. Initially, the parent firm manufactures products for the home market; as demand for the products grows in foreign countries, the firm begins exporting. Subsequently, the firm begins local manufacturing abroad, first in advanced countries such as in Europe, and then in less-developed countries as in Asia. In this view, foreign subsidiaries are passive recipients of R&D.

This conventional wisdom about the division of labour between parent companies and their foreign subsidiaries is now being challenged. Foreign subsidiaries increasingly develop new products and new production equipment; they even transfer innovations to parent companies or other foreign subsidiaries. The transfer of R&D can follow three patterns: orthodox, reverse and horizontal transfer. Under the orthodox pattern, parent companies transfer the results of research to foreign subsidiaries; technology transfer usually follows this orthodox pattern. In reverse transfer, the foreign subsidiary sends R&D results to the parent company. Horizontal transfer occurs among foreign subsidiaries. As R&D at foreign subsidiaries increases, the second and the third types of transfer of R&D results can be expected to rise.

TRANSFER OF PRODUCTION SYSTEMS

Production systems are composed of production equipment, production management and organizational culture. Production equipment is the hardware of the production system including machines, belt conveyers, tools, test instruments or jigs. Because the machinery industry is generally undeveloped in most Asian countries, foreign firms have difficulties in securing the necessary hardware in local markets. Core production equipment, which is often designed and fabricated in-house by the parent firms, is transferred to foreign subsidiaries. Less-important machines such as conveyers, instruments and tools are sometimes secured in local markets.

As pointed out above, parent companies can rarely achieve the complete transfer of production facilities to foreign subsidiaries (Yamashita 1991; Itagaki 1997). Production in developing countries is generally characterized by the following:

- small-scale production;
- low wages;
- unskilled workers;
- insufficient maintenance;
- shortage of engineers, technicians and managers;
- underdeveloped supporting industries; and
- underdeveloped infrastructure.

Such conditions demand that companies adapt their production equipment, and such adaptation may be pursued in various ways. Some companies scale down or simplify their operations; others employ equipment that requires little maintenance. Robots, computer-controlled machines and other sophisticated equipment typical at the factories of the parent firm appear less frequently in the factories of foreign subsidiaries. However, this is changing. Recently, many multinationals have introduced the newest production equipment in their Asian subsidiaries as they emphasize quality over cost.

The second element of the production system is production management. The factories of the parent firm usually have a mother–daughter relationship with the plants of foreign subsidiaries. This relationship is especially strong in the case of Japanese companies. Subsidiaries depend on the mother plants in the home countries not only for the facilities necessary for production, but also for production management know-how. Parent factories provide instruction based on manuals while the firm organizes workers in the subsidiary much as it organizes workers at the parent firm. The physical layout of machines, belt conveyer and other production equipment in the subsidiaries mirrors the layout of the mother plant; and the company introduces quality control methods from the parent factories to subsidiary plants abroad. Many Japanese foreign factories have quality control circle activities that were originally developed at the home country's plants.

Thirdly, parent firms tend to transfer their organizational culture to foreign plants. For Japanese manufacturers, organizational culture emphasizes cleanliness and discipline, egalitarianism, *genbashugi* (management on the spot), team-play and information sharing. European firms also try to transfer their organizational culture to foreign plants although often to a lesser degree than their Japanese counterparts.

OWNERSHIP POLICY

From the standpoint of ownership, we should first distinguish between wholly-owned subsidiaries and joint ventures. Joint ventures themselves are classified as majority-owned joint ventures, 50–50 joint ventures and minority-owned joint ventures. Issues of control, corporate resources and government policy can shape the strategic decisions regarding ownership.

Control is most complete in the case of wholly-owned subsidiaries. Companies that choose this arrangement most often cite freedom from interference by partners as their reason for opting for complete ownership. Corporate resources necessary for doing business in foreign countries include foreign language ability, knowledge of local conditions, methods of management appropriate to the culture of local employees, marketing in local markets, and the ability to negotiate effectively with local governments. Foreign firms operating in Southeast Asia often lack an efficient way to gather these kinds of resources on their own. In joint ventures, foreign firms may expect local partners to provide these resources.

The issues of control and corporate resources come together when the company confronts government policy. In Southeast Asian countries, the importance of good relations with the local government continues to be a concern (Stopford and Wells 1971; Yoshihara 1997). Generally speaking, the governments of developing countries in Asia prefer joint ventures to wholly-owned subsidiaries. They encourage majority ownership by local partners, a characteristic reflected in the many minority shares foreign companies hold in joint ventures in the region today.

In the 1990s, host governments gradually relaxed constraints on foreign ownership, and particularly since the start of the economic crisis in 1997 they have increasingly accepted full foreign ownership. For firms investing in high-technology or export-oriented enterprises, relaxation of controls on ownership has been especially evident. This trend has been most obvious in the cases of supporting industries, undeveloped rural regions, and investment involving medium- and small-sized firms. Southeast Asian countries welcome this investment because they expect it to contribute to the development of domestic industries.

ASIA IN GLOBAL PRODUCTION

Relative Importance of Asia

In formulating a production strategy for Asia, managers must decide how important Asia or a single Asian country is within their global production network. For Japanese firms, Japan, Asia, the USA and Europe are important sites for production. Until the 1970s, Japan occupied a dominant position in these four locations before Asia and then the USA rapidly increased in importance. Recently, China has become a very important place of production for Japanese companies competing with Southeast Asia for investment in an increasing number of industries.

For most European firms, Asia has been of less importance in their production location portfolio to date. Will European companies increasingly emphasize Southeast and Northeast Asia in their global production strategies? Will they increase investment in China? In making these decisions on the importance of Asia as a site for production, European firms will probably have to compare the merits of production in Asia with the merits of production in Eastern European countries.

International Division of Production

The international division of production between parent companies and their Asian subsidiaries has several dimensions reflecting decisions about where the company produces its products, the integration of the production process, and the distribution of technology between the parent company and the subsidiary. In making production strategy decisions for Asia, it is important to consider all of these dimensions. Before the 1990s, Asian subsidiaries mainly produced mature products while parent companies concentrated on new products. There were basically two reasons why mature products were produced in Asia, the first reason being costs. Production costs are an important factor for mature products and low wages in Asia have always been very attractive. The second reason is technology. In general, the production technology of mature goods is standardized which means this kind of technology is more certain, more stable, and thus easier to handle.

Generally, parent company factories took the lead in innovation for a number of reasons. Production costs are less important in new products because buyers of these products pay attention to new features rather than price. Also, constant communication between the producer and early buyers is necessary to improve the products. By definition, innovative production technology is more uncertain and vulnerable, thus requiring well-trained technicians and workers. Such workers are more available in developed countries than in the developing economies of Asia. Smooth production, without interruption, is critical in realizing low-cost production. Direct labour costs usually amount to about 10 per cent of total manufacturing costs, and production interruptions greatly increase total costs. Products rejected by customers require additional labour, time and equipment for their repair, thus raising costs. Companies should therefore not introduce new and unstable production technology to foreign subsidiaries at too early a stage.

Production integration constitutes the second dimension of the international division of production. The production process consists of stages ranging from material production to parts production and the final stages of assembly or processing. The recent change from so-called screwdriver plants to more integrated methods of production cannot be overemphasized. Also, companies are switching to in-house production where no local suppliers are available. When manufacturers do not produce parts in-house, they try to procure them from local suppliers. To do so, foreign firms sometimes provide technical guidance to local parts manufacturers. Japanese firms provide such technical guidance through Japanese-affiliated supplier companies because sometimes the parent companies do not have the necessary technology and knowledge.

Technology is the third dimension of the international division of production. As mentioned above, the distinctions in this area have become less clear as home parent companies spread the use of advanced production technology to subsidiaries. Today, Asian subsidiaries of Japanese and Western firms manufacture new products and use advanced production technologies.

Production in Asia and in the Home Country

Managers must balance production in the home country with production in Asia when making strategic decisions. Increasing production in Asian subsidiaries may decrease production by the parent company and lead to the so-called hollowing out in the home country. This is a fairly recent development for Japanese companies, more so than is the case with European companies (see Legewie 1999). However, hollowing out is not inevitable.

One strategy to avoid hollowing out is to change (mainly upgrade) the products that the parent firm manufactures. Products manufactured at foreign subsidiaries are low-priced and technologically mature. To compensate for a decrease in production of such goods at home, parent firms must increase production of technologically sophisticated, newly developed products. In a second approach, companies can avoid the ill effects of sending production abroad by developing new products. Thus parent firms maintain production of new products at their home plants while shifting the production of mature products to their foreign factories.

A third strategy is to increase production of parts and components. Under this approach, foreign subsidiaries produce finished products and parent firms produce parts and components for these finished goods. The implementation of this division will gradually change parent firms from assembly-oriented manufacturers to manufacturers of components. This kind of change is widely observed in Japanese and European companies, where some firms now resemble machine-tool manufacturers. They sell equipment fabricated for their own production on the open market, a practice that in turn opens up new lines of business.

Finally, a diversification strategy is required to prevent the hollowing out of parent firms. One approach is for companies to enter related product-market fields. For example, consumer electronics firms may diversify into industrial electronics. In another approach, a company may jump into an unrelated business; an iron and steel firm, for example, might produce semiconductors or enter non-manufacturing businesses.

CONCLUDING REMARKS

In light of the strategic concerns of firms reevaluating their approach to production in Southeast Asia as outlined above, there are five points that bear emphasis:

1. Managers must decide whether or not the current economic crisis in Southeast Asia will continue. If they decide that the economy of Southeast Asia will recover in the short term, then Japanese and European firms should not change their basic production strategies; they should instead respond to the economic crisis by adapting their production operations.
2. Understanding the past development of production in Southeast Asia is a useful basis for conceiving production strategies for the future. Despite rapid changes in Southeast Asia and its environs, managers can still learn from historical developments.
3. Managers should take a broad view of the problem of implementing production strategies. Besides focusing on production operation, they must attend to R&D and the procurement of materials and parts.
4. The analysis of any Southeast Asian country should include the broader context of Asia as a whole. China and Northeast Asian countries like Korea and Taiwan have intimate relationships with Southeast Asian countries.
5. The importance of Southeast Asia seems to remain different for Japanese and European firms. The physical proximity of Japanese companies to their Southeast Asian subsidiaries (compared to European firms and their subsidiaries in the region) influences perceptions. Japanese firms see the subsidiaries as a close extension of their domestic manufacturing process. In contrast, European firms tend to see Southeast Asia as a remote, untapped frontier that is growing in importance as a market.

References

ASEAN Centre (1998) *ASEAN–Japan Statistical Pocketbook*, Tōkyō: ASEAN Centre.

Bartlett, C. A. and S. Ghoshal (1989) *Managing across Borders: The Transnational Solution*, Boston, Mass.: Harvard Business School Press.

Ishida, H. (1999) *Kokusai keiei to howaito kara* [International Management and White-collar], Tōkyō: Chūō Keizai-sha.

Itagaki, H. (ed.) (1997) *The Japanese Production System: Hybrid Factories in East Asia*, London: Macmillan.

Keizai Kikakuchō (1997) *Ajia keizai 1997* [The Asian Economy 1997], Tōkyō: Ōkurashō Insatsukyoku.

Legewie, J. (1999) 'The Impact of FDI on Domestic Employment: The Phenomenon of Industrial Hollowing Out in Japan', in N. Phelps and J. Alden (eds), *Foreign Direct Investment and the Global Economy: Corporate and Institutional Dynamics of Global-Localisation*, London: The Stationery Office/Regional Studies Association, pp. 179–99.

Masuyama, S., D. Vandenbrink and S. Y. Chia (eds) (1997) *Industrial Policies in East Asia*, Tōkyō: Tōkyō Club Foundation for Global Studies.

Sakakibara, K. (1995) *Nihon kigyō no kenkyū kaihatsu manejimento* [Management of R&D by Japanese Firms], Tōkyō: Chikura Shobō.

Stopford, J. M. and L. T. Wells, Jr. (1971) *Managing the Multinational Enterprise*, New York: Basic Books.

Vernon, R. (1971) *Sovereignty at Bay: The Multinational Spread of U.S. Enterprises*, New York: Basic Books.

Yamashita, S. (ed.) (1991) *Transfer of Japanese Technology and Management to the ASEAN Countries*, Tōkyō: University of Tōkyō Press.

Yoshihara, H. (1997) *Kokusai keiei* [International Management], Tōkyō: Yuhikaku.

5 Production Strategies of Japanese Firms: Building up a Regional Production Network

Jochen Legewie

INTRODUCTION

The immediate effect of the Asian economic crisis has been a clearly negative one for most manufacturers in Southeast Asia, and Japanese affiliates in ASEAN countries are no exception to this observation. Two questions arise immediately regarding the short-term measures of Japanese manufacturers to overcome the negative impact of the crisis, and their long-term strategic responses to strengthen their position in the region for the medium and far future. The analysis of both short- and long-term reactions are important and interesting for at least two reasons.

First, Japanese companies have built up a strong and leading production presence in many regional industries which makes their attitude towards production in Southeast Asia crucial for the further development of the manufacturing sector of that region. In the FY 1996 (fiscal year, April 1996 to March 1997) just before the crisis, the production value of Japanese affiliates in Southeast Asia for the first time exceeded 10 trillion yen. This is four times more than in 1989 and represents more than 60 per cent of the total overseas production volume of Japanese firms in Asia (see Table 5.1).

Second, the early start of production by Japanese manufacturers in Southeast Asia and the strong production linkages that exist between these affiliates and Japan have so far made Japanese regional production strategies distinctively different from their European and American counterparts. Whether and in which form such differences will continue to exist in the future, are highly relevant questions not only for Southeast Asian countries and Western competitors but also for the academic discussion dealing with national differences in the

74

Table 5.1 Production value of Japanese foreign affiliates in Asia by industry
in FY 1996

	ASEAN 6		NIEs 3		China		Asia total	
	bn yen	%	bn yen	%	bn yen	%	bn yen	%
Electronics	4 629	44.6	1 669	34.5	442	34.9	6 742	39.6
Transport equip.	2 244	21.6	833	17.2	318	25.1	4 121	24.2
Gen. machinery	394	3.8	456	9.4	99	7.8	961	5.7
Precision instr.	100	1.0	253	5.2	71	5.6	424	2.5
Iron & steel	400	3.8	157	3.2	28	2.2	496	2.9
Non-ferrous metals	303	2.9	105	2.2	8	0.6	415	2.4
Chemicals	723	7.0	389	8.1	81	6.4	1 222	7.2
Textiles	302	2.9	525	10.9	123	9.7	952	5.6
Foodstuffs	275	2.6	192	4.0	19	1.5	485	2.9
Others	1 014	9.8	255	5.3	76	6.0	1 190	7.0
Total	10 384	100	4 834	100	1 265	100	17 008	100

Note: ASEAN 6 = Singapore, Malaysia, Thailand, Indonesia, Philippines,
Vietnam. NIEs 3 = Taiwan, Korea, Hong Kong.
Source: TSS (1999a, p. 159).

internationalizing strategies of multinational firms (Yip, Johansson
and Roos 1996; Birkinshaw and Hood 1998; Buckley and Casson 1998;
Bartlett and Ghoshal 1989; and Young in this volume).

   To tackle the question regarding the strategic response by Japanese
manufacturers to the economic crisis in Southeast Asia from both the
short-term and long-term points of view, this chapter will be divided
into three main sections followed by concluding remarks. The next
section briefly explains the direct effects of the crisis on Japanese
affiliates in the region with special reference to existing procurement
and sales linkages. We then describe the direct short-term countermeasures taken by Japanese firms in the first two years since the start
of the crisis in the summer of 1997. Following this, in the main part of
the chapter, we provide an analysis of the long-term regional reorganization of production by Japanese companies. The analysis focuses on
the shift from domestic to regional production strategies that started
well before the crisis but which is still far from being totally implemented. Identifying the main characteristics, including the strengths
and weaknesses, of these new regional production strategies allows us
to draw conclusions regarding the future behaviour and performance
of Japanese manufacturers not only in Southeast Asia but within the
whole Asian region.

DIRECT EFFECTS OF THE ASIAN CRISIS ON JAPANESE PRODUCTION IN SOUTHEAST ASIA

Figure 5.1 presents the results of a survey conducted by the Export–Import Bank of Japan among 352 Japanese affiliates in Malaysia, Thailand, Indonesia and the Philippines in the summer of 1998. It provides a good overview of the extent to which the Asian crisis has affected Japanese manufacturers in ASEAN countries in general, and the differences between single industries and firms.

81.7 per cent of all manufacturing affiliates suffered either adverse or substantially adverse effects, while only a mere 6.1 per cent stated a positive overall influence for their company. A different picture emerges when we look at single industries. Manufacturers of automobiles or automobile parts, steel and chemicals suffered the most from the crisis with more than 90 per cent of them citing at least adverse effects, while not a single firm stated a positive impact. On the other hand, Japanese companies of the electronics and textile sectors did not only endure less substantial adverse effects (65–75 per cent), but even sometimes confirmed a positive overall impact as did 14.3 per cent in the case of electronics assemblers. Hence, there were not only different effects between single industries, but also between single firms within the same industry.

Both the overall negative picture but also the inter- and intra-industry differences can be mainly explained by the structure of sales and procurement linkages of Japanese affiliates in Southeast Asia as given prior to the crisis (see Tables 5.2 and 5.3). Table 5.2 illustrates the striking differences between industries immediately before the crisis. The very low export ratios for automobiles, steel and chemicals were the main reasons that these industries were hit the hardest by the Asian crisis through the enormous drop in local and regional demand.

Affiliates of Japanese electronic companies, by contrast, benefited from their high export ratio to non-Asian markets (58.5 per cent in FY 1996) which allowed them to profit from devalued ASEAN currencies and a subsequent rise in competitiveness over other regions. These eventual gains were, however, limited by their low local procurement ratio of 33.3 per cent and their strong dependency on imported parts and components from Japan, to be paid for in either US dollars or Japanese yen.

In addition, this intensified competition resulting from an over-supply led to a deterioration of prices in regional and world markets affecting even the profit performance of export-oriented companies

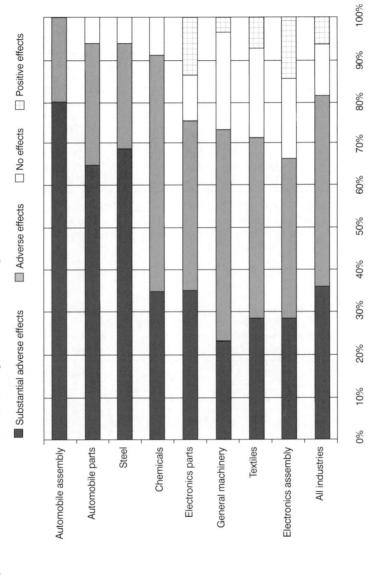

Figure 5.1 Effects of the Asian crisis on Japanese manufacturing affiliates in ASEAN 4

Note: ASEAN 4 = Malaysia, Thailand, Indonesia, Philippines.
Source: Nihon Yushutsunyū Ginkō (1999, p. 53).

Production Strategies of Japanese Firms

Table 5.2   Procurement and sales linkages of Japanese affiliates in
ASEAN 4 in FYs 1995/96

	Source of procurement (%)				Direction of sales (%)			
	Local market	Other Asia	Total Asia	Japan	Local market	Other Asia	Total Asia	Total export
Electronics	33.3	27.4	61.1	37.7	34.9	21.6	56.5	65.1
Transport equip.	40.1	0.7	40.8	57.0	92.1	0.4	92.5	7.9
Gen. machinery	39.7	8.5	48.2	51.5	50.4	9.2	59.6	49.6
Precision instr.	67.1	1.9	69.0	28.6	31.6	0.0	31.6	68.4
Iron & steel	27.4	5.1	32.5	58.6	94.0	2.8	96.8	6.0
NF metals	37.9	16.1	54.0	24.1	57.8	17.4	75.2	42.2
Chemicals	48.9	15.5	64.4	27.7	82.7	10.6	93.3	17.3
Textiles	55.1	6.3	61.4	27.1	48.6	14.7	63.3	51.4
Foodstuffs	97.9	0.9	98.8	1.0	33.7	7.4	41.1	66.3
Total average	41.3	12.7	54.0	42.0	62.6	10.9	73.5	37.4

Note: ASEAN 4 = Malaysia, Thailand, Indonesia, Philippines; Asia does not include Japan. All data given here were calculated as average figures for two years (FYs 1995 and 1996) to avoid extreme one-year figures.
Source: TSS (1998, 1999a).

Table 5.3   Procurement and sales linkages of Japanese affiliates in
ASEAN 4 in FY 1992 and FY 1996

	Source of procurement (%)				Direction of sales (%)			
	Local market		Total Asia		Local market		Total Asia	
	FY 92	FY 96	FY 92	FY 96	FY 92	FY 96	FY 92	FY 96
Electronics	39.7	35.3	55.6	60.0	19.7	21.0	29.8	41.5
Transport equip.	51.4	44.5	52.7	45.0	92.3	90.7	92.8	91.1
Gen. machinery	42.6	43.0	42.6	47.6	37.3	64.7	48.5	71.2
Precision instr.	26.3	69.8	26.3	69.8	19.7	42.4	19.7	42.4
Iron & steel	41.5	38.7	66.6	42.7	93.9	92.5	94.1	97.8
NF metals	65.3	39.6	68.5	61.3	52.5	59.4	66.9	79.8
Chemicals	57.9	59.8	62.1	76.1	83.8	83.7	93.2	92.8
Textiles	40.8	74.1	50.9	75.0	51.3	46.1	65.4	58.3
Foodstuffs	94.8	98.2	97.9	98.7	36.2	73.7	46.4	77.8
Total average	50.0	44.7	57.2	56.8	65.1	58.9	75.2	70.5

Note: See Table 5.2.
Source: TSS (1994, 1999a).

like electronics component-makers and assemblers. Although the sales volume of Japanese affiliates in electronics, precision instruments, general machinery and textiles, which are all export-oriented industries, rose in all ASEAN 4 countries by more than 10 per cent in FY 1997, profits decreased over the same time in all those countries (TSS 1999b, pp. 68–9), a picture that did not change much in 1998. Due to a very bad performance in Thailand and Indonesia in FY 1997, Japanese manufacturing affiliates even turned in a total operating loss of 68 billion yen in the ASEAN 4. This presents a dramatic turn to the former years when the ASEAN 4 had been the most profitable region for Japanese firms abroad (TSS 1999b, p. 30).

The analysis of the procurement and sales structure of ASEAN affiliates of Japanese manufacturers as described in Tables 5.2 and 5.3 thus helps us to understand the immediate impact of the Asian crisis on sales and profits of Japanese firms in this region. This structure is also significant for the understanding of short-term countermeasures to the crisis as well as long-term regional production strategies that will be discussed in more detail in the next two sections. At least a few points deserve to be highlighted here.

First, despite a remarkable decline of the local procurement ratio in most industries since FY 1992, the ratio for regional procurement stayed stable at about 57 per cent on average (Table 5.3). This implies that Japanese firms have succeeded to some extent in shifting from local to regional suppliers, thus making some progress in implementing a regional strategy in terms of procurement. At the same time, though, the overall degree of dependence on non-regional suppliers (mainly from Japan) remained the same indicating that parts and components from Japan will continue to play a pivotal role for any production system of Japanese firms in Southeast Asia.

Second, within sales, a regional (other Asia) export ratio of only a little more than 10 per cent (Table 5.2) shows that most of the Japanese production in Southeast Asia is either oriented to domestic or to overseas markets in North America, Europe or Japan. Other ASEAN markets or other parts of Asia like Taiwan, Korea or China still play a very small role as export destinations. While this implies a large market potential for future regional strategies directed at Asian markets, any growth expectations must not be exaggerated.

Third, looking at different industries reveals that one industry clearly stands apart from the overall picture of weak regional procurement and sales linkages. Japanese electronics affiliates not only strongly procure on a regional basis (27.4 per cent in FY 1995/96), they also sell more than 20 per cent to other Asian countries (Table 5.2). No other industry gets close to this level of regional production and sales networks. Thus, any analysis of the present and future behaviour of Japanese manufacturers in Asia has to take into account this characteristic that might also serve as some kind of model for changes to be expected in other industries over the next years.

SHORT-TERM COUNTERMEASURES BY JAPANESE MANUFACTURERS

Dealing with the direct countermeasures to the crisis taken by Japanese manufacturers since 1997, we will first look at recent changes in procurement. In general, cost reductions are possible by a shift to cheaper raw materials and/or by an increase of local or regional procurement. A shift to new input materials is one of the aims of the recently increasing number of regional research and development (R&D) centres of Japanese firms, but it is difficult to achieve in the short run. Thus, we will deal with this measure only in the next section. Within procurement, Japanese machinery industries achieved a remarkable rise of 3 percentage points on average in regional purchases in the first year after the start of the crisis (TSS 1999b, p. 71). An especially successful example is the automotive parts maker Denso that raised its ASEAN procurement ratio from 30 per cent in 1996 to 41 per cent in 1998, while at the same time reducing imports from Japan by 18 percentage points. Overall, though, persisting quality problems with suppliers in ASEAN limit the scope of a fast increase of the localization ratio within the next few years.

Second, on the production line, defensive measures have dominated so far. These range from cutting down on working time, cuts in salary or the freezing of salary increases of rank-and-file workers, forced vacation leave up to the laying-off of personnel, and the temporary or permanent closure of single plants. The most prominent examples can be found in the automobile industry where all Japanese car makers halted, at least temporarily, production at some plants (*Jidōsha Geppō* 159, pp. 8–13). In some cases single plants might remain closed forever, for example one of the two plants of Mitsubishi Motors in Thailand. The delay or cancellation of new investments is another defensive measure that Japanese manufacturers widely made use of in 1997 and 1998 (Nihon Yushutsunyū Ginkō 1999, pp. 7–11; TSS 1999b, pp. 73–5).

Countermeasures to the crisis of a more offensive nature are those that change and upgrade the structure of the goods to be produced at the affiliates in ASEAN. In some cases, Japanese companies of the automobile and electronic industries have accelerated the shift of production from Japan to their affiliates in Southeast Asia to help these firms to stay in business but also to take advantage of the new exchange rate situation. However, such efforts were limited from the start not only by the ongoing exchange rate fluctuations and a restrengthening of local ASEAN currencies since the fall of 1998, but also by persisting quality problems in local production. Even if solved, most quality shifts in production require an increase in imported components and materials and thus are not yet feasible in terms of cost.

Still, one measure stands out as typical for many Japanese firms in coping with the problem of dropping regional sales and underutilized production capacities: the shift of production from Japan to their ASEAN affiliates for export to Japan. Here we turn to the sales side. For the time being, due to the stagnating demand within Southeast Asia (and other parts of Asia) any additional production has to be exported to overseas markets in Europe, North America and Japan. Obviously, for Japanese affiliates the first country to turn to is Japan. And indeed – despite the recession in Japan – there has been a substantial increase of exports of components and final products in all industries but textiles from Japanese affiliates to Japan (TSS 1999b, p. 71).

In 1998 Honda, for example, raised parts imports from its Thai subsidiary to Japan by 150 per cent from the 1997 level (*Nikkei Weekly* 21 December 1998, p. 22). In 1997 Toyota started to increase the amount of imported parts from its ASEAN affiliates to Japan from 2.5 billion yen to eventually more than 14 billion yen in 2000 (*Nikkei Weekly* 5 October 1998, p. 18). Both cases present textbook examples for the ability of globally-active companies to shift production among their international production sites, but also for the determination to strengthen affiliates that are regarded as important links in their global production network. However, this phenomenon has been naturally limited to large companies and cannot be expected to continue in the long run without further changes in the Asian production system that will be discussed later.

A fast export shift to regions other than Japan turned out to be difficult not only for cost and quality reasons, but also because of different product specifications and technical requirements as in the case of the automobile industry. Therefore, a significant export increase of automotive components and cars has so far been restricted to only a few countries in Asia and Oceania (*Jidōsha Geppō* 159, pp. 8–13).

Finally, turning to financial and other measures we encounter the second distinctive behaviour of Japanese firms. So far, cases of mergers and acquisitions (M&A) in Asia by Japanese companies have been very rare compared to their Western counterparts. As for these Western firms, they have been involved in more than 150 cases – although not all in manufacturing – in Southeast Asia between January 1998 and April 1999 (Goad 1999, p. 38). Japanese firms, by contrast, have shown a strong financial commitment and support to already existing affiliates and subsidiaries.

The most striking feature has been the injection of additional capital into joint ventures whose local partners are financially distressed. In many cases, this capital influx has changed the position of Japanese companies from minor stakeholders to that of owning the majority of shares of their affiliated companies and sometimes even wholly owning the subsidiary. Between November 1997 and January 1999, out of 244 approved capital increases in Thailand, Japanese firms accounted for 53 per cent. Measured by value, their share even rises to 63 per cent of total additional foreign investment (Uehara 1999, p. 20). Most of these examples took place in the automobile sector but they can be found in other industries as well as in other countries. In Indonesia, for example, Toshiba and Hitachi each bought out a local joint-venture partner that could not meet its financial obligations.

These capital injections were financed to a large extent by an official aid programme of the Japanese government-owned Export–Import Bank that paid out more than one trillion yen to Japanese companies and their subsidiaries in Asia in 1998 (Sender 1999, p. 52). Thus, rather than really expanding and upgrading operations, these capital injections sometimes merely reflect the Japanese government's strong intention to keep Japanese companies in Asia afloat.

However, this strong commitment is noteworthy in the light of recent investment figures, as an isolated interpretation of the figures shown in Table 5.4 can easily lead to an underestimation of the Japanese firms' interests in Southeast Asia. A comparison of Japanese foreign direct investment (FDI) in ASEAN countries to that of European and US companies shows the drop of investment activity by Japanese firms since 1996 to be significantly larger than that of their Western counterparts. In some countries, firms from Europe and the USA even showed an anti-cyclic investment behaviour by clearly

Table 5.4 FDI flows to ASEAN countries from Japan, Europe and the USA, 1996–98

	Singapore (mn US$ and index)				Malaysia (mn ringgit and index)				Thailand (bn baht and index)			
	1996	'96	'97	'98	1996	'96	'97	'98	1996	'96	'97	'98
Total value	5 716	100	103	91	17 056	100	67	77	321	100	77	48
Japan	1 960	100	104	91	4 607	100	47	40	136	100	92	40
Europe	1 389	100	103	79	2 571	100	88	61	66	100	65	54
USA	2 262	100	105	100	2 397	100	83	222	70	100	91	31

	Indonesia (mn US$ and index)				Philippines (mn US$ and index)			
	1996	'96	'97	'98	1996	'96	'97	'98
Total value	29 931	100	113	45	25 381	100	231	147
Japan	7 655	100	71	17	1 516	100	245	184
Europe	5 230	100	224	102	3 864	100	828	302
USA	642	100	159	88	868	100	1 199	691

Note: Data for Singapore, Malaysia and Thailand show the manufacturing sector only; those for Indonesia and the Philippines include other sectors as well.
Source: Country statistics (EDB, MIDA, BKPM, BOI).

stepping up their presence as US investors did in Malaysia and the Philippines, and as European investors did in Indonesia and the Philippines. However, most of these increases took place in the service and especially in the utilities sector, but not within manufacturing where Japanese firms continue to concentrate their engagement.

Beside these capital measures, Japanese firms, especially automakers, extended strong financial and other kinds of support to their core suppliers and dealers to keep them in business. These measures have ranged from shouldering the cost of raw material purchases and offering letters of credit, to extended payment terms and other direct and indirect means. Similarly, they eagerly tried to pursue a non-layoff policy to keep their trained personnel. This included extended training of ASEAN workers in Japan. A case in point is Toyota where the number of trainees in 1998 was increased from 250 to 500 while the length of their stay was extended from three to six months (*Jidōsha Geppō* 157, p. 6). These training programmes are strongly supported by the official development assistance scheme AOTS (Association for Overseas Technical Scholarship) by the Japanese government.

In general, all measures described above aim at short-term survival and long-term strengthening of already strong market positions of Japanese affiliates, and are thus far from any strategy of retreat. Although – due to the prolonged problems of the Japanese domestic economy – most Japanese companies lack the power and motivation for an offensive expansion strategy (Sender 1999, pp. 52–4), measures taken so far constitute the clear will to defend and strengthen existing positions. Only two measures, the production shift to ASEAN for exports to Japan and the strong injection of additional capital into existing affiliates (as opposed to M&A), set Japanese firms distinctively apart from Western competitors in their short-term reaction to the crisis in Southeast Asia. Both measures are to be found mainly in the case of large and financially sound parent companies in Japan. Companies struggling at home and suffering under heavy losses and debt in Japan were rarely among those that have strengthened their position in ASEAN by capital increases or other offensive means (Tōyō Keizai 1999).

Whether the FDI figures in Table 5.4 indicate a long-term trend towards a reduced production activity of Japanese firms and a stronger production engagement of Western firms in Southeast Asia is still unclear. The future activities of Japanese companies in the region will mainly depend on their long-term regional strategies that have, in some cases, just started to be formulated, and in others, only recently commenced in their implementation. The next section will describe these strategies and look in detail at the different elements constituting and characterizing them. So far, the regional economic crisis seems to have worked to accelerate the implementation process.

LONG-TERM REGIONAL REORGANIZATION OF PRODUCTION BY JAPANESE FIRMS

Any long-term strategic reorientation of Japanese or other multinational firms in Southeast Asia is greatly influenced by the rapid environmental changes that have taken place in this region since the early 1990s. The three most important factors constituting such a reorientation are the regional market growth, the regional trade liberalization and the gradual lift of investment restrictions that all started well before the crisis and that are all expected to prevail in the long run.

Southeast Asian countries did not only grow rapidly until 1996/97, but are also anticipated – after overcoming the immediate crisis effects from the year 2000 onwards – to return to a strong growth path though probably not to the high growth rates of before the crisis (World Bank 1998; ADB 1999). Hence, this region is increasingly gaining interest not only as a production base but also as an important regional market on its own. The same holds true for the trend towards regional trade liberalization. This trend only started in earnest in 1992 with the idea of establishing an ASEAN Free Trade Area (AFTA), and it is still facing many obstacles (Legewie 2000b). Importantly, however, the crisis so far has not reversed the trend – at the sixth ASEAN summit in Hanoi in December 1998 it was even decided to advance the start of AFTA by one year to January 2002. Similarly, the easing of investment restrictions like capital and ownership regulations continued and was sometimes even accelerated by ASEAN governments after 1997.

These factors have created an environment increasingly suited to a stronger regional division of labour than was feasible until recently. In addition, the emergence of trade blocs in Europe (EU) and North America (NAFTA) has added to the perception of many multinational companies that Asia will rapidly develop to form a third trade bloc probably with ASEAN at its core (Teranishi 1999, pp. 4–6). This perception of an emerging Asian trade bloc became even stronger in 1998 and 1999 exacerbated by the problems and failures of trade liberalization efforts at the APEC and WTO level. In total, Japanese like other multinational firms increasingly feel the need for a regional corporate strategy to be built around regionally oriented production activities.

This need for a regional production strategy requires a fundamental strategic reorganization for most Japanese firms that have directed their production strategies either to domestic or overseas export markets in the past. The keyword for such new strategies is 'economies of scale', within a new regional production portfolio that is to be decided upon considerations regarding cost, quality and risk. There are three main elements that constitute such regional production strategies which are being increasingly implemented by Japanese companies, namely the spatial concentration and specialization of production, the increase of regional R&D and the establishment of regional headquarters.

Production: Focus on Concentration and Specialization

The first and most obvious element of the emerging regional production strategies is the concentration of certain production activities at one site. Most electronics companies started to follow this strategy in the 1970s by the establishment of single-product companies in Singapore and Malaysia. Since then, a diversified regional production network of suppliers has developed facilitating the far-reaching regional procurement of parts and components as seen earlier (p. 78). However, these single-product companies were aimed exclusively at exports to overseas markets.

At the same time most of the electronic assemblers still run multi-product companies in every Southeast Asian country serving closed domestic markets and producing a variety of goods, though in each case with a small production capacity. Now these domestic-market-oriented multi-product companies and the single-product companies geared for overseas markets have to be integrated into a new regional production network with a stronger horizontal division of labour to facilitate the attainment of scale economies. This new division of labour will be an extension of existing production networks in the electronics industry and has to go beyond the level already achieved for many parts and components (Chia 1997; Teranishi 1999). A similar transformation process of former multi-product companies can also be observed in other industries such as automobiles or chemicals.

The best-known example of the ongoing reorganization process in the electronics industry is probably the case of Matsushita Electric

Industrial. Since the late 1960s, this company has established the so-called Mini-Matsushitas in most Asian countries to serve local markets. The term 'Mini-Matsushita' describes Asian affiliates of Matsushita that produce nearly the whole range of Matsushita products at one company. They are probably the most extreme form of multi-product companies. These Mini-Matsushitas have been built up by Matsushita all over Asia to serve closed markets with local production though with a very small output for every single product. These local affiliates lost their competitive edge in the 1990s and are now regarded as 'minus assets of Matsushita in Asia' (Gomi 1999). Even in 1998, Matsushita, for example, still had seven companies in different Asian countries producing television sets (even more when including facilities in China). This production split continues to prevent Matsushita from enjoying economies of scale and is just one example of the radical change and transformation required to achieve optimal production allocation while avoiding production duplication. As a first step in this transformation process, Matsushita succeeded in 1998 to convert its Mini-Matsushita in Thailand into a holding company with eight independent firms each specializing in different products.

In the automobile industry, the larger Japanese assemblers started in the early 1990s to concentrate their production of certain components in single countries, like transmissions in the Philippines or steering gears in Malaysia (see Table 5.5). The volume of the resulting regional intra-firm trade of Japanese car-makers rose more than six times between 1992 and 1996, with Taiwan and Australia playing an important role in most of these complementation schemes (Kamo 1999, pp. 188–93; Legewie 2000). A similar strategy is pursued by Denso that in 1995 started to concentrate the production of key components like starters, compressors or instrument clusters in different ASEAN countries (Table 5.5). The successful increase of the regional procurement ratio by Denso since 1996 (described in the previous section) can be partly explained by this new production pattern.

In the chemical industry, Lion, a maker of household products, is another telling example. Until recently this company's production in Southeast Asia was divided among factories in Thailand, Malaysia and Indonesia each serving domestic markets with the same products (export ratios between 5 and 9 per cent). This changed in 1998 when the production of Lion's body-soap line *Shokubutsu Monogatari* was started in Southeast Asia after being a big success in the Japanese market. In Southeast Asia, the production is concentrated solely in Thailand from where it is exported to other ASEAN countries and

Table 5.5 Regional pattern of parts production and trade of Japanese car manufacturers within ASEAN

	Toyota	Mitsubishi	Honda	Nissan	Denso
Thailand	Diesel engines, stamping parts	Casting parts, suspensions	Stamping parts	Engine parts, stamping parts	Starters, alternators
Malaysia	Steering gears, suspensions	Steering gears, stamping parts	Plastic products, suspensions	Steering gears, stamping parts	Air-conditioner relays, flashers
Indonesia	Gasol. engines, cylinder blocks	Engine parts	Cylinder heads, cylinder blocks	Engine parts	Compressors, spark plugs
Philippines	Transmissions, transm. parts	Transmissions	Casting parts	Transmissions, stamping parts	Instrument clusters
Intra-regional trade volume (bn yen)					
1992	<2	<0.5	<0.5	<0.2	0.01
1996	20	3	4	1	<0.5
2000	90	>20	>20	20	6

Note: The estimates for the year 2000 date to mid-1997, and thus to the time before the Asian crisis; hence they have to be reduced significantly – Toyota, for example, scaled back expectations for 2000 to 60 billion yen.
Source: Toyota, Mitsubishi, Honda, Nissan, Denso.

Taiwan. Lion plans to transform its two Thai factories into its Asian production hub by 2005 and to raise its export ratio from 8 per cent to more than 20 per cent.

Similar examples can be also found in other industries with concentration measures aiming at a reduction of costs by achieving economies of scale in production. However, concrete implementation still faces many problems. For example, Matsushita is still in the midst of its reorganization process in all other ASEAN countries except Thailand. The main problems are resistance by local joint-venture partners and governments and by capital restrictions that permit wholly-owned subsidiaries only for export-oriented companies. In other areas like automobiles, chemicals, textiles or foodstuffs, the remaining tariff walls still limit the scope for further production concentration or confine it to the area of parts and components.

In general, relative latecomers to the region (including most Western firms but also Japanese manufacturers like Sony or Pioneer Electronics) seem to benefit from the current situation as they are mainly free from 'minus assets' hindering the development of an optimal regional production network. Most ASEAN affiliates founded after 1980 are majority-owned subsidiaries and thus their transformation into new organizational entities is comparatively easy. This was shown by the recent large-scale reorganization of Sony affiliates in Malaysia that even included the closure of some plants and companies.

Procurement and Product Development: Increase of Regional R&D

The second trend is an obvious increase of regional R&D which is especially noteworthy as Japanese firms in general still lag well-behind Western companies in the internationalization of their R&D activities (OECD 1998, p. 37). Between FY 1996 and FY 1997, Japanese companies increased their R&D expenses in all of Asia (excluding Japan) from 18.4 billion yen to 24.1 billion yen which represented 8.6 per cent of all overseas R&D expenses by Japanese firms (TSS 1999b, p. 55). Singapore and the ASEAN 4 account for roughly a third of Japanese R&D in Asia with an overwhelming part concentrated in the electronics industry (TSS 1998, p. 365).

Matsushita has established regional R&D centres for air-conditioners in Malaysia and for multimedia products and semiconductors in Singapore. Its audio headquarters in Singapore even serves on an equal footing with its R&D facility in Japan and might soon become the only R&D centre for audio products of Matsushita worldwide. Toshiba has already moved all its VCR operations including product development from Japan to Singapore where Hitachi is conducting research on memory chips. Honda established R&D centres for motorcycles in Bangkok in 1998, and is considering opening a similar R&D company for automobiles in Thailand (Shimizu 1999, p. 19). Similar examples can be found in other electronics companies but also within chemicals, textiles or foodstuffs in companies like Sumitomo Chemical and Kao, Teijin and Toray or Ajinomoto and Nissin Foods.

The main aim of such regional R&D is either research for cheaper local inputs and thus for a reduction of costs, or the development of product applications to adjust to local tastes and customers and hence to better serve regional markets (Teranishi 1999, pp. 8, 12). The great importance of highly effective means of procurement has been mentioned before: it directly complements any efforts in the area of production concentration and thus represents a crucial part in any regional production strategy. Consequently, focusing more on the 'D' than the 'R', these R&D centres are mainly restricted to research on local materials as in the case of R&D for air-conditioners and TVs in Singapore and Malaysia, or for chemical products and foods/beverages in Malaysia, Thailand or Indonesia.

A relatively new development is the emphasis on the development of products tailored for regional markets and consumers. The best-known examples for this new trend towards regional products are probably the so-called Asian cars *City* and *Soluna* that were developed by Honda and Toyota in Thailand for sales only in Asian markets outside of Japan. The food company Kikkoman is another interesting example. For the first time in history, this company decided to alter the worldwide identical formula for its soy sauce and develop a regional brand called 'Special Fragrance' in Singapore. In the spring of 1999, this product was launched on the Singaporean market from where it will be exported to other Southeast Asian countries in the case of market success.

Accelerated by the crisis, there is a growing interest in products that are reasonable in terms of function, shape and price. Despite the need to be affordable, which is the first consideration, these products must appeal to local people and thus go beyond the so far dominating types that were mainly just cheaper versions of products sold in Japan. Accordingly, Japanese firms are stepping up their regional R&D facilities and increasing the number of their local engineers, for example Sharp in Malaysia will increase the number of its engineers from 100 in 1998 to 250 in 2001, and Matsushita in Malaysia from 372 in 1999 to 750 in 2004 (Shimizu 1999, p. 19).

R&D in manufacturing technology is mainly missing in Southeast Asia as most production lines have so far been transferred from Japan to ASEAN countries without major technical changes. The consumer electronics manufacturer Aiwa presents one of the rare examples where R&D on engineering has already been partially transferred to a large R&D centre in Singapore. The obvious reason for this is the large production share of Asia that accounts for about 80 per cent of the worldwide (including Japan) production of Aiwa. The number of local training facilities for the development of personnel in Southeast Asia has been steadily increased making them a prominent characteristic of larger Japanese companies of the electronics and automobile industries. These training facilities reflect the increasing need for skilled workers as the result of a continuous upgrading of local production.

Basic research activities of Japanese affiliates in Southeast Asia are relatively seldom and can be found only in consumer electronics, mainly in the cases of white goods (refrigerators, microwave ovens, air conditioner, and so on), audio and video products. A closer look at these product categories that have regional R&D centres reveals that they mainly consist of 'sunset' industries where production already peaked out in the mid-1990s and where high profits and added-value are not expected in the future (see Table 5.6).

In 'sunrise' industries such as information processing and telecommunications equipment (but also in categories such as digital TV) the R&D of Japanese companies is still conducted nearly exclusively in Japan. This can be explained by both the strong technological capabilities of Japanese companies at home and the need to conduct leading edge R&D close to the industrial lead-customers who are still found to a much larger degree in Japan than in Southeast Asia.

However, the reluctance to shift R&D, other than that on input materials and product development, to Asian affiliates remains a characteristic of Japanese companies. While regional R&D increasingly complements regional production strategies, it still remains largely separated from the basic R&D conducted in Japan. It is also mainly conducted on a national level with few connections between R&D sites of the same parent company in different ASEAN countries. Hence, with regard to R&D, a strategy comprising the whole region is only slowly emerging with especially Japan far from becoming an

Table 5.6   Production figures of selected electronic products in ASEAN 5
(100 000 units)

	1991	1992	1993	1994	1995	1996	1997	1998
Microwave ovens	19	26	25	31	38	**44**	42	42
Air conditioners	37	41	47	48	56	52	**58**	53
Stereo sets	140	170	203	252	**278**	242	251	238
Radio-cassette players	**244**	187	192	200	168	117	75	69
Headphone stereos	179	166	166	**238**	194	141	158	155
Car audios	115	114	105	160	169	**189**	189	186
Color TVs	185	192	205	253	**280**	263	215	191
VCRs	75	118	130	259	**289**	237	222	219
TV/VCR sets	–	–	–	18	27	**41**	38	43
Personal computers	32	63	82	88	111	109	125	**149**
Floppy-disk drives	160	247	412	563	623	596	851	**891**
Hard-disk drives	153	277	375	546	633	803	913	**1 122**
CRT monitors	10	18	44	108	152	175	**189**	182

Note: Peaks of production in bold.
Source: Teranishi (1999), pp. 19–22.

integral part of such a strategy for Southeast Asia or other parts of
Asia.

Functional and Regional Coordination: Establishment of Regional Headquarters

Finally, the establishment of regional headquarters stands out as a
third indicator for a shift to regional strategies requiring a functional
and regional coordination of production activities. Once again, electronic companies are leading the trend with most of them building up
regional headquarters in Singapore since the late 1980s/early 1990s.
From the automobile sector, only Toyota, Hino and Denso have followed so far while others still coordinate their regional activities mainly
from Japan; Yamaha Motor also established a regional headquarters
in Singapore in 1998. A third group comprises a few companies from
the chemicals sector like Sumitomo, Dainippon Ink or Eisai. Regional
headquarters of companies in other industries are still an exception.
Kao, Lion or Ajinomoto, for example, still coordinate most of their
Asian activities from their headquarters in Japan (Tōyō Keizai 1999).
   Interestingly, all existing regional headquarters have in common
that they do not only cover the ASEAN region but also neighbouring

countries including Taiwan, Korea or sometimes even India and Australia. However, they are never in charge of China which is still regarded as a region of its own. This is due not only to the special characteristics of the Chinese market, but equally to the strong regulations and import restrictions that continue to set China apart from the rest of Asia.

The main function of these regional headquarters is the coordination of international procurement including cost and quality control for production facilities in the region. Additionally, logistic and financial support are increasingly provided on a regional basis as well as marketing activities. In some cases all functions are combined in one company, in other cases functions are divided among two, three or four companies specializing in either regional procurement, logistic, financial or sales activities as in the case of Toshiba or Sony (Tōyō Keizai 1999).

An effective regional coordination of marketing and sales activities is, however, still the exception. In most cases regional sales activities have developed from expanding the scope of former national sales subsidiaries and are thus often limited in scope and coordination power. Although this has also been the case with Sony Marketing International, founded in Singapore in 1973, this company was recently assigned far-reaching regional marketing and sales authority for the audiovisual equipment market. This makes it one of the first Japanese companies in Southeast Asia with the function of a strong regional headquarters in the area of regional marketing and sales.

Another striking feature of Japanese regional headquarters is the low degree to which they are organized along business segments or product divisions. In most cases regional procurement or sales functions are executed by just one or two companies over all business segments. In the electronics industry such a separation is mostly made into consumer electronics on the one hand and electronic devices on the other. Western companies, by contrast, tend to follow a much stronger divisional approach even separating regional headquarters functions of different product divisions by countries (see Yip, Johansson and Roos 1996).

In general, Japanese firms seem to be lagging behind Western firms in establishing and efficiently operating regional headquarters. This holds true regardless of whether Western or Japanese firms have been the respective latecomers to the region (for example the electronic and automobile industry versus the chemical and food industry). A comparison of companies like Unilever or Nestlé with their Japanese competitors like Kao or Ajinomoto is especially interesting as – contrary to most industries – here Kao and Ajinomoto are the relative latecomers to Southeast Asia as compared to their Western counterparts.

While most Western companies started their business in Southeast Asia with regional sales subsidiaries, Japanese firms either used to control all activities from Japan or transferred only limited authority to nationally operating units. Even today, large companies like Kao or Ajinomoto seem hesitant to transfer power from their Japanese headquarters to their Southeast Asian affiliates and subsidiaries while companies like Unilever or Philips run highly autonomous regional headquarters in Singapore (Singh, Putti and Yip 1998, pp. 175–7). Although this reluctance to establish regional headquarters might be partially explained with the relative geographical closeness of Southeast Asia to Japan, such a lack of autonomous regional coordination entities might become a barrier for the implementation of far-reaching regional production strategies.

Regarding the overall trend towards regionalization and regional production strategies, in some industries like consumer packaged goods the slow development of regional marketing activities of most Japanese companies threatens to become a significant weakness as it prevents scale economies within sales. However, in most industries, established brand names and domestic sales channels still present a strong asset for Japanese firms. But there is certainly a strong threat to the large number of smaller Japanese companies. These affiliates can no longer rely on established *keiretsu* channels for the sales of industrial goods and are hence under particular pressure due to the intensified competition resulting from the Asian crisis. As these firms used to depend nearly exclusively on sales relations established in Japan, they did not even develop national marketing functions, not to speak of any regional marketing functions (CKSKK 1999, pp. 138–40). This lack makes them especially vulnerable to other (often Asian) competitors that possess much stronger and more aggressive marketing networks in ASEAN countries.

CONCLUSIONS

Summarizing the findings, we can state that the immediate effects of the Asian crisis on Japanese manufacturers in ASEAN countries have been more or less the same as for other multinational firms active in the region. Accordingly, Japanese firms have in the main taken the same short-term countermeasures to the crisis as their Western competitors, ranging from cost-cutting measures in the areas of procurement and production to increased efforts to raise exports.

Only two direct support measures were found to be distinctively Japanese. One is a substantial shift in production from Japan to ASEAN affiliates for re-export to Japan, a move, however, which is mainly restricted to large companies. The other is a strong injection of capital into existing affiliates as opposed to M&A, which could be identified as an additional investment method preferred only by Western firms.

The general background for long-term production strategies in Southeast Asia is the same for all players. It is characterized by three developments that started well before the crisis and that are expected to continue in the long run, namely regional market growth, regional trade liberalization and the gradual abolition of investment restrictions. All three factors create an environment suited to an enforced regional division of labour and hence to the implementation of regional production strategies at the micro-level of single companies regardless of their nationality.

Although concrete production strategies differ between countries, between industries and between companies, two factors can be identified that set apart most Japanese affiliates in Southeast Asia from those of European and US firms. One is the relatively early start of many Japanese production operations in the region that resulted, among others effects, in a strong domestic-market orientation and a high percentage of affiliates organized as joint ventures with local partners. The other characteristic is the usually strong linkage of Japanese ASEAN affiliates to their headquarters in Japan and their relatively low level of decision-making autonomy. This can be explained by the relative closeness of Southeast Asia to Japan but also by the general reluctance of Japanese managements to transfer power abroad.

Both factors are found to influence the implementation of regional production strategies of Japanese firms in Southeast Asia in each of the three main constituting steps which are the concentration and specialization of production, the increase of regional R&D and the establishment of regional headquarters. The traditionally strong domestic-market orientation of Japanese affiliates so far hinders the smooth establishment of regional headquarters with strong regional functions. Furthermore, it has become a major obstacle in transforming existing production sites into new ones aiming at economies of scale as it inevitably comes with the closure of single plants. This threat has led to strong resistance by local joint-venture partners complicating, especially, the transformation of old, long-established affiliates that are often the biggest and most important ones of Japanese companies in each single country.

The strong bias of Japanese ASEAN affiliates to headquarters in Japan is equally a barrier to the establishment of effective regional headquarters as it often prevents the necessary transfer of authority. This bias often denies regional headquarters of Japanese firms the degree of flexibility and responsiveness needed to effectively supplement the production side with the regional coordination of marketing and sales activities. The so far limited role of regional R&D centres is also partly an outcome of the reluctance of transferring power abroad. Whether the strong concentration of R&D in Japan will be advantageous or disadvantageous for Japanese companies in the long run is not easy to foresee and will probably differ by industry.

In conclusion, we can state that a shift to a regional production strategy is clearly underway with most Japanese manufacturers active in Asia, though it comes with strong differences between single industries and firms. These strategies have in common that they are geared to a region that does not only consist of Southeast Asia, but also of other Asian-Pacific countries like Taiwan or Australia. However, for the time being this region does not include either China or Japan itself.

Within such a 'larger' Asia, the clear focus of Japanese manufacturers is on achieving a cost-efficient regional production network, both for serving regional markets but also for exports to the rest of the world. The still low level of regional procurement and sales linkage shows that this process has just started. Even in the electronics sector, Japanese MNCs still have a long way to go in achieving production networks that are not only regionally integrated, but that also go beyond the mere manufacturing process. Besides building up regional production networks, manufacturing and other functions located in Asia must increasingly be regarded as an integral part of the whole value chain of each company – not only in Asia but also globally.

Regarding this requirement, it is important to note that basic R&D and also most non-national marketing activities are still kept clearly concentrated in Japan. Therefore, with regard to their strategy in Asia, Japanese manufacturers remain the 'reluctant multinationals' (Trevor 1983), or in other words the 'global' company type as opposed to the 'multinational' and 'international' to borrow the classification of Bartlett and Ghoshal (1989). Whether this strategy and the strong focus on production efficiency will prove to be the right approach for Japanese companies to survive in a globalizing economy remains to be seen.

Notes

The author extends his special gratitude to all company and government representatives who spared their precious time for long interviews with him in Singapore (S), Malaysia (M), Thailand (T) and Japan (J) between February and December 1999; in alphabetical order: Aiwa (J), Ajinomoto (M, J), Asia Matsushita Electric (S), Asian Honda Motor (T), BASF (J), British Chamber of Commerce (T), Board of Investment (T), DaimlerChrysler (T), Denso (S), Deutsche Securities Asia (S), Droege (S), EBIC (M), EBIC (T), EDB (S), Fujitsu (J), German Embassy (M), German–Thai Chamber of Commerce, Hitachi (J), Hitachi Consumer Products (S), JETRO (T, M, S, J), Kao (J), Kikkoman Trading (S), Lion (J), Matsushita Electric Industrial (J), Mediocredito Centrale (S), Merck (J), Mitsubishi Electric (J), Mitsubishi Motors (J), MMC Sittipol (T), National/Panasonic (M), NEC (J), NEC Semiconductors Singapore, Nichirei (J), Nihon Keizai Shinbun (T), Nihon Keizai Shinbun (S), Nippon Steel (J), Pioneer Electronics Asiacentre (S), Sanyo (S), Shiseido (J), Siemens Power Generation (M), Siew-National (T), Snow Brand Siam, Sony (M), Sumitomo Chemical (J), Teijin (T), Toyota (J), TMSS Toyota (S), Toshiba (J).

References

ADB Asian Development Bank (1999) *Asian Development Outlook 1999*, Hong Kong: Oxford University Press.
Bartlett, C. and S. Ghoshal (1989) *Managing Across Borders: The Transnational Solution*, Boston, Mass.: Harvard Business School Press.
Birkinshaw, J. and N. Hood (1998) *Multinational Corporate Evolution and Subsidiary Development*, London: Macmillan.
Buckley, P. and M. Casson (1998) 'Models of the Multinational Enterprise', *Journal of International Business Studies*, vol. 29(1), pp. 21–44.
Chia, S. Y. (1997) 'Singapore: Advanced Production Base and Smart Hub of the Electronics Industry', in W. Dobson and S. Y. Chia (eds), *Multinationals and East Asian Integration*, Singapore: Institute of Southeast Asian Studies.
CKSKK Chūshō Kigyō Sōgō Kenkyū Kikō (1999) *Ajia chūshō kigyō no genjō ni kansuru chōsa kenkyū, tai-hen* [Survey Research on the Current State of Small and Medium Enterprises in Asia, Volume Thailand], Tōkyō: Chūshō Kigyō Sōgō Kenkyū Kikō.
Goad, G. P. (1999) 'Optimism vs Medicine', *Far Eastern Economic Review*, 17 June, pp. 38–9.

Gomi, N. (1999) *Going National, Regional or Global – Corporate Strategies for Southeast Asia after the Crisis*, Presentation at the DIJ Conference 'Economic Crisis and Transformation in Southeast Asia: Strategic Responses by Japanese and European Firms' in Tōkyō, 17–18 June).

Kamo, K. (1999) 'Kokusai bungyō no shinten to jidōsha sangyō [The Development of the International Division of Labour and the Automobile Industry], in Y. Maruyama, T. Sago and H. Kobayashi (eds), *Ajia keizaihen to kokusai bungyō no shinten* [The Asian Economic Region and the Development of the International Division of Labour], Tōkyō: Minerubua Shobō.

Legewie, J. (2000a) 'Driving Regional Integration: Japanese Firms and the Development of the ASEAN Automobile Industry', in V. Blechinger and J. Legewie (eds), *Facing Asia – Japan's Role in the Political and Economic Dynamism of Regional Cooperation*, München: Iudicium, pp. 217–46.

Legewie, J. (2000b) 'The Political Economy of Industrial Integration in Southeast Asia: The Role of Japanese Companies', *Journal of the Asia Pacific Economy*, vol. 5(3) (October).

Nihon Yushutsunyū Ginkō (1999) *1998 nendo kaigai chokusetsu tōshi ankēto chōsa kekka hōkoku* [Report on the 1998 Survey on Foreign Direct Investment], Tōkyō: Nihon Yushutsunyū Ginkō.

Organization for Economic Cooperation and Development (1998) *Internationalisation of Industrial R&D: Pattern and Trends*, Paris: OECD Publications.

Sender, H. (1999) 'Stemming the Flood', *Far Eastern Economic Review*, 29 July, pp. 52–4.

Shimizu, Y. (1999) 'Japanese Companies Take New Approach to Rest of Asia', *Nikkei Weekly*, 26 July, pp. 1, 19.

Singh, K., J. Putti and G. Yip (1998) 'Singapore – Regional Hub', in G. Yip (ed.), *Asian Advantage – Key Strategies for Winning in the Asia-Pacific Region*, Reading: Addison-Wesley, pp. 155–9.

Teranishi, K. (1999) *Tsūka kiki ato no ASEAN seisan kyoten* [ASEAN as a Production Base after the Currency Crisis], Tōkyō: Goldmann Sachs Investment Research.

Tōyō Keizai (1999) *Kaigai shinshutsu kigyō sōran '99, kunibetsu-hen* [General Survey of Japanese Companies Abroad '99, Volume by Countries], Tōkyō: Tōyō Keizai Shinpōsha.

Trevor, M. (1983) *Japan's Reluctant Multinationals: Japanese Management at Home and Abroad*, London: Frances Pinter.

TSS Tsūshō Sangyōshō (1994) *Kaigai tōshi tōkei sōran, dai 5-kai* [Statistical Overview on Overseas Investment, no. 5], Tōkyō: Ōkurashō Insatsukyoku.

TSS Tsūshō Sangyōshō (1998) *Kaigai jigyō katsudō kihon chōsa, dai 6-kai* [Basic Survey on Overseas Business Activities, no. 6], Tōkyō: Ōkurashō Insatsukyoku.

TSS Tsūshō Sangyōshō (1999a) *Wagakuni kigyō no kaigai jigyō katsudō, dai 27-kai* [Overseas Business Activities of Domestic Firms, no. 27], Ōkurashō Insatsukyoku.

TSS Tsūshō Sangyōshō (1999b) *Kaigai jigyō katsudō dōkō chōsa gaiyō, dai 28-kai*[Outline on the Basic Survey on the Trend of Overseas Business Activities, no. 28], Tōkyō: Sangyō Seisakukyoku Kokusai Kigyōka.

Uehara, M. (1999) 'Japanese Companies Gave Most Aid to Thai Joint Ventures Amid Crisis', *Nikkei Weekly*, 14 June, p. 20.

World Bank (1998) *Global Economic Prospects and the Developing Countries*, downloaded from www.worldbank.org.

Yip, G., J. Johansson and J. Roos (1996) 'Effects of Nationality on Global Strategy in Major American, European, and Japanese Multinational Companies', MSI Working Paper no. 96–126, Cambridge, Mass.: Marketing Science Institute.

6 Production Strategies of European Firms: Between Retrenchment and Expansion Opportunities

Corrado Molteni

INTRODUCTION

How does the crisis in Southeast Asia affect the strategies and the operations of European manufacturers in the region? Are they retreating, restructuring or in other ways revising their regional production plans? Or are they aggressively expanding thanks to the opportunities generated by falling asset prices and exchange rates, and the weakness of local competitors and partners? Is it possible to identify different patterns reflecting the characteristics of the sectors, the strategies pursued in the past, and the countries where companies operate? And how do the European firms' strategic responses compare to those of their Japanese competitors?

These questions shall be addressed in this chapter. Previous studies (Kumar and Mohr 1999; Lasserre and Schuette 1999a) have analysed the crisis' implications and consequences for European firms from a theoretical point of view. In this chapter, we will provide data and concrete examples to support preliminary findings. However, at this stage, scarce empirical evidence and an understandable managers' reluctance to disclose critical information on recent changes have not made the author's task an easy one. This has been particularly true in the case of small and medium-sized enterprises that have established manufacturing units in the Southeast Asian region, or have started the outsourcing and licensing of a part of their production to local partners. As a result, what follows is a still blurred picture of European companies' reactions to the crisis, focused on manufacturing investment in some countries of the region (Thailand and Singapore, in particular) and the experience of a selected group of firms. Nevertheless, even if there are still wide gray areas, it is possible to identify some distinctive features of the European response to the crisis.

In particular, what is clearly discernible is the fact that many European firms have reacted more boldly and assertively than their Japanese competitors. Rather than retreating or retrenching, they are trying to acquire new positions in the regions or, at least, to consolidate those already existing. In this respect, they have certainly benefited from their competitors' weaknesses, as Japanese (and Korean) firms have been greatly affected by the unprecedented contraction of their domestic economies and the dramatic conditions of their financial systems. But European firms have also taken advantage of their latecomer status (on the delay of European companies involvement in Asia see Robinson (1997) and UNCTAD and European Commission (1996)). As such they had been less involved in Asia before the crisis, but they have also been less affected by the subsequent economic and financial turmoil. Thus, what was portrayed as a major weakness before the crisis might turn out to be an advantage supporting European firms' manufacturing strategies as active players in the region.

EUROPEAN FIRMS' PERCEPTION OF THE CRISIS AND ITS IMPACT ON THEIR STRATEGIES

European perceptions and reactions to the Asian crisis differ greatly. The companies most concerned and affected are those threatened by the rapid surge of low-cost Asian exports into European markets. Almost daily in 1998, the Italian financial newspaper *Il Sole 24 Ore* carried long articles on the deteriorating balance of trade, the aggressive policies of Asian competitors and the loss of market share, revenues and employees by domestic producers in sectors like leather products, footwear and textile machinery: the traditional strongholds of Italian manufacturing capability. For companies in these sectors – particularly small and medium-sized companies manufacturing intermediate and final products for the lower segments of the market – the Asian crisis has transformed a fear into a real threat.

On the other hand, companies exporting to or producing in Southeast Asia are concerned but, in general, more positive about the future of the region, its economy and its relations with Europe. Indeed, as pointed out by a Malaysian economist, the crisis has created a larger investment need. Many undertakings and projects in manufacturing, infrastructure development and services require the injection of fresh capital to maintain their viability and, in this regard, European companies could play an important role (Mahani 1999, p. 47). Moreover, for those companies that consider the region's potential for growth unabated the crisis could be an opportunity to establish, acquire or expand production facilities, taking advantage of the currency depreciation, the decline of asset prices and the temporary lead on actual or potential competitors. The crisis as an opportunity is even more evident in the case of those companies that look at Southeast Asia as a resource base or an export platform. The reduction of factor costs have made these countries particularly attractive places for producing and exporting goods, especially when the export destination is outside of the region, in less-affected markets like Europe or North America (Kumar and Mohr 1999, p. 7).

An extensive survey of German companies' views of the Asian crisis carried out in 1998 on behalf of the German Business Association of Singapore by Droege & Comp., an international consulting company, provides an interesting picture of how German companies perceive and face the crisis. Although this survey has been conducted only among German companies, the results seem to be representative for other European MNCs, at least to a certain extent, as well. The survey was carried out with the participation of 1500 subsidiaries of German companies operating in 10 Asian countries and the German headquarters of 500 companies. Of the 1500 subsidiaries more than 70 per cent are manufacturers in the following sectors: machinery (36 per cent of the total), chemicals (18 per cent), electronics (11 per cent) and consumer goods (3 per cent). (The author gratefully thanks Droege & Comp. Singapore Pte Ltd. for authorizing the use of the survey's results.)

As shown in Figure 6.1, while 46 per cent of the managers in the 1500 Asian subsidiaries see the crisis as a threat, 33 per cent of them consider it as an opportunity (the remaining 21 per cent see their situation as unchanged). What is interesting is the response of the headquarters of German companies: 55 per cent of the respondents neither see the crisis as a threat or an opportunity, only 4 per cent see the crisis as a threat and 41 per cent see it as an opportunity. This definitely presents an overall more 'optimistic view'. Of course, the large perception gap between the centre and the periphery reflects the different impact of local realities on those in the field and on those in the far-away, sheltered environment of the headquarters. Yet, the high percentage of positive replies by managers in the German headquarters

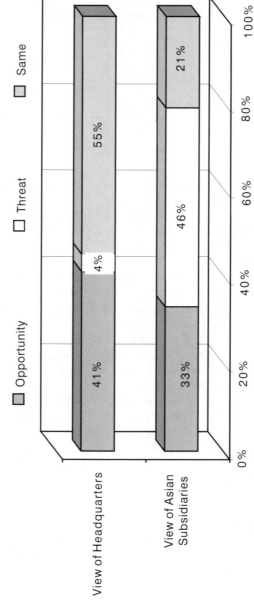

Figure 6.1 German companies' perceptions of the Asian crisis

Source: Droege & Comp. (1999).

Table 6.1   German companies' views on future business in Asia

	Increasing	Unchanged	Declining
Future importance of Asia			
Headquarters' view	96%	3%	1%
Asian subsidiaries' view	81%	18%	1%
Own future presence in Asia			
Headquarters' view	84%	15%	1%
Asian subsidiaries' view	78%	16%	6%

Source: Droege & Comp. (1999).

also shows how a large number of companies have great expectations and remain firmly committed to Asia.

Another interesting result of the survey are the expectations about the future importance of Asia and about the future presence of German companies in this region (Table 6.1). Here the positive image of Asia (not only Southeast Asia) remains as strong as ever. Indeed, 96 per cent of the managers in Germany see Asia's importance growing and 84 per cent see an expanding German presence in the region. This view is not only a German one but common throughout Europe which is confirmed by other surveys and by the author's own interviews with several managers of Italian and French companies operating in Asia. According to Lasserre and Schuette, 'the overall perception among Asian businessmen and representatives of the MNCs remains surprisingly positive' (1999b, p. 10).

The real issue, however, is when will the Asian recovery gain momentum and how strong will it be. Different perceptions imply different strategies. If the time horizon for a robust recovery is more than five years from the outburst of the crisis – that is after 2002 – companies might choose or have already chosen to retreat, closing operations or leaving only a small manufacturing outpost in the region. If the recovery is expected to happen within the next three to five years, then the option might be to retrench, restructure and streamline operations, but to maintain a significant presence. An even shorter timeframe would justify instead an increased commitment including new greenfield investments or acquisitions (also see Lasserre and Schuette 1999a).

The majority of the European companies seem to consider the second scenario of an economic recovery within three to five years the most plausible, but there is also a significant number of companies aggressively targeting Asian markets. According to a survey conducted by the UNCTAD Secretariat and the International Chamber of Commerce in February/March 1998, only 12 per cent of 198 multi-national companies were planning to reduce their investment in the region, while 62 per cent planned to maintain their presence stable and 26 per cent planned to expand their investment in East and Southeast Asia in the short to medium term. Firms from Europe are distinctly above the average as 34 per cent of them have responded that they expect to increase their direct investment to the region, 55 per cent intend to maintain their position unchanged and only 11 per cent plan to reduce their presence (UNCTAD 1998a, pp. 222–3).

Manufacturers, in particular, are not reversing their commitment to the region. Companies do not want to relinquish the capabilities and the tangible and intangible assets (human capital, networks of suppliers, institutional linkages, and so on) acquired in the region in the last decade. In particular, they are concerned with the loss and the dispersal of trained personnel. Their recruitment and training has been particularly costly, and their absence is considered the main hurdle when trying to establish a manufacturing presence. Moreover, in many cases foreign companies already in the region have to invest additional capital in order to take over part or the whole quota controlled by financially distressed local partners. Thus, as a whole, European investment in the region has not declined, showing how companies remain strongly committed to the region.

Obviously, strategies differ depending on each country's conditions and prospects. In some countries like Indonesia, where the prospects of a rapid and sustained recovery are weaker, the retreat or the slow-down is more pronounced. On the other hand, in countries like Thailand, Malaysia and Singapore investment flows have registered only a smaller contraction, as will be shown in the next section.

RECENT TRENDS IN EUROPEAN DIRECT INVESTMENT IN SOUTHEAST ASIA

The flow of direct investment to Southeast Asian countries has not been interrupted by the financial crisis. The fragmented statistics and evidence available confirm this point. The 1998 UNCTAD *World Investment Report* points out that in 1997, despite the financial crisis, foreign direct investment (FDI) in Asia and the Pacific rose by about

8 per cent and, as in the past, an overwhelming proportion of the investment was directed to East and Southeast Asia. In 1998, FDI inflows to Asia and the Pacific were down by 11 per cent to US$ 85 billion but still above the level of 1996. FDI to Southeast Asia decreased by 23 per cent to US$ 22 billion but still well above the average of annual flows recorded during 1991–95 (UNCTAD 1999, pp. 52–8).

Detailed data (Tables 6.2 and 6.3) provided by Thailand's Board of Investment (BOI) show how applications and approvals of European investment projects in this country have actually increased in 1997 and 1998 both in terms of number and investment value (although the latter is obviously inflated by the local currency depreciation). The Bank of Thailand statistics provide a similar picture, although the amounts are considerably smaller. The central bank statistics show only the actual net flow of funds related to FDI.

Table 6.2   Foreign direct investment in Thailand during 1995–98 (applications)

	1995	1996	1997	1998
Total foreign and domestic investment*	1 408	1 198	992	881
Total foreign and domestic investment value	936 384	834 673	490 792	283 788
Total foreign investment*	716	692	606	659
Total foreign investment value	527 913	439 130	344 382	258 697
Total European investment*	126	112	144	166
Per cent value on total foreign investment	17.6%	16.2%	23.8%	25.2%
Total European investment value	65 988	105 373	121 713	118 769
Per cent value on total foreign investment	12.5%	24.0%	35.3%	45.9%
Ownership:				
Wholly-owned European subsidiaries*, share	14%	25%	38%	52%
Wholly-owned European subsidiaries, inv. value	4 666	18 454	5 887	29 795

Notes: Values in million baht; * = number of projects.
Source: Board of Investment (Thailand).

Table 6.3   Foreign direct investment in Thailand during 1995–98 (approvals)

	1995	1996	1997	1998
Total foreign and domestic investment*	1 205	974	920	713
Total foreign and domestic investment value	586 044	529 428	482 892	303 386
Total foreign investment*	621	545	577	551
Total foreign investment value	414 526	355 863	333 250	272 528
Total European investment*	99	99	123	135
Per cent value on total foreign investment	15.9%	18.2%	21.3%	24.5%
Total European investment value	60 461	69 017	110 425	137 625
Per cent value on total foreign investment	14.6%	19.4%	33.1%	50.5%
Ownership:				
Wholly-owned European subsidiaries*, share	11%	22%	37%	44%
Wholly-owned European subsidiaries, inv. value	6 588	16 405	4 100	23 017

Notes: Value in million baht; * = number of projects.
Source: Board of Investment (Thailand)

What is important to note, however, is the strong expansion of the European share of the total FDI. This has grown from 17.6 per cent in 1995 to 25.2 per cent in 1998 in terms of the number of applications, and from 12.5 per cent to 45.9 per cent in terms of the value of the investment. The same, strong upward trend can be seen in Table 6.2 regarding approved investments. In this case, European investment in 1998 accounted for more than 50 per cent of the total value of approved foreign investment. Even if some of these investments could be delayed, postponed or reconsidered, the data clearly show how aggressively and positively European firms have reacted to the crisis, overtaking their Asian and American competitors at least as potential investors. If this trend is maintained and strengthened in the future, European companies in Thailand could indeed play a role comparable to that of Japanese and American firms.

In terms of sectors, as shown in Tables 6.4 and 6.5, note should be taken of the growth in the number and value of manufacturing investment in export-oriented sectors such as light industries and textiles (yarn spinning and manufacture of garments), and the relative

Table 6.4 European approved direct investment in Thailand by sector, 1995–98

	1995		1996		1997		1998	
	No. of projects	Invest. value	No. of projects	Invest. value	No. of projects	Invest. value	No. of projects	Invest. value
Agricultural Products	9	815	16	2 586	15	3 457	16	5 190
Minerals/Ceramics	6	31 730	11	22 286	7	15 104	4	567
Light Ind./Textiles	10	606	6	344	13	969	20	5 497
Metal Prod./Machinery	14	3 208	20	2 203	22	3 088	13	1 929
Electric/Electronics	14	6 063	19	22 445	10	3 156	19	12 285
Chemicals/Paper	25	9 490	17	16 168	17	17 248	13	9 974
Services/Utilities	21	8 549	10	2 985	39	67 404	50	102 179
Total	99	60 461	99	69 017	123	110 425	135	137 625

Note: Values in million baht.
Source: Board of Investment (Thailand).

Table 6.5   Export-oriented European-approved direct investment in Thailand, 1995–98

	1995		1996		1997		1998	
	No. of projects	Invest. value	No. of projects	Invest. value	No. of projects	Invest. value	No. of projects	Invest. value
Agricultural Products	4	359	5	866	3	256	10	4 825
Minerals/Ceramics	0	0	0	0	1	207	1	97
Light Ind./Textiles	3	41	3	79	10	651	16	4 319
Metal Prod./Machinery	5	1 347	5	365	3	298	6	1 241
Electric/Electronics	11	5 820	17	22 255	7	2 420	18	12 123
Chemicals/Paper	2	3 191	4	321	3	3 968	5	5 963
Services/Utilities	0	0	1	30	0	0	0	0
Total	25	10 758	35	23 916	27	7 801	56	28 568

Note: Values in million baht; export-orientation $\geq 80\%$.
Source: Board of Investment (Thailand).

decline in industries like chemicals and paper. Investment in the electric and electronics sectors (more than half in the manufacturing of electronic parts) have maintained the second position, although the amount of investment has sharply fallen if compared with the pre-crisis level.

Excluding direct investment in the service and utilities sectors, the strong export-orientation of recent European investment is confirmed by the fact that 56 out of 85 projects in 1998 are classified by Thailand's Board of Investment (BOI) as projects that are planning to export more than 80 per cent of their production. By sector, the highest concentration of export-oriented investment is to be found, as expected, in the electric and electronics industries, and in the textile and light industries.

As for the ownership pattern of new investments, a strong increase has been registered in European wholly-owned projects (see Tables 6.2 and 6.3), although it is reported that European participation has become considerably larger also in the case of joint ventures. This is an obvious outcome given the financial conditions of domestic firms adversely affected by capital and liquidity constraints.

Turning our attention to Singapore, we can see, as in the case of Thailand, a contraction of foreign direct investment in 1998. As shown in Table 6.6, FDI in Singapore has in fact decreased from S$ 5.9 billion in 1997 to S$ 5.2 billion in 1998. But in the case of Singapore,

Table 6.6   Investment in the manufacturing sector in Singapore by country 1990–98

	1990	*1991*	*1992*	*1993*	*1994*	*1995*	*1996*	*1997*	*1998*
USA	1 055	969	1 201	1 452	2 452	2 076	2 262	2 366	2 262
Japan	708	713	858	779	914	1 153	1 960	2 033	1 794
Europe	435	684	619	882	907	1 526	1 389	1 424	1 040
UK	90	187	306	358	525	771	398	445	9
Netherlands	73	216	43	8	176	391	518	385	44
Germany	166	60	106	205	92	184	247	121	523
France	60	75	34	125	54	141	60	272	139
Italy	–	70	27	43	39	13	54	175	90
Total foreign	2 218	2 461	2 733	3 177	4 327	4 852	5 716	5 908	5 226
Total local	267	473	748	746	1 437	1 957	2 369	2 580	2 574
Overall total	2 487	2 934	3 481	3 923	5 765	6 809	8 085	8 488	7 800

Note: Values in million Singaporean dollars (S$).
Source: Economic Development Board (Singapore).

European investment also has declined. In 1998, EU firms' investment accounted for S$ 1 billion, or 30 per cent less than the previous year. What is important to note, however, is the fact that even in 1998 EU firms invested a conspicuous amount, well above the levels of the early 1990s. Thus, Singapore has also succeeded in keeping high the interest and the involvement of European companies, particularly in those high-tech and export-oriented sectors like semiconductors, computer peripherals and pharmaceuticals. These sectors have benefited not only from the availability of skilled labour and managerial resources, but also from the lower Singaporean dollar and the active stance of the government that has promptly adopted cost-cutting and investment-promotion policies.

As for Malaysia, the other major country in the region attracting a large amount of foreign investment, here too, despite the difficult economic conditions and the controversial economic policies adopted, equity investment from European countries has remained at a relatively high level. Applications for the establishment of manufacturing projects with foreign participation actually registered an increase (507 in 1998 against 494 in 1997), though the investment value was 12 per cent lower than the year before. In particular, expansion or diversification projects recorded a sharp increase (130 per cent), against a fall (−44.9 per cent) in applications for new projects. According to the Malaysian Industrial Development Authority, a large number of foreign-owned companies have used retained earnings to finance expansion and diversification projects.

In terms of countries, the USA have taken the lion's share with 51 per cent of the total, while Japan's investment has contracted considerably both in absolute and relative terms (from 3.2 million ringgit or 22.3 per cent of the total in 1997 to 1.1 million ringgit or 9.0 per cent in 1998). On the other hand, European countries, except Germany, have shown a strong interest with the Netherlands and the United Kingdom registering a large increase compared with past records. The commitment of the Netherlands (1.1 million ringgit) is particularly noteworthy as it is the same as that of Japan. (The high level of Dutch investment in 1998 is due to two large projects in the chemicals sector and a major expansion project in microelectronics.)

Thus, the trends in the three Southeast Asian countries show that European investors have not been deterred from investing in the region despite the economic and financial turmoil and the selective exchange controls introduced by Malaysia. Many investors with an established presence in the region have actually increased their commitment, expanding or upgrading their operations. Also, as a whole, European firms appear to be more active and ready to grasp the opportunities than their Japanese competitors.

A CLOSER LOOK AT THE POLICIES AND BEHAVIOUR OF EUROPEAN COMPANIES

According to the scattered information and evidence available so far only a few companies have completely closed their manufacturing operations in Asia. They have restructured and streamlined their activities, but not abandoned the region. Electrolux, the Swedish MNC manufacturing electric home appliances, has announced the lay off of hundreds of workers in Thailand and Indonesia to face the contraction in demand. Novartis, the Swiss pharmaceutical giant born from the merger of Ciba and Sandoz, is implementing a global restructuring plan to rationalize its global activities. It foresees the closure of 35 plants, many of them in Asia. Yet these companies are not going to stop manufacturing activities.

Other companies have postponed their expansion plans, but avoided dismissals or plant closures. Among these are several small manufacturing units set up by enterprising individuals and small and medium-sized enterprises in Indonesia and the other countries of the region (*Il Sole 24 Ore* 15 March 1999; Molteni 1998, pp. 198–205).

A third group of companies has adopted instead a more aggressive policy of investment expansion in order to take advantage of the decline in asset prices and the depreciation of the currency. These investments can be regrouped into three types: (1) those in export-oriented industries, (2) those in fast-growing and innovative sectors, and (3) those aimed at increasing the company's market share in mature industries that still have a large potential in emerging markets like those of Southeast Asia.

Good examples of the third type of investment are those currently considered by Volkswagen, BMW, Renault and FIAT in Thailand, a country where Japanese car-makers have so far controlled about 90 per cent of the market (*Nihon Keizai Shinbun* 5 July 1999). In 1998, FIAT, the Italian car-maker, in particular, announced the establishment of a joint venture with a local partner (PNA) in Thailand. According to the plan, the new joint venture will start the production of FIAT models from 2001, using the existing facilities of the Thai partner. In 1999 Renault announced a tripartite joint venture with the participation of Nissan and Thai interest for the manufacturing of *Clio*, a compact model that has been very successful in the European market. BMW is currently building in Thailand its first plant in Asia to start operations in 2001 while Volkswagen production is using a license agreement with a local partner. In this way, European companies are preparing themselves to compete with both Japanese and American firms when, as expected, the local market will resume its growth (*Nihon Keizai Shinbun* 5 July 1999).

An investment with similar objectives has recently been announced by Ciment Français, a French company controlled by the Italian Italcementi group. Ciment Français will acquire the control of Asia Cement, the fourth Thai producer of cement, affiliated to the powerful Sophonpanich group (Bangkok Bank). Through this investment the Thai side will be able to dispose of its foreign debt, but the French-Italian side will own and manage (together with the Thai partner) one of the most modernized and efficient companies in a sector that still has a strong growth potential in Thailand (*Il Sole 24 Ore* 24 July 1999). As also shown by this case, European companies appear to be more prone than their Japanese competitors to acquire Asian companies (on this point see also Legewie in this volume and Lasserre, 1999).

As for the second type of investment (those in fast-growing, innovative sectors), a notable example is the one recently announced by Philips Semiconductor, that will establish a joint venture with Taiwan Semiconductor Manufacturing Company, the leading Taiwanese semiconductor manufacturer. The two companies will set up a wafer plant in Singapore with an investment of S\$ 1.2 billion. When fully implemented by the year 2000 the plant will employ 900 people to produce advanced logic chips for the consumer electronics and telecommunications industry (*Singapore Investment News – Sectoral Supplement* April 1999, p. 4). A second example is that of Gemplus, the world's largest smart card company set up in 1988 by five engineers from the French multinational Thomson (Lasserre and Schuette 1999, pp. 49–58), that will invest S\$ 20 million to set up its regional manufacturing centre for smart cards and micromodules. This is a growing market with a huge potential that it is likely to attract powerful Japanese and Korean competitors (*ibid.*, p. 5).

Other examples can be found in the life-sciences industries in which, despite the current economic woes, there are expectations of double-digit growth over the next few years. To these belongs the investment by Glaxo Wellcome that in 1999 opened a S\$ 80 million new manufacturing and product development facility in Singapore. Also relying on the future growth of the Asian market are Genset of France, which has established Genset Singapore Biotech, a joint venture with the Singaporean Bioprocessing Technology Centre, and Roche Vitamins of Switzerland, which has set up a major plant for blending vitamins and micronutrients (*ibid.*, p. 7).

The Case of Pirelli Cables & Systems

An interesting case is that of Pirelli Cables & Systems, a company of the Pirelli group, producing electrical cables for power transmission and telecommunications which is one of the two core business of the group (the other is the manufacturing of tires). (This section is based on material published by Pirelli (annual reports, press releases, and so on) and interviews at the company's headquarters.) The company has 49 plants in 14 countries, including two in China and one in Indonesia (PT Pirelli Cables Indonesia), opened in March 1997, just a few months before the crisis erupted. These new investments were the result of the management's decision in the early 1990s to focus on the emerging countries of Asia. As for Indonesia, the company was established in 1994 as a joint venture with a local partner (GT Kable Indonesia), although the management was completely entrusted to Pirelli through a shareholders' agreement. Recently, however, due to the financial crisis, Pirelli has agreed to acquire the local partner's entire share and thus gain full control of the company.

The plant in Indonesia, a greenfield investment with less than 200 employees, is located in Bukit Indah, in an industrial park near Jakarta. It produces optical cables for telecommunications and medium-voltage cables, reputed to be the most advanced available in the entire Asian area. The factory became completely operative at the end of 1997, but the dramatic economic conditions have not made it possible to fully utilize the installed capacity for the domestic market, as it was originally envisaged. The company has been trying to increase export to other countries in Asia and in Latin America, but in Asia it is facing increased competitive pressure from Asian manufacturers and other non-Asian competitors. Efforts to raise exports have also been hampered by the fact that the drastic depreciation of the Indonesian currency has reduced labour costs (accounting for 20 to 30 per cent of the total cost) but has increased the prices of other inputs like raw materials that have to be imported. The result is that gains in price competitiveness are quite negligible. Thus, just after the end of the inception phase, the company had to curtail output, while keeping the number of employees at the same level. A high-ranking manager explained that a 'no laying off policy' was adopted in order to avoid the dispersal of human resources trained at a high cost on the job.

The difficulties encountered in Indonesia have induced the management to postpone other initiatives already planned for Thailand, Malaysia and Vietnam. Pirelli is in fact convinced that only by acquiring a 'local identity' it is possible to play a leading role in a market dominated by public utilities that prefer to deal with domestic-based producers. The local presence is also necessary to compete in a very fragmented industry, in which it coexists with Western and Asian MNCs but also a huge number (more than a thousand in China alone) of small companies manufacturing an extremely diversified variety of products.

However, for the Pirelli managers these expansion plans will be resumed fairly soon, as they expect the region to recover within one or two years. In the case of Indonesia, they expect that within two years the country will be back at the pre-crisis level. An even faster recovery is expected in the cases of Thailand and Malaysia.

The Case of STMicroelectronics

In the electronic industry, another truly European and global company that is planning an additional investment in Singapore is STMicroelectronics (formerly SGS-THOMSON Microelectronics), established in the Netherlands in 1987 as a result of the merger of Italian SGS Microelettronica and the non-military business of the French Thomson Semiconducteurs, and currently listed on the New York Stock Exchange, on the Paris Stock Exchange and on the Milan Stock Exchange. The company, the No. 9 manufacturer of semiconductors and discrete devices in the world in 1998 and the No. 2 in Europe after Philips, has had a strong Asian presence since the early 1980s. (This section is based on material published by STMicroelectronics (annual reports, press releases, and so on) and interviews with Mr Guido Zargani, former Vice-President of STMicroelectronics for Asia.)

Indeed, the history of the company in Asia goes back to the end of the 1960s, when the Italian SGS – at the time a company of the Olivetti group – set up an assembly and testing unit (a back-end unit to use the industry's jargon) at Toa Payoh in Singapore. This was a labour-cost savings investment (at that time labor costs in Singapore were about one-twelfth of those in Italy) and also a 'follow-the-leader' type of investment, as it was undertaken following the transfer of manufacturing activities in Southeast Asia by American competitors (Texas Instruments and Fairchild).

Later, in 1984, the Italian firm established a second production unit in the city-state at Ang Mo Kio, where the regional headquarters of STMicroelectronics are now located. This was the first manufacturing unit to start so-called front-end production (wafer fabrication) in Southeast Asia (Molteni 1977, pp. 67–72). The decision to locate strategic manufacturing activities in Singapore was due to the far-sightedness of the management that clearly saw the opportunities provided by the rapid economic growth of Southeast Asia as well as the upgrading of the region's managerial, technological and manufacturing capabilities. Other investments followed and by 1999 STMicroelectronics employed more than 8000 people in four manufacturing units in Asia: one in China (Shenzen), a joint venture with Shenzen Electronics Group inaugurated in June 1998 with about 600 employees; one in Malaysia (Muar) with 3350 employees; and two in Singapore with more than 3700 people. 23 per cent of the production is actually taking place in Asia. As a result, STMicroelectronics has obtained a market share of about 5 per cent in the region, while net revenues in Asia Pacific (excluding Japan) have climbed from US$ 243 million (17.7 per cent of total revenues) in 1991 to US$ 1.1 billion (26.8 per cent) in 1997.

The strong commitment in the region has also enabled the company to overcome current difficulties. In fact, revenues and market shares have continued to grow thanks to the localization of activities in Asia, continuous efforts in research and development, a focus on the manufacturing of differentiated products for specific applications such as smart cards (a growing and rewarding segment of the market), and strong integration with local suppliers, most of them located in South Korea, Taiwan, Hong Kong and Malaysia. Thus, even in 1998, when the world market for semiconductors shrank by more than 8 per cent due to the Asian economic crisis and excessive capacity worldwide, STMicroelectronics was able to increase revenues in the Asia-Pacific region by more than 16 per cent to US$ 1.3 million (global revenues have increased by 5.7 per cent to US$ 4.2 million). Indeed, according to preliminary results, in the second quarter of 1999 sales in the Asia-Pacific region registered a further, strong increase, accounting for 31.4 per cent of the total. These are significant achievements, reflecting the underlying strength of the European company that has recently decided to restart the building of a new plant in Singapore that was temporarily suspended. In addition, STMicroelectronics plans rather to increase than to reduce investment in both production facilities and R&D.

CONCLUSIONS

Focusing on investment strategies in manufacturing, we have seen how the effects and the reactions to the crisis by European firms are extremely diversified. Although the great majority of firms remain confident in the region, there are significant differences according to the sector, the strategic objectives of the investment, the mode of entry, the country and also the time horizon considered.

The Asian crisis obviously favours export-oriented and resource-seeking investments. On the other hand, it discourages domestic or regional-market-oriented FDI, although there are major differences among sectors. In fact, if the investment is envisaged in a fast-growing, innovative sector, Asia remains a very attractive region. As noted by Jean-Pierre Dhanis, President of BASF's Polyurethane/PVC Division, 'in spite of the current crisis, Asia will be the biggest growth market (for polyurethane) within the next ten years' (*Singapore Investment News* March 1999, p. 1). Thus, it is normal that in these sectors investment in manufacturing facilities continues and will continue to grow, taking advantage also of the opportunities that the crisis has generated.

Yet, also in mature and less-dynamic sectors, competitive European companies with high-quality products, advanced manufacturing capabilities and managerial resources are striving to benefit from the current turmoil in order to enhance their position. We should not forget that in many 'mature' sectors (motor vehicles, electrical household appliances, and so on) there are still ample opportunities for growth in Southeast Asia. In these sectors, the companies that have strengthened their position during the crisis will most probably be the companies benefiting most once high economic growth resumes.

As for the mode of entry, lower asset prices, the removal of entry barriers and the adoption of FDI promotion policies by the local governments favour greenfield, wholly-owned FDI. But, on the other hand, the reduced financial capabilities of domestic entrepreneurs and firms and their acute need for capital injection allow European companies to enter Southeast Asian markets through the partial or total acquisition of existing undertakings. Indeed, in this phase European companies have adopted, in comparison to their Japanese competitors, a more assertive and determined attitude towards investment in general, and acquisitions in particular.

In terms of countries, those that are politically stable and economically stronger attract more FDI than others. Yet, changing realities and perceptions could easily modify the order of preferences. Finally, it should be noted that the Asian crisis is also changing the manufacturing strategies and the production system in Europe. Many European companies in sectors affected by the severe contraction of exports and the concurrent increase of low-cost imports have been forced to restructure and rationalize their activities. Such is the impact that even the celebrated Italian 'industrial districts' have been shaken and are undergoing a process of reorganization. In places like Prato, in Tuscany, the textile district exporting about 70 per cent of its production, authorities and entrepreneurs are openly discussing the need to rethink the traditional production system. This traditional system is based on an extensive, integrated network of 8000 highly-specialized small businesses and subcontractors with an average of 5.5 employees, that so far has provided both the technological and managerial capabilities as well as the organizational flexibility necessary to compete in the global market. The Asian crisis, however, has shown that the industrial district has to evolve in order to survive. To guarantee high-quality standards and the control of technological innovations, firms will have to grow and consolidate their activities, as the small dimension is becoming more a liability than an asset. At the same time, however, the low value-added parts of the production process have to be localized abroad, albeit in the countries of Eastern Europe rather than Asia.

References

Chen, E. K. Y. and P. Drysdale (eds) (1995) *Corporate Links and Foreign Direct Investment in Asia and the Pacific*, Pymble, Australia: Harper Educational.

Chia, S. Y. (1995) 'The International Procurement and Sales Behaviour of Multinational Enterprises', in E. K. Y. Chen and P. Drysdale (eds), *Corporate Links and Foreign Direct Investment in Asia and the Pacific*, Pymble, Australia: Harper Educational, pp. 227–61.

Droege & Comp. (1999) *Seeing Eye to Eye? A Comparison of Views on the Asian Crisis from German Companies at Home and their Subsidiaries in Asia*. Singapore: Droege.

European Business Information Centre (EBIC) Malaysia (1998) *Directory of European Companies in Malaysia 1998/99*, Kuala Lumpur: EBIC.

Kumar, B. N. and A. Mohr (1999) *Strategies of Western Firms for Transformation in Asia*, Paper presented at the LVMH Conference on Crisis and Transformation in Asia: Implications for Western Corporations, Fontainebleau: INSEAD Euro-Asia Centre.

Lasserre, P. (1999) *Managing Acquisitions in the Asia Pacific Region*, Paper presented at the LVMH Conference on Crisis and Transformation in Asia: Implications for Western Corporations, Fontainebleau: INSEAD Euro-Asia Centre.

Lasserre, P. and H. Schuette (1999a) *Strategies for Asia Pacific: Beyond the Crisis*, London: Macmillan.

Lasserre, P. and H. Schuette (1999b) *Strategy and Management in Asia Pacific*, London: McGraw-Hill International.

Mahani, Z. A. (1999) 'The Significance of the Economic and Currency Crisis on ASEAN–EU Trade and Investment Relations', in C. Suthiphand, C. Filippini and C. Molteni (eds), *ASEAN–EU Economic Relations: The Long-term Potential Beyond the Recent Turmoil*, Milano: EGEA, pp. 47–75.

Ministry of Trade and Industry (1998) *Economic Survey of Singapore 1997*, Singapore: MITI.

Molteni, C. (1997) 'Italian Firms in ASEAN Countries: Direct Investment and Non-equity Linkages between Asian and Italian Firms', in J. Slater and R. Strange (eds), *Business Relationships with East Asia: The European Experience*, London: Routledge, pp. 65–72.

Molteni, M. (ed.) (1998) *Strategie in concerto: sedici casi di successo discussi da giovni imprenditori*, Milano: EGEA.

Robinson, G. (1997) 'Is Europe Missing the Asia Boat? An Overview of EU–Asia Pacific Relations', in J. Slater and R. Strange (eds), *Business Relationships with East Asia: The European Experience*, London: Routledge, pp. 73–84.

UNCTAD and European Commission (1996) *Investing in Asia's Dynamism: European Union Direct Investment in Asia*, Luxembourg: Office for Official Publications of the European Communities.

UNCTAD United Nations Conference on Trade and Development (1998a) *World Investment Report 1998 – Trends and Determinants*, New York and Geneva: UN.

UNCTAD United Nations Conference on Trade and Development (1998b) *Handbook on Foreign Direct Investment by Small and Medium-sized Enterprises – Lessons from Asia*, New York and Geneva: UN.

UNCTAD United Nations Conference on Trade and Development (1999) *World Investment Report 1999 – Foreign Direct Investment and the Challenge of Development*. New York and Geneva: UN.

Part III
Marketing

7 Options for Strategic Change: Exploration or Exploitation in Marketing for New Wealth Creation*

Tomoaki Sakano, Arie Y. Lewin
and Naoko Yamada

OVERVIEW

In this chapter, we set out to present a framework for understanding changes in marketing practices by European, Japanese and US companies in Southeast Asia after the Asian economic crisis. How organizations evolve and adapt to their environments continues to be a central theme of organization and strategic change theories (Burns and Stalker 1961; Lawrence and Lorsch 1967; Thompson 1967; Donaldson 1996; Rajagopalan and Spreitzer 1997). Lewin, Long and Carroll (1999) have developed a model of new wealth creation, and following them we classify changes in marketing practices into two types: exploration and exploitation. The model assumes that the historical pattern of organization adaptations establishes a firm-specific path dependence which enables and restricts future adaptations, and that the long-term survival of the organization requires both exploitation and exploration adaptations (Levinthal and March 1993). Also, the nation-state form of capitalism creates a system of constraints which affects the type and direction of changes in marketing practices after the crisis (Lewin, Long and Carroll 1999).

* This research was made possible by the Japanese Government Ministry of Education Grant for Scientific Research (09630124) and Waseda University Grants for Special Research Projects (97C-009 and 97A-295) and also by the generous support of the IBM Consulting Group, Fuqua Centre for International Business Education and Research (CIBER) and the National Science Foundation Grant #NSF-SBR-9411218.

EXPLORATION–EXPLOITATION THEORY

March (1991, 1995) has described two fundamentally distinct, yet complementary, ways by which organizations can affect changes in their performance distributions. They may do so through 'exploration' and through 'exploitation'. Exploration involves the development of or trial-and-error experimentation with new technologies, strategies, processes, competences, new opportunities and organization forms. In contrast, exploitation involves the extension, elaboration, routinization or rationalization of extant technologies, strategies or processes. In short, the former involves pursuit of 'new possibilities' while the latter entails the elaboration and extension of 'old certainties' (March 1991, p. 71).

Other important differences between exploration and exploitation have to do with their goals and objectives and the means by which they are accomplished (Lewin, Long and Carroll 1999). The objective of exploration is the attainment of flexibility and the development of new knowledge and means of solving problems which the organization faces. It is associated with and accomplished by way of complex search, basic research, invention, risk-taking, relaxed control and loose discipline. The goals of exploitation are typically more objective and particular; for example, to meet clearly-defined, short-term objectives and immediate targets, to achieve short-run efficiency and improvements, to reduce slack, and to improve reliability, accuracy, precision or control. Exploitation is achieved by or associated with the standardization of procedures, problemistic search, relatively tighter control and discipline, risk-aversion, the emulation of successes (for example benchmarking), institutionalization, systematic reason, and acting in appropriate ways.

The effects of exploration and exploitation are realized in categorically distinct changes in the performance distribution of the firm. The benefits or returns to exploration are uncertain, more distant in time, highly variable, and often with a negative expected value. Returns to exploitation are more predictable, proximal in time, and less likely to deviate significantly from the mean of the performance distribution. Thus, exploration increases the likelihood of achieving levels of performance significantly different from historical levels – either above or below it – by its impact on the variance of the distribution. Exploitation, however, maintains performances at or near current levels.

According to the theory, organizational survival is dependent upon the ability of a firm to engage in 'sufficient' exploitation to ensure the current viability of the organization while exploring 'enough' to ensure its future viability (March 1991, p. 71). Exploration pursued in excess, at the expense or to the exclusion of exploitation, is said to lead to a condition where the firm has too many undeveloped ideas and too little distinctive competences. Exploitation pursued in the extreme jeopardizes the organization's survival by creating a 'competency trap' – the continued elaboration of capabilities that are increasingly obsolete. Thus, unlike some other notions of innovation, exploration–exploitation theory does not have a 'pro-innovation' bias. Instead it argues that long-term survival requires a sustained balance of exploitation and exploration (Levinthal and March 1993; Lewin, Long and Carroll 1999). However, it has not yet been empirically determined what ratio of exploration to exploitation constitutes 'enough' to ensure survival. Moreover, managers have an asymmetric preference for exploitation and, therefore, few firms develop the capability to simultaneously balance exploitation and exploration (Lewin, Long and Carroll 1999). Most firms realize negative returns from exploration because their explorations occur randomly or infrequently.

APPLICATION OF EXPLORATION–EXPLOITATION THEORY TO MARKETING PRACTICES IN SOUTHEAST ASIA AFTER THE CRISIS

Exploration–exploitation theory has clear applicability to the changes in marketing practices by European, Japanese and US companies in Southeast Asia after the economic crisis. Those marketing activities which involve the extension, modification or upgrading of existing practices, and are intended primarily to achieve cost savings or slack, would be consistent with the theoretical construct of exploitation. Examples are reducing the number of product items, reducing inventory, increasing local content, reformulating the product to obtain a lower price, slowing down the pace of new product introduction, and reducing promotional activities. Conversely, marketing activities which involve experiments or new approaches intended to innovate, develop or to help discover new knowledge and competences for the firm would be consistent with the construct of exploration. Examples are viewing the countries of Southeast Asia as a single market and launching new major products for the region, and establishing new forms of marketing organization such as new distribution channels.

In the aftermath of the financial crisis, firms greatly intensified exploitation marketing responses relative to exploration responses.

The immediate action taken by many European, Japanese and US companies was to slash their costs. Matsushita cut its budget for advertising and sales promotion in the region. Nike laid off about 2000 non-manufacturing employees in Asia, and it also replaced some expatriate staff in Asia with people hired on local terms. Reebok reduced its production capacity by at least 10 per cent to cope with shrinking demand in the Asian region. Marks & Spencer laid off about 50 workers in the Asia-Pacific region while some staff faced pay cuts. The company also shelved its marketing exploration initiative in China by closing its Shanghai representative office which was to prepare for the entry into the mainland.

Price had become much more important after the crisis (Meyer-Ohle and Hirasawa, and Davies in this volume). For example, most of Kao's products were little affected by the economic crisis because they were not luxuries. However, many companies had to increase prices because of the changes in currency values. For example, Matsushita and Sharp increased their wholesale price of home appliances imported into Thailand by 5–10 per cent because of the devaluation of the baht. Those products included TV, DVD players, cellular phones, and so on. Matsushita had to raise local retail prices of its products in Indonesia such as air conditioners and mini audio sets (mini-compo), which more than doubled in price (relative to price levels in September in 1997). Similarly locally-produced products such as TV sets also increased in price by 80 per cent. Following the initial price adjustments companies tried to raise local content as a way to reduce prices. For example, Sharp tried to shift its sourcing to overseas local suppliers with lower costs. The company organized a committee to raise the local procurement rate and staffs were expected to intensify their search and certification of parts-makers in Southeast Asia. It established a quality-authorization centre in Malaysia to check and monitor the quality of parts procured in the region. The company also started to produce its high-tech, main products such as mini disc players in order to test the possibility of effective local procurement of high-tech parts.

Changes in price have been a major tool for European and US companies too (Davies in this volume). For example, Coca-Cola avoided raising prices by shifting more production to returnable cans and bottles in Indonesia. By the middle of 1998 these containers represented about 85 per cent of the business (Hamilton 1998). Nike cut its sales prices in Thailand by 50 per cent for the first time to encourage teenagers to buy its shoes. The company had changed its original marketing strategy of not entering the low-end of the market, and developed marketing strategies aimed at increasing the frequency of people engaged in sports (Jitpleecheep 1999). Reebok shared its profit margin with regional distributors, who were expected to pass the benefit on to consumers, thus making Reebok products affordable. Unilever launched new soaps and detergents under the Sunlight name in Indonesia and Surf in Thailand at discounts of up to 30 per cent (Madden 1998). Unilever priced the single-use packets at only 250 rupiah (33 US cents) and marketed to Indonesian consumers who were unable spend a week of wages on a full-size bottle. The marketing goal of Unilever was to make high-quality goods affordable to poor people by earning a small margin on broad-based sales, and building a consumer base that would stay loyal as it grew more affluent. The company had previously used this strategy in rural developing markets for decades, and it was effectively applied in the more developed markets during a time of economic downturn. To slash packaging costs in Indonesia, it had put Sunsilk shampoo in plastic bags instead of the more expensively decorated bottles. It also introduced bulk sales of tea and laundry detergent, which allowed customers to scoop the quantity they could afford or needed (McDermott and Warner 1998). Adidas assembled its sandals in Malaysia as a way of making them more affordable to domestic consumers and succeeded in reducing the retail price by 15 to 20 per cent. The Marks & Spencer local franchisee in Singapore offered average retail price reductions of 15 per cent. The business model changed from low turnover and high margins to high turnover and low margins; and analysts concluded that the shift to the new business model had no effect on total profits (Jain 1998).

In addition to pricing, companies have tried to implement various defensive measures. Some companies launched products which were previously successful in home countries or other regions of Asia. For example, Kao launched the Biore Pore Pack, a facial treatment product that was quite successful in the Japanese domestic market, in Taiwan, Hong Kong, Indonesia and other regional markets in Asia. The company was confident that products popular in Japan could sell well in the region even if they carried prices close to those in the Japanese market. Procter and Gamble launched new anti-aging products in Thailand because this sector had good prospects in the other Southeast Asian countries. The company expected to expand its customer base in this market and enhance its market share in skin-care products by 5 per cent in 1998. Other companies have refocused on brand equity and brand image, and streamlined their brands. For example, Reebok focused resources on the brands that had been showing strong growth and adjusted its marketing strategy by separating its products into two segments. Some companies have customized their products. For example, Nike launched a new shoe especially for the Asian market, intending with this entry-level footwear to target customers who had not yet purchased their brand.

Many companies have tried to strengthen their distribution channels. For example, Procter and Gamble in a joint venture with a local Vietnamese partner, expanded its retail network to the tiny shops and roadside stalls where most Vietnamese buy their household goods (Warner 1998). Coca-Cola restructured its distribution network from supermarkets back to traditional outlets such as mom-and-pop stores and street vendors (Hamilton 1998). Unilever has expanded its direct distribution networks to reach remote villages by eliminating wholesalers and their product markups. The Unilever independent and exclusive distributors aggressively campaigned for the expansion of outlets, dispatching sales staff directly to stores, sidewalk stalls and tiny corner shops. The data received by Unilever's national sales manager from the 290 000 outlets visited by the distributors' direct sales staffs, when analysed, showed this number to be about six times the reach of other multinationals such as Pepsi and Nestlé (McDermott and Warner 1998). Adidas strengthened its dealer network and redesigned sales outlets in Thailand and terminated distribution contracts with 20 local dealers that had financial problems. The company also developed same-look Adidas stores throughout Asia to stimulate sales especially in tourism-dependent countries such as Singapore and Hong Kong (Rungfapaisarn 1999).

Companies have tried to streamline consumer awareness media. For example, Coca-Cola launched its first localized advertising campaign to suit the Malaysian lifestyle (Li 1999). Nike launched a marketing campaign created specifically for Thailand as it took control of its Thai operations from Sports Ace, which had served as its distributor for 12 years (Warner 1997). Similarly, the company shifted from distributors to wholly-owned subsidiaries in many markets in the region, appointing its own advertising agencies to develop campaigns reflecting local sports and athletes (Wentz 1997). Levi Straus also created an advertising campaign specifically for Asia for the first time ever, although it still featured strong American themes (Warner 1997). Adidas launched its first TV commercial in Malaysia emphasizing local lifestyles and atmosphere.

As expected, the exploration type of marketing activities attempted by European, Japanese and US companies in Southeast Asia following the crisis have been rare and infrequent. Some companies have re-defined their view of the Southeast Asian markets and their strategies, for example by shifting towards viewing the countries of Southeast Asia as a single market and totally restructuring marketing activities accordingly (Meyer-Ohle and Hirasawa in this volume). Nestlé has divided Asia into four sub-groups and countries according to simi-larity of consumption patterns, and designated its Thailand factory as the headquarters for the Indochina sub-region. The stated goal was to aggregate the group's activities and develop its brands and products on a regional basis (Rungfapaisarn 1999). Nestlé also eliminated 10 regional warehouses and set up a high-tech national distribution centre in Malaysia to centralize its entire warehousing and distribution net-work for both domestic and export markets in over 40 countries.

This centre is expected to house all of Nestlé's brands and products and is being equipped with the most advanced warehouse management system, 24-hour stock transfer operations and bar-code product-tracking features. In a similar move Procter and Gamble established a regional exporting centre in Thailand; and in 1998 they also invested an additional 1 billion baht in production facilities in Thailand to dramatically improve production efficiency. The factory became a major sourcing centre for skin and hair-care products, as well as for diapers and sanitary napkins for distribution to over 10 countries. Nestlé, moreover, started to build a database in Asia with detailed information on consumption patterns, lifestyle, race, religion and feel-ings about specific brands. The company's global strategy is to make Malaysia a suitable pilot for an Asian rollout utilizing information from the database by building a one-on-one marketing communication programme (Bidlake 1998).

Some companies have tried to introduce global products. Kao focused on its most strategic products in Japan to make them into global brands. For Asian markets, it increased exports and strength-ened distribution channels for Sofina cosmetics and Biore product lines. By introducing highly competitive products into Asian markets from the domestic market with globally uniform brand names, Kao expected to improve income on a consolidated basis. Kao chose a Japanese department store as its first outlet for the Sofina brand in Taiwan, where the products were sold only through counselling by sales associates.

THE MEDIATING EFFECT OF FORMS OF CAPITALISM

Whether country history, culture, managerial ideologies or the institutional system affect organization form, management practices and strategies continue to be subjects of much research. However, many researchers have noted that the specific nation-state form of capitalism is reflected in the governance structures, employment relationships, and management practices of enterprises (see discussion in Lewin, Long and Carroll 1999). Lewin, Long and Carroll (1999) show that the collective enactment of a nation's culture, values and history is represented in the development of specific political institutions, social compacts, educational systems and institutional structures which legitimize the particular business system and property rights, and specific management practices (Whitley 1992, 1994; Hofstede 1993).

Following Lewin, Long and Carroll (1999), we expect that the specific nation-state form of capitalism creates a system of constraints that affect the type and direction of organizational restructuring and strategic change. To illustrate the differential effect of country differences on the marketing strategies of companies in Southeast Asia after the crisis, we first contrast the nation-state forms of capitalism in Germany, Japan and the USA, and Table 7.1 represents a comparison of institutional factors and management practices for those countries.

Japanese companies generally have not been engaged in radical strategic changes, such as pulling out of markets, even after the crisis. Also, they have not been very actively involved in taking over local partners, or changing their shares in joint ventures. In fact, there have not been any radical changes in the way Japanese companies operate in Southeast Asia; they have primarily focused on incremental adjustments to their marketing activities in terms of products, promotions, price and distribution channels (Meyer-Ohle and Hirasawa in this volume). This is consistent with the findings of Sakano and Lewin (1999) that CEO succession in Japan is not associated with radical strategic and organization changes, but, rather, is related to Japanese companies' preference for evolutionary organization and strategic changes.

In contrast, as in the case of CEO succession, US companies did initiate drastic strategy changes during and after the crisis. For example, Reebok downsized by eliminating management layers and combining business units as their way of coping with the difficult industry conditions (Auerbach 1998). Reebok eliminated the international division and replaced it by four regional divisions: USA and

Table 7.1 Comparison of institutional factors and management practices in Germany, Japan and the USA

Institutional factors	Germany	Japan	USA
Role of government	• Extensive involvement • Detailed regulatory environment	• Industrial policy • Embedded government guidance	• Relatively *laissez-faire*
Rule of law	• Highly developed • Central role for government and parliament • Transparent	• More general • Administrative guidance	• Highly developed • Decentralized • Transparent
Structure of capital markets	• Restrictive • Banks major long-term equity owners	• Very restrictive • Market for divestiture/M&A very limited	• Very competitive • Sophisticated, large-scale, very liquid markets
Culture: individualism/collectivism	• Moderate individualism • Institutionalized communitarianism	• Collectivism	• Individualism
Educational system	• Centralized • Uniform • Vocational system • Meritocracy	• Centralized • Uniform • Meritocracy determines entry level into socioeconomic status	• Decentralized • Heterogeneous • No vocational system • Path to socioeconomic system

Table 7.1 (contd.)

	Germany	Japan	USA
Management practices			
Governance structure	• Supervisory board considers employees, society and state	• Company managed for employees and shareholders • Inside directors • Stable cross-shareholding • Main bank	• Company managed for shareholders • Board responsible to shareholders • Outside directors • Diversified ownership • Hierarchy
Authority and control	• Hierarchy • Top-down	• Top-down • Bottom-up • Consensus-based decision-making	• Top-down • Individual centred decision-making
Employment relationship	• Long-term commitments • Layoffs/downsizing/ severance pay tightly regulated by social legislation	• Life-time employment • Entry-level hiring • Internal labour markets	• Employment-at-will • External labour markets • High internal and external mobility
Compensation		• Seniority-based • No stock options	• Performance-based • Stock options
Strategic paradigm	• Related diversification • Infrequent exit-entry of lines of business • Long-term orientation • Risk-seeking	• Related diversification • Most joint ventures with group • Long-term orientation • Risk-seeking	• Exit-entry of lines of business • Short-term orientation • Less risk-seeking
Knowledge	• Tacit: low, high for master craftsmen • Explicit: high	• Tacit: high • Explicit: moderately low	• Tacit: low • Explicit: high

Canada; Latin America; Europe, Africa and the Middle East; and Asia-Pacific. US companies have also been actively involved in many mergers and acquisitions. For example, the Coca-Cola company has increased its equity in bottling operations in Southeast Asia. In Thailand, the company paid 1.9 billion baht for an additional 5 per cent equity in Thai Pure Drink, increasing the company stake to 49 per cent in the Coca-Cola bottler. At the same time, it sent a new management team from the USA to assume greater control over its bottling operations in the crucial Thai market. It also acquired four local bottlers in South Korea in 1997 under its worldwide strategy of consolidating bottlers (Slater 1998). Nike moved from distributor arrangements in Asia to wholly-owned subsidiaries to run marketing and sales operations (Wentz 1997). Also, many of the European companies which had entered Southeast Asia in earlier times exited the market through divestitures and often sold out to American companies. US companies, however, are more likely to abruptly pull out of a market, reflecting their sensitivity to short-term earnings pressures and their belief that they could re-enter the market anytime.

In the USA, the capital markets are instrumental in exerting direct and continuous pressures on company management to undertake short-term cost reductions. In contrast, Japanese capital markets are not as fluid and competitive because of the extensive cross-holding of shares, main bank relationships, the interrelated structure of corporate groups known as *keiretsu*, and the absence of outside directors. The less-competitive characteristics of the capital markets in Japan operate to buffer Japanese companies from short-term market pressures, suggesting that they should be under less pressure to make radical strategic changes in the short term than their US counterparts.

The structure of the capital markets in most European countries is more similar to Japan, the exception being the London markets. The size, efficiency and liquidity of the highly competitive capital markets in the USA have served to focus management attention on maximizing shareholder value, and for many American managers this focus has intensified a short-term orientation. In addition, the scale, liquidity and diversity of the US capital markets make resources available for the full range of strategic options such as mergers, acquisitions, leverage buyouts and initial public offerings. In contrast, Europe and Japan operate under a more 'patient' capital structure and scale, liquidity and diversity of investors are far less developed. For example, in Germany the major banks have controlling equity positions (as well as key roles as lenders) in almost all the publicly held companies. In

Japan, cross-holding arrangements of equity among companies belonging to a *keiretsu*, as well as major bank ownership of equity, have a similar effect (Sakano and Lewin 1999). In either case, managers are relatively more insulated from the monitoring of the capital markets, can adopt a longer-term strategic orientation and can be less concerned with short-term fluctuations in reported performance.

Therefore, like Japanese companies, European managers are likely to have a longer perspective in marketing strategy even during or after the crisis. For example, Adidas has been patient in maintaining its one local distributor in Malaysia to ensure high quality products as well as affordable pricing. Similarly, a joint venture between Adidas and G. S. Gill Malaysia has remained very stable and currently commands a 30 per cent market share in the local sports goods market. The company continues its more than 20 franchised concept shops nationwide.

However, authority and control of European companies is more hierarchical and top-down than is the case in Japanese counterparts; also, the strategic planning process is more formalized. Therefore, European companies are more likely to initiate drastic strategy changes and restructuring from the top than Japanese companies. And European companies are more often engaged in mergers and acquisitions than Japanese companies. For example, Unilever has for some time been involved in a wide-ranging major restructuring of its worldwide operations. Under strong CEO leadership, the company has been restructured to a few core categories – ice creams, margarines, teas, detergents, skin-care products and prestige cosmetics and fragrances. In the Asian markets, it is focusing on acquisitions to better exploit the untapped growth potential of the region because of the high cost of acquiring companies in North America and Europe (Beck 1998).

A MODEL OF NEW WEALTH CREATION

The distinction between exploration and exploitation would not be useful if it did not relate to performance. A major potential contribution of exploration–exploitation theory is its implication for resolving the question of how each type of marketing activity can improve or alter organizational performance. There have been few empirical tests of the theory, an exception being Hunter's study (1999), which does involve a direct empirical test of the theory. Using the event study method, Hunter found that investments in information technology classified as explorations had significant and positive abnormal returns, whereas those classified as exploitations yielded positive but non-significant returns. Also, the variance in the returns to explorations was greater than that of exploitations.

Lewin, Long and Carroll (1999) developed a model of new wealth creation generalized from March's (1991, 1995) theory of exploration and exploitation. Survival of the firm over time is realized in changes in the firm's wealth creation performance, which Lewin, Long and Carroll (1999) hypothesize to be the joint outcome from returns to (1) exploitation (2) exploration and (3) legacy (returns to reputation, market position and capabilities built up from a history of exploitation and exploration adaptations). Figure 7.1 depicts the recursive interplay between exploitation, exploration, legacy and a firm's wealth creation.

Exploitation adaptations are imitable and any advantages are likely to be competed away. Therefore, in the long run, returns to exploitations cannot be a significant source of above average returns. The returns to explorations, however, have the potential to result in above average returns and to provide the primary input to new wealth creation. Because exploration involves the search for, identification of, and investment in new opportunities (which expand and replenish legacy), long-run returns to a sustained strategy of exploration are realized in new wealth creation and above average returns.

The cumulative effect of exploitation and exploration adaptations is reflected in the firm's legacy, which is both an industry and a firm characteristic. Consequently, industries and firms will differ in terms of their legacy decay rates and in terms of the contribution of legacy to performance.

The enactment of exploration adaptations and the likelihood of achieving above average returns is moderated by, among other things, the availability of slack resources (Cyert and March 1963; Singh 1986). Other moderating factors involve absorptive capacity for assimilating new knowledge (Boer, van den Bosch and Volberda 1999; Cohen and Levinthal 1990; Lane and Lubatkin 1998) and path dependence. Path dependence is the firm's unique historical profile of exploitation and exploration adaptations and managerial intentionality, such as strategic intent to invest slack resources in exploration (Lewin and Wong 1998) and top management (for example, the CEO) preference for risk seeking (Lewin and Stephens 1993; Finkelstein and Hambrick 1996)

Many European and US companies have actively increased their marketing budgets. Coca-Cola, for example, recognizing that a crisis is a good time for increasing advertising as media space is cheaper and

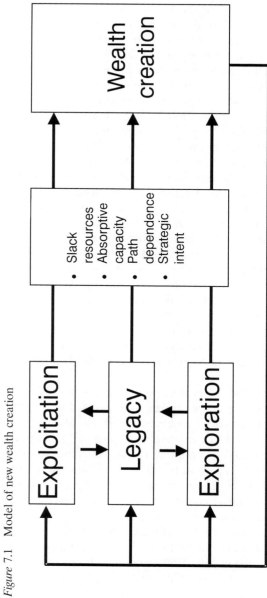

Figure 7.1 Model of new wealth creation

competition is sparser, increased its marketing budgets in Southeast Asia by 25 per cent to 50 per cent for certain brands (Slater 1998). And European retail companies have quickly expanded their presence in Southeast Asia (Davies in this volume). In contrast, Japanese companies are nowadays not so active in their investments in Southeast Asia, this being partially explained by the difference in their commitment to this region. Japanese companies have had a long history of Asian investments, whereas European and US companies are in a catch-up mode and their active promotions represent necessary entry costs at this point due to their late arrival. Another explanation may lie in the lack of slack resources; Japanese companies are not able to maximize the opportunities created by the crisis due to financial difficulties of their parent companies in Japan.

Since the relationship between exploration/exploitation and new wealth creation is moderated by absorptive capacity (among other factors), many companies have tried to increase absorptive capacity, and accumulate core competences. For example, Coca-Cola brought into Southeast Asia a team of experts in financial, operating and marketing matters to help affiliates and subsidiaries and to explore new business opportunities. The team provided expertise to improve efficiency and tackle problems in the region. The company's aim was to combine the best experiences and practices from different markets, and incorporate key lessons learned during the economic downturn in Mexico (Rungfapaisarn 1998). The company moved very fast to deploy lower-cost returnable packaging, to launch smart promotions and give attention to distribution and to continue investment (Hamilton 1998). Furthermore, Levi Straus restructured its executive teams to place a new leadership team throughout the company's Asia-Pacific division in order to leverage learning and integrate best practices. For example, a one-to-one relationship marketing expert was assigned from Canada to a Levi Straus marketing position in the Philippines subsidiary.

CONCLUSIONS

Many European, Japanese and US companies have changed their marketing practices in Southeast Asia since the economic crisis. Some of their actions have been audacious and bold, and some mimetic and incremental. We have set out to present a framework for understanding these changes.

Following Lewin, Long and Carroll (1999), we classify these changes in marketing practices to two types: exploration and exploitation. Exploration and exploitation have categorically distinct effects on company performance, especially on the mean and the variance of the distribution. Since exploration involves searching for, identifying and investing in new opportunities, the expected returns are to be realized over a longer time-horizon, and are predicted to exceed the returns from exploitation. However, because of the risk and uncertainty, the variance of returns to exploration are greater than for exploitation. Since exploitation involves the refinement, elaboration or incremental improvement of existing capabilities, the expected returns are smaller, but the likelihood of underperformance is reduced. Because of the lower risk and lower variance in the returns to exploitation, companies have a strong preference for and engage more frequently in exploitation.

We also claim that the nation-state form of capitalism creates a system of constraints which affects the type and direction of changes in marketing practices by European, Japanese and US companies in Southeast Asia following the crisis. Because of the less-competitive characteristics of capital markets in Japan, Japanese companies were unwilling or unable to engage in radical changes such as exiting entirely out of markets after the crisis. In contrast, US companies were able to or had to effect radical strategy changes and organizational restructuring largely due to the short-term orientation of managers reflecting preferences of capital markets in the USA. Since the structure of the capital markets in European countries is more similar to that of Japan, European companies are more likely to adopt a longer-term perspective in marketing strategy after the crisis. However, since authority and control of European companies are more hierarchical and top-down, the strategic planning process can be expected to be more centralized and formalized. European companies are more likely to initiate radical strategic actions such as mergers and acquisitions and drastic organizational restructuring than their Japanese counterparts.

References

Auerbach, J. G. (1998) 'Reebok Set to Take a $25 Million Charge for Restructuring Plan', *Asian Wall Street Journal*, 4 February, p. 10.
Beck, E. (1998) 'Unilever Aims to Restructure Across Globe', *Asian Wall Street Journal*, 11 February, p. 23.

Bidlake, S. (1998) 'Nestle Builds Database in Asia with Direct Mail: Malaysia Pilot Shows Success of Defining Market Full of "Peculiarities" ', *Advertising Age International*, 1 January, p. 34.

Boer, M. de, F. A. van den Bosch and H. W. Volberda (1999) 'Managing Organizational Knowledge Integration in the Emerging Multimedia Complex', *Journal of Management Studies*, vol. 36(3), pp. 379–98.

Burns, T. and G. M. Stalker (1961) *The Management of Innovation*, London: Tavistock.

Cohen, W. M. and D. A. Levinthal (1990) 'Absorptive Capacity: A New Perspective on Learning and Innovation', *Administrative Science Quarterly*, vol. 35, pp. 128–52.

Cyert, R. M. and J. G. March (1963) *A Behavioral Theory of the Firm*, Englewood Cliffs, NJ: Prentice-Hall.

Donaldson, L. (1996) 'The Normal Science of Structural Contingency Theory', in S. R. Clegg, C. Hardy and W. R. Nord (eds), *Handbook of Organization Studies*, London: Sage, pp. 57–76.

Finkelstein, S. and D. Hambrick (1996) *Strategic Leadership: Top Executives and Their Effects on Organizations*, St Paul, Minn.: West Publishing Company.

Hamilton, M. M. (1998) 'Coke Keeps Afloat in Asia; Mexico Experience Offers Blueprint for Crisis Management', *The Washington Post*, 22 August, p. E1.

Hofstede, G. (1993) 'Cultural Constraints in Managerial Theories', *Academy of Management Executive*, vol. 7(1), pp. 81–95.

Hunter, S. (1999) *Which Investments in Information Technology Increase the Market Value of the Firm?*, Paper presented at the Workshop on Information Systems in Economics, Charlotte, North Carolina, 12 December.

Jain, A. (1998) 'Robinson Cuts Prices at Retail Outlets – Move at Marks & Spencer Division is Not Expected to Increase Profits', *Asian Wall Street Journal*, 11 May, p. 8.

Jitpleecheep, S. (1999) 'Sporting Products: Nike, Pan Enlist Starts in Price War to Woo Teens', *Bangkok Post*, 27 August, p. 10.

Lane, P. J. and M. Lubatkin (1998) 'Relative Absorptive Capacity and Interorganizational Learning', *Strategic Management Journal*, vol. 19, pp. 461–77.

Lawrence, P. and J. Lorsch (1967) *Organization and Environment*, Boston, Mass.: Harvard School of Business Administration Press.

Levinthal, D. A. and J. G. March (1993) 'The Myopia of Learning', *Strategic Management Journal*, vol. 14 (Winter), pp. 95–112.

Lewin, A. and C. U. Stephens (1993) 'CEO Attitudes as Determinants of Organization Design: An Integrated Model', *Organization Studies*, vol. 15(2), pp. 183–212.

Lewin, A. and S. Wong (1998) *Organization Adaptation: Relationship of Strategic Intent on Performance*, Working Paper, Center for Research on New Organization Forms, The Fuqua School of Business, Duke University, Durham, North Carolina.

Lewin, A., A. Okumura and T. Sakano (1998) 'Managing Global Competition: Japanese Companies in Transition', *Seoul Journal of Business*, vol. 4(2), pp. 1–25.

Lewin, A., C. Long and T. Carroll (1999) 'The Co-Evolution of New Organization Forms', *Organization Science*, vol. 10(5), pp. 535–50.

Li, K. S. (1999) 'Coke Goes Fully Malaysian', *Business Times*, 5 May, p. 15.

Madden, N. (1998) 'Asian Crisis: Marketers Rely on Survival Tactics: Lower Prices, Recession-proof Products Offered as Recovery Looks Bleak for 1999', *Advertising Age International*, 19 October, p. 3.

March, J. G. (1991) 'Exploration and Exploitation in Organizational Learning', *Organization Science*, vol. 2(1), pp. 71–87.

March, J. G. (1995) 'The Future, Disposable Organizations, and the Rigidities of Imagination', *Organization*, vol. 2(3/4), pp. 427–40.

McDermott, B. and F. Warner (1998) 'Unilever Thinks Small to Cope in Asia', *Wall Street Journal Europe*, 26 November, p. 4.

Rajagopalan, N. and G. Spreitzer (1997) 'Toward a Theory of Strategic Change: A Multi-lens Perspective and Integrative Framework', *The Academy of Management Review*, vol. 22(1), pp. 48–79.

Rungfapaisarn, K. (1998) 'Coke Sends Experts to Aid Asian Affiliates', *The Nation* (Thailand), 5 February.

Rungfapaisarn, K. (1999) 'Local Nestle now Indochina HQ', *The Nation* (Thailand), 26 February.

Rungfapaisarn, K. (1999) 'Adidas Revamps as Sales Stay Pegged', *The Nation* (Thailand), 24 May.

Sakano, T. and A. Lewin (1999) 'Impact of CEO Succession in Japanese Companies: A Co-Evolutionary Perspective', *Organization Science*, vol. 10(5), pp. 651–71.

Singh, J. V. (1986) 'Performance, Slack and Risk Taking in Organizational Decision-Making', *Academy of Management Journal*, vol. 29(3), pp. 562–85.

Slater, J. (1998) 'Companies: Keeping its Cool: Coca-Cola Splurges to Boost Itself in Asian Markets', *Far Eastern Economic Review*, 21 May, p. 56.

Thompson, J. D. (1967) *Organization in Action*, New York: McGraw-Hill.

Warner, F. (1997) 'Asian Marketing', *The Asian Wall Street Journal*, 15 December, p. 11.

Warner, F. (1998) 'Stall Speed: Aimed Spats, P&G is Losing it', *Asian Wall Street Journal*, 26 February, p. 4.

Wentz, L. (1997) 'Nike Steers Creative to Local Asia Agencies', *Advertising Age*, 8 December, p. 49.

Whitley, R. (1992) *European Business System*, London: Sage.

Whitley, R. (1994) 'Dominant Forms of Economic Organization in Market Economies', *Organization Studies*, vol. 15(2), pp. 153–82.

8 Marketing Strategies of Japanese Firms: Building Brands with a Regional and Long-term Perspective

Hendrik Meyer-Ohle and Katsuhiko Hirasawa

INTRODUCTION

In April 1997, an article entitled 'Production in Asia, from Asia to Asia' appeared in the leading Japanese business newspaper, the *Nihon Keizai Shinbun*. It stated that:

> With the onset of the cheap yen and the rising strength of local currencies in Malaysia, for example, the price competitiveness of some Asian countries and areas has decreased. Companies were pushed to review their production locations to sustain low costs. 'Products have emerged that could be produced less expensively in Japan' says one large electronics manufacturer.
>
> However, the trend by large manufacturers to relocate production back to Japan has been rather limited. A notable example are large screen 29-inch television sets which were once produced by Matsushita in Malaysia.
>
> The reason behind this is Asia's growing importance as a consumer market. Though it used to be an 'export base focussed on Japan', it has changed to a 'provision base for neighboring consumer markets.' (*Nihon Keizai Shinbun* 28 April 1997, p. 8)

This article, written only three months before the crisis hit Southeast Asia in the summer of 1997, reflected the attitude of Japanese companies at the time. They harboured great hopes for the development of consumer markets in a Southeast Asia they no longer saw as a mere production base. However, the devaluation of the Asian currencies, starting with the Thai baht, dashed these hopes as it hit financial markets all over Asia. Drops in income and rising unemployment derailed the development of consumer markets and disrupted marketing strategies.

This chapter discusses how the onset of the crisis affected the marketing strategies of Japanese multinational companies in local consumer markets in Southeast Asia. We shall concentrate on manufacturers of consumer electronics, household goods and foods and retail companies with the exclusion of automobile manufacturers. First we describe major characteristics of the activities of Japanese companies in the area to date, followed by an examination of how the crisis effected marketing activities. We then look at strategic changes, beginning with methodological observations and then turning to the question driving this study: how did Japanese companies respond to the crisis in Southeast Asia and what are the long-term strategies for this market? The chapter concludes with reflections on the importance of Southeast Asian consumer markets for Japanese firms.

BACKGROUND: LONG EXPERIENCE AND HIGH EXPECTATIONS

Mention of the activities of Japanese companies in Southeast Asia often conjures up images of export-oriented production. However, this has not always been the case; most companies began by selling products in the region before setting up production facilities. In order to understand the current situation of crisis and change one must understand the characteristics of earlier marketing activities, the development of consumer markets and the attitudes Japanese companies held towards those markets before the crisis.

The earliest engagement of Japanese companies in Southeast Asia commenced in the 1920s, yet it was not until the second half of the 1960s that the main initiative of Japanese companies to sell in these markets began. Companies involved ranged from large Japanese electronics manufacturers to producers of household goods and foods. For example Kao, a producer of detergents and other household goods, advanced into Thailand in 1963, Singapore in 1965 and Malaysia in 1973. It built up a presence in the region that at that time was considerably stronger than its presence in Europe or America. The household electronics manufacturer Sanyo established affiliates in Singapore in 1967, in Thailand in 1969 and in the Philippines in 1971. In foods, Ajinomoto established a base in the Philippines in 1958, in Thailand in 1960, and in Malaysia in 1961. Retailers, especially department stores, also embarked on early initiatives. In 1964, Daimaru opened a store in Bangkok. Isetan and Yaohan opened in Singapore in 1970 and 1974 respectively. While the second half of the 1970s did not see many openings of new stores, activities picked up in the early 1980s and really took off in the second half of the 1980s. Supermarket operators joined all the major department stores and expanded into the region (Okamoto 1999).

Decades of involvement have enabled companies to establish a strong position in the region. Unsurprisingly, Japanese consumer electronics companies clearly dominate local markets. However, Japanese companies are major players in other sectors, too. In personal and household goods, Lion and Kao compete on an equal footing with Unilever, Procter & Gamble or Colgate and even lead some categories. Ajinomoto challenges Nestlé and Coca-Cola and has even clinched the lead in certain market segments such as canned coffee. Finally, Japanese department stores dominate the shopping districts in many Asian capitals.

Two points about their marketing activities must be emphasized here. First, trade barriers caused companies to develop separate subsidiaries or affiliates with marketing and production facilities in every country of the region. Second, companies included a local partner when setting up affiliates. Governments in the region permitted the holding of majority stakes in joint ventures only to companies that restricted their activities to exports. At the same time, they applied stricter regulations to companies that targeted local markets. Generally, governments restricted foreigners to minority stakes in order to protect local competitors (Masuyama, Vandenbrink and Chia 1997).

The role of local partners differed. While Japanese companies always provided products and production knowledge, their partners sometimes limited their involvement to the role of silent investor. More often the partners provided marketing capabilities and took an active position in the distribution of goods. By focusing on one country, these organizational characteristics hindered the development of region-wide strategies. They are also a major factor behind the very different weight one company might have in the different markets of Southeast Asia.

The last point to be discussed in this section is the development of markets for consumer goods. Consumers in the area enjoyed relatively steady increases in household income in the 1990s (Table 8.1). While not comparable in absolute terms, increases in household income and demand in the countries in Southeast Asia stood out against stagnation in Japan.

Table 8.1   Change in household income (1986 = 100)

	1991	1996	1997
Singapore	136	177	186
Malaysia	104	132	134
Thailand	108	165	164
Indonesia	132	153	158
Philippines	114	133	146
Japan	115	122	119

Source: Calculations based on data assembled by Asian Demographic Limited.

Table 8.2   Reasons for the importance of Asia as a consumer market (excluding China)

Reason	Relative importance (%)
High growth	73.4
Large population	14.3
Established markets	40.5
Stable political and economic environment	4.8
Existing manufacturing base	23.8
Existing sales base	11.9
No trade conflicts	0.0
Stable exchange rates	2.4
Existing historical relations	2.4
Other	2.4

Source: Nihon Keizai Shinbun Nikkei Sangyō Shōhi Kenkyujo (1996, p. 17).

This constant increase in household incomes raised the interest of Japanese companies. A report published by *Nihon Keizai Shinbun* in 1996, titled 'Asia's consumer markets and the response by Japanese Companies', described the large expectations of Japanese firms in the 1990s. First, it stated that sales of goods in developing Asia accounted for only 5 per cent of the total sales of Japanese companies to date. Survey results showed the perceptions of Japanese managers towards the markets of Asia: China attracted Japanese companies mainly for its large population, enabling companies to profit by focusing on high-income consumers; the much smaller ASEAN countries, however, mainly appeared attractive for their rapid growth (Table 8.2). Strong growth was expected to create a growing middle class and by extension new stable mass markets with needs that would go far beyond everyday products to include high-class, high-tech and high-fashion goods.

The crisis of 1997 ended the long period of rapid growth in the area and affected the strategies of companies involved in Southeast Asian markets.

EFFECTS OF THE CRISIS

For companies marketing products in the region the economic crisis created three main impacts: a drop in consumer demand, economic instability, and growing political inference in the economic sphere. The most important area is consumer conduct. Consumers in the region had to cope with what onlookers described as a double punch (*Nihon Keizai Shinbun* 2 November 1997); household incomes stagnated or fell due to lower wages or unemployment, and at the same time the devaluation of local currencies caused a rise in prices. Faced with unemployment, people who had moved to the cities returned to their hometowns.

For companies the double punch led to a sudden drop in demand for their products. Two factors made it difficult to analyse this effect in detail. First, many companies raised prices for their goods, so that the actual demand was often even lower in volume than reflected in sales data. Second, companies had planned many activities like the launch of new products well before the crisis. It is impossible to say how successful these moves would have been had the crisis not interfered.

In the area of consumer electronics the Industrial Bank of Japan conducted a survey of Singapore, Malaysia, Thailand and Indonesia. It estimated a drop in demand for Thailand and Malaysia close to 20 per cent for air conditioners and 30 per cent for colour televisions. Indonesia was most affected with a drop in demand of over 50 per cent (NKGSC 1998, p. 172). In interviews conducted by the authors companies reported drops in sales from 5 per cent to 30 per cent. (The authors interviewed subsidiaries of Japanese companies in Singapore, Malaysia and Thailand in March 1999. Interviews in headquarters in Tōkyō followed in May, June and July 1999. Altogether, the authors included about 15 companies from household electronics, household goods and cosmetics, foods and the retail sector in this interview series. The interviews corroborated reports in newspapers and provided information and background on overall strategies.) However, most companies claimed that their market share had remained unaffected. In general, the crisis had less of an effect on the consumption of daily products in the household goods and foods sector than it did on consumer durables, especially high-tech and fashion products.

For example, Aiwa reported a 35.8 per cent drop in sales during fiscal year 1998 in Asia outside of Japan. Sales in the region accounted for 13 per cent of total sales; a sharp decline from the 19.3 per cent reached a year earlier (Aiwa *Annual Report* 1999, p. 30). In Singapore sales of the department store company Isetan dropped from 6 to 8 per cent in 1998 compared to 1997 (*Business Times* 22 January 1999). In sharp contrast, the household goods producer Lion Malaysia achieved a 40 per cent increase in sales in Malaysia. The managing director explained: 'The economic crisis proved to be a blessing for us, because consumers were trying to stretch their ringgit, and we offered them quality, value-for-money products' (*New Straits Times* 28 May 1999).

Sudden currency changes destabilized companies in many ways. They faced currency instabilities when importing merchandise, and problems arose in financing their operations. Before the crisis many subsidiaries and affiliates had relied on dollar-denominated foreign debt and had not hedged the currency risks. Many companies also faced problems with joint-venture partners that had problems in their core businesses or illiquid distributors on whom they relied to distribute their products. The debt of Lion Thailand rose from 700 million to 1.2 billion baht (*Bangkok Post* 13 November 1998), and in 1998 the operator of supermarkets Jaya Jusco reported an exchange-rate-related loss of 48.5 million ringgit in Malaysia (*New Straits Times* 9 June 1998).

Finally, politics intruded in markets. On the one hand governments intervened in activities of companies, and on the other hand the overall political situation in the region became increasingly unstable. In Thailand, prices for many basic goods were still in 1999 controlled by central and local governments slow to allow price increases after currency changes. Malaysia introduced ceiling prices in the retail sector for basic packaged foodstuffs (*Business Times* 13 January 1998), and most countries initiated buy-local campaigns. Under the slogan 'Made in Malaysia' the government in Malaysia urged companies to develop products with high local content for local consumption. In November 1997, post offices joined in the government campaign by stamping post with the motto 'Buy Malaysian Goods' (*New Straits Times* 19 April 1999). In May 1998 Wacoal, like other Japanese firms, closed its office and factory in Indonesia temporarily and ordered its Japanese employees to return to Japan (*Nihon Keizai Shinbun* 19 May 1998).

Finally, the impact of the crisis was not the same in all countries (see Davies in this volume). While Indonesia was hit the hardest, Singapore weathered the crisis relatively well and Thailand and Malaysia lie between these extremes. In some respects the crisis had a major and sudden impact on consumer markets. In other respects it only exacerbated existing trends. For example, a slow-down in Thailand's consumer markets had begun well before the currency crisis set in by fall 1997.

REACTIONS BY JAPANESE COMPANIES

Companies changed their marketing strategies in response to the crisis: changes can be measured in terms of the areas of change, the extent and importance of the changes, and sources of change.

The basic international marketing decision-making process (for example Kotler, Leong, Ang and Tan 1996, p. 496) is the best tool for understanding areas of change. This process is faced by every organization when entering a foreign market. It begins with the decision to enter the market, on to the analysis of how to operate in the market, the development of a marketing programme, and the establishment of an international marketing organization. Decisions have to be reviewed continuously to keep pace with changes in overall corporate strategy and resources, and changes in the environment. In view of the crisis in Southeast Asia it seems appropriate to analyse decisions on all levels of this process.

Areas of change must be evaluated on the basis of their extent and relative importance, with tactical and strategic decisions being distinguished. Tactical decisions are short-term and operational, while strategic decisions have a long-term impact and a high level of uncertainty. In this regard Boulas, Fryling and Buchanan (1999) identified three levels of corporate reactions in times of crisis: damage control, creative risk management, and creating and exploiting new game opportunities. Damage control focuses on managing the immediate effects of the crisis, creative risk management aims at stabilizing the organization in its political and economic environment in order to reduce its vulnerability to future crises. The third level, creating and exploiting new game opportunities, means seeing a crisis not as a threat, but as an opportunity. This level is the most challenging because it requires that actors understand the discontinuities the crisis may trigger in the economic and political marketplace.

Finally one can look for sources of change. Sakano *et al.* (in this volume) follow 'March's Theory of Organizational Learning' in distinguishing between strategies based on existing capabilities and those based on experimenting with new ideas, paradigms or technologies. Sakano *et al.* calls measures based on existing technology exploitation, and measures which involve experimenting with the new, exploration. The following sections are organized according to the marketing decision-making process; after describing reactions to the crisis the other perspectives will be taken into account to evaluate changes.

Stay in or Exit the Market

The first question companies must answer when a crisis occurs is whether to reduce or to sustain their presence in the market or enter a market if they have not yet done so. Statistics on Japanese direct investment in Southeast Asia show a drop in new direct investment after the crisis (ASEAN Centre 1999). While this may be interpreted as a postponement of new activities, it is difficult to draw solid conclusions. Investment statistics do not distinguish between investment in facilities for export-oriented production and investments for local marketing, therefore, the aim of foreign investments is unclear.

Most companies present in the region at the time of the crisis continued their overall engagement in local markets, and Japanese companies still believe that the markets of Southeast Asia constitute an area of future growth. Some companies have even stepped up their engagement. Many companies point to the demographic situation of these countries as a reason for their continued engagement, and the high share of young persons promises future growth, contrasting sharply with aging Japan. Furthermore, Japanese companies point to the proximity of Southeast Asia as a potential competitive advantage over American or European competitors.

Japanese retailers are the exception in the midst of overall confidence and continued engagement. Under pressure at home from stagnant consumer markets and increasing competition as a result of deregulation, retailers decided to close down unprofitable outlets in Southeast Asia. Reasons for the failure of these stores varied. Some, such as the pioneer department store in Thailand, Daimaru, were no longer competitive after three decades of retail change (*Bangkok Post* 26 June 1998). In other cases, however, stores opened in the early

1990s did not produce results in their early years. Here, the crisis may have been the final incentive to close flagging stores and correct previous mistakes.

As example, the manufacturer of household goods Lion decided to stay in the region and stepped up its engagement citing the high regional potential for sales in the future. The company set aside funds to construct new production facilities in Indonesia and Malaysia, and expanded its capacities in Thailand to become the centre of its activities in the region (*Nihon Keizai Shinbun* 22 April 1999; *Bangkok Post* 4 December 1997). The producer of processed foods and seasoning Ajinomoto invested in a plant for the production of canned coffee in Thailand in cooperation with the Japanese company Calpis after sales remained relatively unaffected after the crisis. So far, the company has left production to a local company (*Nihon Keizai Shinbun* 17 July 1998).

As for retailers, the Tokyu group closed its store in Singapore after only six years; the store had recorded net losses of about 2 million Singapore dollars a year from its opening. Tokyu also liquidated operations in Thailand (*Straits Times* 17 September 1998). The retailer Ryōhin Keikaku abandoned its Mujirushi Ryōhin outlets in Singapore due to the crisis in Southeast Asia, and also closed its stores in Hong Kong and decided to focus on Europe and the US market instead (*Straits Times* 9 December 1998). Jusco, by far the most active Japanese company in the development of supermarkets in the region, slowed down the pace of new construction and will not reach its planned target of 10 stores in Malaysia by the year 2000 (*Nikkei Ryūtsū Shinbun* 10 November 1998). In June 1999, Hankyu Department Stores ended its relationship with an Indonesian company in which Hankyu had supplied management know-how. The company cited instability in the country and the decision of its local partner not to carry out the terms of the agreement (*Nikkei Ryūtū Shinbun* 10 June 1999).

Organization of Marketing Activities

How to enter and operate in a foreign market might be the most discussed issue in international marketing literature. For the most part, sales affiliates of Japanese manufacturers in the region operate as minority partners in joint ventures with local companies. In spite of changes in government regulations and the financial difficulties that have beset local partners, relatively few Japanese companies have taken over control of sales affiliates. There have been no reports of

Japanese retailers putting to use new investment regulations that allow foreigners to hold a majority share in joint ventures. This is in strong contrast to European retailers; Europeans are expanding their presence in the region, taking over local companies in the process (see Davies in this volume). Japanese companies may be reluctant to take higher shares in joint ventures because the parent companies in Japan lack the resources to do so. They may also be satisfied with their long-established relationships with existing partners. In explaining the need for these continuing relationships, they point to complex local distribution systems and the importance of good relationships with local governments. Japanese manufacturers did not take over local competitors to either enter a new market or increase their market share.

There have been a few exceptions. Some companies have taken control of affiliates, to which they plan to give a major role in coordinating marketing and production activities for the whole region in the future. For example, after the Thai government changed investment rules, Lion raised the share in its sales company to 51 per cent, a move which reflects Lion's plan to concentrate regional activities in Thailand (*Nihon Keizai Shinbun* 22 April 1999). Aiwa also took advantage of the new Thai regulations to cut ties with its local distributor. It has established a wholly-owned sales subsidiary that will market its goods in neighbouring countries, too (News Release, Aiwa 14 May 1999).

Marketing Programmes

Companies mainly responded to the crisis by adapting their marketing programmes. Measures used covered all fields – products, prices, distribution and promotion – and were of different strategic importance, but with two primary aims. *Cost-cutting* measures, which were operational, countered the first effects of the crisis. The second aim, *adapting to new customer needs*, had strong tactical aspects on first sight, but these measures must be seen in the framework of long-term strategies, too.

Products

Following the crisis, companies analysed their product lines, and changes reflected the following trends. First, companies cut down product lines, reducing the number of items; although they continued the introduction of new products, they slowed down the pace of doing so. They also narrowed there focus to particular products or product lines in order to build up brands with long-term profitability. In household goods, marketers shifted to global brands; and where companies had developed products for single local markets in the past, they introduced products successful in Japan, the ultimate goal being to develop these products as global brands.

However, not all companies in the region adopted the global approach, as is evident in the introduction of new regional brands. Especially companies with high-priced products seem to have realized that it will take time for the markets of Southeast Asia to develop a high and stable demand for their products. To broaden their customer base, Japanese companies have introduced products especially designed with consumers in emerging markets in mind.

In the area of household and food products, most of these measures were not taken in direct reaction to the crisis but were initiated earlier. Companies felt, however, that these strategies became more important after the crisis and therefore stepped up their implementation. Companies pushing global brands want to establish a long-term image in the market and thereby become more stable in the event of future fluctuations in demand.

In electronics, most companies reduced high priced product lines. While companies had introduced new products in Southeast Asia shortly after their introduction in Japan, demand for some of these products has fallen considerably. For example, companies no longer harbour hopes of selling large numbers of 29-inch television sets in the region in the short term. In contrast to other product categories, electronics manufacturers developed products in direct response to the crisis, featuring slightly reduced specifications thereby enabling lower prices.

Examples Lion Thailand has reported that it reduced the number of items by 20 per cent (*Bangkok Post* 13 November 1998), and has also regrouped categories and put them under the control of one manager. It will also strengthen its product lines other than detergent, where competition on prices is very intensive. With this move the company is putting more and more emphasis on its so-called global product lines in its main areas of washing lotion and mouth care.

In November 1997, Shiseido introduced a new product line, Za New York. This line was developed for the emerging middle-class markets in Asia and is not sold in Japan. Products under this name do not bear the Shiseido trademark, and are sold through mass distribution channels at a considerably lower price than Shiseido's branded products (only sold over the counter), enabling it to reach a group of younger consumers unable to purchase its normal high-prestige, high-priced Shiseido brands (Mizuō 1999, p. 51; *Nihon Keizai Shinbun* 3 July 1999).

Kikkoman for the first time in company history has allowed a change of its core product: soy sauce. In Singapore, it introduced a brand called Asian Taste that is priced lower than the high-priced, Japanese-style product it sells successfully in all other countries. Doing so, the company tries to reach a broader range of consumers. Although Kikkoman began the development of this product before the crisis, it now regards it as an important means to position itself after the crisis.

Matsushita developed products for local markets in Thailand and Malaysia. With the aim of saving on production costs and offering lower prices, Matsushita Thailand introduced a new television set in which a reduced maximum volume output enabled the company to save on inputs by using a less vibration-resistant frame. In Malaysia, Matsushita joined a government-led 'Made in Malaysia' campaign to promote products that have high local content and are designed with the Malayan consumer in mind. The company brought together local marketers, dealers, engineers and designers to develop a refrigerator that was launched in early 1999 (*New Straits Times* 19 April 1999).

Isetan Singapore, citing positive experience from the last consumption crisis in 1985, has introduced a whole range of new high-priced labels into its department stores. The aim is to be well-established as a fashion leader once demand picks up again (*Straits Times* 10 October 1998).

Price

Price became more important during the crisis. Companies confronted a difficult situation: on the one hand most faced drastically increased prices for imported products or raw materials; on the other hand, they faced consumers with lower incomes who even demand lower prices. Thus, the flexibility of companies to adapt their prices depended on the country of origin of their products. Companies that had to import all of their products from Japan or other non-ASEAN countries were hit hardest by the crisis, and in order to counter the impact of the crisis they had to resort to drastic price increases. With the exception of the few companies that targeted Japanese expatriates or other high-income groups, these increases resulted in decreases in volume demand. Companies with local production facilities and a high percentage of locally-sourced raw materials were able to keep prices stable. However, this distinction was not always clear, since most companies sell a mix of locally-produced and imported products.

To support the demand for their products, most companies shouldered part of the cost of currency fluctuation themselves, and tried to share the rest with wholesalers, retailers and consumers. However, firms were not always free to change their prices. In Thailand, the government controls prices for many basic goods and it was sometimes slow to allow higher prices or did not allow prices to follow currency changes to the full extent. This further increased the burden on companies (*Bangkok Post* 26 September 1997).

To prepare for future currency fluctuations, most companies reduced imports of materials and raised local content. To stay profitable they also engaged in reorganization and cost reduction. As demonstrated by the examples of Shiseido, Kikkoman and Matsushita, new product lines developed for Asian markets are often lower priced to stimulate demand and to build up a more stable consumer base for these products. Finally, companies that had relied on comparatively stable currency exchange rates in the past, and had concentrated their efforts on production or marketing, upgraded their activities in the areas of financial risk management.

Examples   Matsushita raised prices for its products in Thailand, Indonesia and the Philippines; price increases were substantial and not restricted to imported products. In January 1998, it increased prices in Indonesia for imported air conditioners and stereo sets by 80 per cent, and prices for locally-produced colour television sets and refrigerators by 50 per cent. While prices have doubled over a short period, sales have fallen by 50 per cent (*Nihon Keizai Shinbun* 10 February 1998). In 1998, Matsushita raised local content in Malaysia in nine of its products by between 1 per cent and 13 per cent (*New Straits Times* 19 April 1999).

Kikkoman tied its prices to the change in import prices for its raw materials. Thus, even though its products became more expensive, the company was not affected seriously by the crisis due to its focus on a small, but high-income group (Yoshida 1999, p. 76).

Ajinomoto Malaysia raised prices for its main seasoning product by 2 to 3 per cent during 1998, and was considering further price increases for 1999. The company imports about 40 per cent of its raw materials and the price of its main ingredient rose by 50 per cent. The company planned to shoulder part of the increases through cost-cutting measures (*New Straits Times* 12 June 1999).

Distribution

Most companies depended heavily on their local partners for the distribution of goods. For Japanese companies the crisis drove them to reconsider their strategies in this area, as it had done in other areas. Due to their long engagement in the markets, companies had developed strong relationships with the dominating companies in the wholesale and retail sector, and had established separate distribution channels for urban and rural areas. To sustain these channels throughout the crisis, manufacturers initially supported dealers that, due to a drop in demand, faced sudden increases in inventories. These same dealers found it more difficult to secure credit-financing for their operations. As the crisis evolved, companies became more attentive to the costs and profits of the different distribution channels and partners, and, on the basis of their analyses, they became more selective in how they distributed their products.

With the introduction of global or regional brands companies took an even more active role in the distribution of their goods. Interest in distribution channels also increased with the rising importance of logistics and modern information-exchange technology. Both areas are increasingly major vehicles of sustaining competitive advantages not only in developed, but also in emerging markets. However, changes and innovations in these areas require high levels of investment that local joint-venture partners are not always able to support. The moves of some companies to claim majority stakes in joint ventures can be read as a response to the local partner's reluctance to invest in new distribution technologies.

The activities of large, international, retail companies are a very important factor for the future development of distribution practices (see Davies in this volume), and European retailers have taken the lead. In spite of, or sometimes even helped by, the crisis they are building up store networks in the region at a fast pace. Meanwhile, many Japanese retailers have postponed plans for expansion. Historically, Japanese manufacturers have profited from the strong presence of Japanese retailers in the region, especially department stores, but European retailers have challenged the Japanese by introducing modern retail formats such as large-scale hypermarkets. In their dealings with manufacturers, they are using the same advanced information-exchange and logistics technologies that they are using in their home markets. In Japan, manufacturers have traditionally relied heavily on wholesalers, even in dealing with large retail chains. As the share of foreign retail chains in the region rises, the ability of manufacturers to deal with retailers directly is becoming vital to their position in the market.

Examples   Ajinomoto built up a strong sales organization in Thailand catering to the different needs of dealers in urban and rural areas. Since 1986 the share of sales through modern retail channels rose from 1 per cent to 10 per cent. While this figure is still low, the new formats constitute a challenge to Ajinomoto's control over retail prices (Ōta 1997, p. 31).

The lingerie manufacturer, Wacoal, has relied on Japanese department stores as a major vehicle for expanding sales in Asia, but due to the closure of many department stores in the wake of the crisis sales have dropped considerably (Yoshida 1998b, pp. 69–70). In order to introduce its new product line, Za, Shiseido has established a sales company in Thailand. Even though the local partner is still involved, Shiseido controls the majority stake. The company plans to market the new product line through mass distribution channels (*Nikkei Sangyō Shinbun* 26 November 1999).

Promotion

Companies responded differently to the crisis in their promotion of goods. While some decided to reduce their promotional activities to save on costs, others increased their promotional activities considerably and actively used the crisis to win market share from local competitors who had to reduce their budgets due to liquidity problems.

At the same time, most companies focused their strategies and concentrated resources on certain media. Promotional activities for example, support the introduction of global or regional products. One company representative described this situation as a move away from traditional, campaign-style promotion to the long-term establishment of brands. Companies recognize that consumers in the Southeast Asian countries increasingly use the same media; this is especially true for Malaysia and Singapore, where consumers share the same television channels. Therefore, they are moving from a national to a regional marketing strategy that establishes a common company or brand image across country borders. In addition to these efforts, companies are also trying to introduce techniques like database marketing to obtain more precise information on their customers.

Japanese retailers were forced to rethink their strategies, too. Due to a drop in tourism, department stores had to appeal to local consumers to widen their customer base. In an increasingly competitive environment, supermarket operators have to concentrate on building up loyalty with customers instead of putting their resources into attracting new customers, as they did in the past.

Examples   To increase customer loyalty, Jusco Malaysia introduced a member's card and will also initiate a cash refund policy for the exchange of merchandise (*New Straits Times* 24 January 1999). Other companies for example Matsushita Malaysia who joined buy-local campaigns initiated by governments, marketed their products as 'Made in Malaysia' (*New Straits Times* 19 April 1999).

Despite the crisis, personal-goods manufacturer Kao launched its Lavenus Shampoo in Thailand with a budget of 400 million baht, nearly three times as high as its largest budget for a product launch so far (*Bangkok Post* 18 August 1998, p. 3).

Lion, which had marketed localized products under different product names, switched to a focus on its company name and the country of origin in establishing its global brand. On its fluid soap Shokubutsu Monogatari (plant story), it is using the same Japanese characters as in Japan and now uses the company logo on all products and in all commercials (Ōsawa 1998, p. 79).

Long-term Strategies

While some of the activities described so far appear to be only short-term adaptations, the crisis will remain a period of special importance and has forced many companies to redefine their view of Southeast Asian markets and their strategies. Confronted with stagnating or even shrinking markets after a long period of growth, many companies had to adapt marketing and rationalize their operations. This was marked by a shift from the dominant goal of future growth to a new goal of achieving profitability and sustaining market share. Overall, companies are better positioned in the market now and better prepared for future fluctuations in demand.

Two trends clearly emerge in the long-term strategies: First, companies increasingly view Southeast Asia as a single market. Second, companies increasingly rely on global or regional brands, where

Table 8.3   Reduction of tariffs for prepared foodstuffs (%, original schedule till year 2003)

Country	1996	1997	1998	1999	2000	2001	2002	2003
Brunei	0.04	0.04	0.04	0.04	0.04	0.04	0.04	0.04
Indonesia	19.24	18.12	15.30	13.98	11.20	10.38	7.93	4.89
Malaysia	5.09	4.50	3.90	3.25	2.60	2.55	2.49	2.27
Philippines	15.39	13.98	12.05	9.27	8.42	6.92	5.50	4.03
Singapore	0.00	0.00	0.00	0.00	0.00	0.00	0.00	0.00
Thailand	22.71	22.71	17.96	17.96	13.33	13.33	9.05	4.91
Vietnam	5.00	5.00	5.00	5.00	5.00	5.00	5.00	5.00
ASEAN	10.13	9.63	7.99	7.32	5.78	5.47	4.17	2.71

Source: The ASEAN Secretariat: www.asean.org

possible. The first trend has been helped along by the ASEAN initiative to lower tariffs on trade between member countries. On the way to the establishment of an ASEAN Free Trade Area, member countries agreed to lower tariffs from current highs – still exceeding 15 per cent in some cases – to below 5 per cent by the year 2003 (Table 8.3). To speed up the process of economic recovery, the members of ASEAN recently adjusted the conversion period up to the year 2002.

It will therefore become attractive to concentrate production in one or two countries and build these up as export bases for the region. However, in this process companies are doing more than just concentrating the production of market-specific products that were formerly produced in several locations. By using new production facilities to produce global or regional brands, they take the pursuit for scale merits one step further. From the outset, they are saving on product design and marketing activities. Although it remains to be seen whether global brands will really dominate in all fields in the future, strong global or regional brands will become more important to counter the growing strength of multinational retailers. In particular, food manufacturers point out that consumer habits are still highly heterogeneous.

Southeast Asia might become a testing ground for the competition between Japanese companies and Western companies that have been leaning on global brands for a long time. Due to their comparatively long experience in Southeast Asia, Japanese companies are able to compete in many areas on more equal terms with Western companies in the region than they can in Europe or the USA. As Figure 8.1 shows,

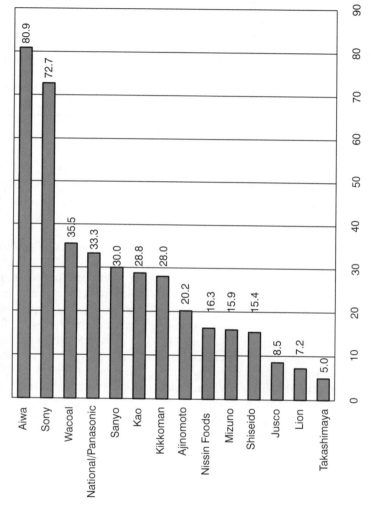

Figure 8.1   Ratio of overseas sales to total sales for major companies (%)

Note: Results for fiscal year 1997, ending for most companies 31 March 1998; Aiwa and Shiseido fiscal year 1998.
Source: Annual reports.

apart from a few manufacturers of consumer electronics, most Japanese companies still depend heavily on the Japanese market for selling their goods. Faced with increasing competition from foreign companies in their home market, Japanese companies are eager to internationalize. Southeast Asia with its relative proximity to Japan is playing an important role in their strategies. Companies might also use Southeast Asia to gain experience for expansion into the growing Chinese markets.

Whether Japanese companies will set up regional headquarters functions for marketing in Southeast Asia, or whether they will continue to make many of the decisions from their headquarters in Japan, remains unresolved. Regional headquarters could take over functions like coordinating promotional campaigns, development of regional products, handling key accounts and coordinating logistics. The answer to this question will depend on the potential the companies see for these markets and how that potential relates to the situation in Japan. At the moment, many European or American companies with regional headquarters in Singapore seem to be nearer to the markets than Japanese companies.

Examples With consumers channel-surfing the television programmes of Malayan and Singaporean broadcasters, Kao views Singapore and Malaysia as one market. In 1998, for the first time, the company launched a major product, Lavenus Shampoo, not in Singapore or Taiwan but in Thailand (*Bangkok Post* 18 August 1998). In 1996, Kao led the market for concentrated detergent in Thailand with a market share of 35 per cent, followed by two products sold by Unilever (19.3 and 16.6 per cent), Colgate-Palmolive (13 per cent) and Lion (10.6 per cent) (*Bangkok Post* 24 September 1997). By 1999, the company had increased its share to 40 per cent, and was ranked third overall in sales of consumer goods, behind Unilever and Procter & Gamble. It aimed to double its share in the hair-care market from 10 per cent to 20 per cent and to increase its share in the skin-care field from 8 to 15 per cent (*Bangkok Post* 5 August 1999).

Sony established a regional headquarters in Singapore for sales and marketing of consumer products in Singapore in March 1999. A Sony representative stated that, 'Maybe someday we will have some products uniquely for Asia' (*Straits Times* 6 April 1998).

A representative of Wacoal is citing the crisis as an opportunity to pull its strongly localized affiliates into one group and reorganize sales and production functions. In times of crisis, such a move encounters less resistance from affiliates than in times of fast growth (Yoshida 1998b).

Finally, Lion is preparing for the reduction of tariffs by standardizing most of its products. These products will allow Lion to swiftly shift to concentrated production when the ASEAN member countries revise their tariffs. The company will produce mouth-care products in Thailand and Indonesia since it sees these markets as having the largest potential. Lion will then export products to other markets where, in the long run, it will only manufacture detergent and other voluminous products (Ōsawa 1998, pp. 79–80).

CONCLUSION AND OUTLOOK

For Japanese companies, the crisis has been a major and sudden event; they have responded by reevaluating their position in the markets of Southeast Asia. While companies knew about deficiencies in their operations before the crisis, many of these went untended in favour of keeping operations smooth in the rapidly growing markets. Rather than retreat, most companies took the onset of the crisis as a situation that eased efforts to restructure operations. They stayed and streamlined both operational and marketing programmes. Their new cost-efficiency makes them better prepared for future fluctuations in demand, and in this sense most companies agree that they will be stronger after the crisis. As one company representative put it: 'Companies are present and have to find solutions, crisis is a chance to develop new ideas'. Another enthused that: 'Business will be done in a more solid way'.

However, the majority of Japanese companies did not view the crisis as an opportunity, in contrast to some European companies who used the crisis to boldly expand their operations. Reserve on the part of Japanese companies can be explained as a lack of resources or a general preoccupation with the situation in their home markets.

Companies once more face the issue of globalization versus localization in the international marketing of their products. At the moment, most companies have opted against strong localisation; although some countries are developing regional brands for emerging markets, others introduce global brands. These strategies promise to be cost-efficient in the short run by introducing scale merits into marketing. Will companies maintain regional or global strategies once markets accommodate for a higher degree of differentiation with renewed growth? The answer extends beyond the narrow bounds of the 1997 crisis. The liberalization of trade, media that transcend national borders, the expansion of global retailers, and the introduction of new information technologies all support current strategies. Asia will remain an important market for Japanese producers of consumer goods even in an age when the international engagement of many Japanese companies is still quite low. As demand in the Japanese market has stagnated over the last few years, most companies realize that to achieve sustainable growth and a strong position against future downturns they need a presence in all world markets. Many companies regard stepping up engagement in the countries of Southeast Asia as a natural choice.

References

ASEAN Centre (1998) *ASEAN–Japan Statistical Pocketbook*, Tōkyō: ASEAN Centre.

Boulas, C., J. Fryling and I. Buchanan (1999) 'New Game Opportunities', *Asian Business Review*, pp. 16–18.

Kotler, P., Leong, S. M., Ang, S. H. and C. T. Tan (1996) *Marketing Management: An Asian Perspective*, London: Prentice Hall.

Masuyama, S., D. Vandenbrink and S. Y. Chia (eds) (1997) *Industrial Policies in East Asia*, Tōkyō: Tōkyō Club Foundation for Global Studies.

Mizuō, J. (1999) 'Kesshōhin mēkā no gurōbaru burando senryaku' [The Global Brand Strategies of Cosmetics Manufacturers], *Māketingu jāneru (Japan Marketing Journal)* vol. 73, pp. 44–56.

Nihon Keizai Shinbun/Nikkei Sangyō Shōhi Kenkyūshō (1996) *Ajia no shōhi shijō to Nihon no kigyō no taiō* [Consumer Markets in Southeast Asia and Responses by Japanese Companies], Tōkyō: Nihon Keizai Sangyō Shōhi Kenkyūshō.

NKGSC Nihon Kōgyō Ginkō Sangyō Chōsabu (1998) *Ajia kiki ato no sangyō chizu* [Chart of Industry after the Asian Crisis], Tōkyō: Nihon Keizai Shinbun.

Okamoto, Y. (1999) 'Waga kuni ryūtsūgyō no Ajia shinshutsu' [The Recent Trend of Japanese Distribution Enterprise in Asian Countries], *Meidai shôgaku ronsô*, vol. 81(3–4), pp. 27–47.

Ōsawa, K. (1998) 'Nihon kigyō no Ajia senryaku – Raion [Asia Strategy of Japanese Companies – Lion], *Jitsugyō no Nihon*, vol. 1, pp. 78–80.

Ōta, S. (1997) 'Ajinomoto no kokusai māketingu' [International Marketing of Ajinomoto], *Keizai ronsō (Kyōto Daigaku)*, vol. 160 (2), pp. 17–34.

Schütte, H. with D. Ciarlante (1998) *Consumer Behavior in Asia*, London: Macmillan.

Yoshida, A. (1998a) 'Nihon kigyō no Ajia senryaku – Kaō' [Asia Strategy of Japanese Companies – Kao], *Jitsugyō no Nihon*, vol. 8, pp. 76–8.

Yoshida, A. (1998b) 'Nihon kigyō no Ajia senryaku – Wakōru' [Asia Strategy of Japanese Companies – Wacoal], *Jitsugyō no Nihon*, vol. 9, pp. 74–7.

Yoshida, A. (1999) 'Nihon kigyō no Ajia senryaku – Kikkōman' [Asia Strategy of Japanese Companies – Kikkoman], *Jitsugyō no Nihon*, vol. 1, pp. 74–6.

9 Marketing Strategies of European Firms: Reconfiguration and Expansion

Keri Davies

INTRODUCTION

Trying to unravel the changes caused by the Asian economic crisis in the marketing practices of European companies in Southeast Asia is not an easy task. There are three main reasons for this: first, even within a relatively narrow geographical focus, the effect of the economic crisis was felt in quite different ways in different countries as a result of different political, economic, social and financial conditions. Second, companies in different sectors have reacted in very different ways and only some of these can be related back to their region of origin. Third, most European companies will differ from many local companies in having a strategy covering the whole of Pacific Asia. Local strategies, and even strategies for the whole Southeast Asian area, have to be seen in the context of this wider arena. We can take each of these issues in turn.

THE VARIABLE EFFECTS OF THE ASIAN ECONOMIC CRISIS IN SOUTHEAST ASIA

Notwithstanding the later claims of commentators to have forecast the bursting of the bubble, one of the most worrying aspects of the Asian economic crisis of the late 1990s was the speed at which events unfolded (Krugman 1999). Within just the last six months of 1997, economic growth in most Asian countries either slowed dramatically or reversed completely (Table 9.1), to be followed in some instances by social, economic and political upheaval.

Table 9.1 Effect of the Asian economic crisis on GDP per capita (US$)

	GDP per capita (US$)		Change 1997–98 (%)	Year-on-year change in real annual GDP (%)		
	1997	1998		1997	1998	1999 (forecast)
People's Republic of China	733	785	7.1	8.8	7.8	8.2
Vietnam	324	303	–6.5	8.2	4.0	
Hong Kong	26 225	24 892	–5.1	5.3	–5.1	–1.0
Malaysia	4 518	3 119	–31.0	7.7	–6.7	3.0
Japan	33 289	30 120	–9.5	1.4	–2.8	0.9
Taiwan	13 065	11 958	–8.5	5.3	–5.1	4.5
Singapore	30 686	26 710	–13.0	8.0	1.5	4.0
Philippines	1 118	866	–22.5	5.2	–0.5	2.4
Thailand	2 540	1 895	–25.4	–0.4	–8.0	1.5
South Korea	10 360	6 908	–33.3	5.0	–5.8	7.0
Indonesia	1 074	380*	–64.6	4.6	–13.7	–1.7

Note: * estimate.
Sources: *Asian Wall Street Journal* 26 October 1998; *Far Eastern Economic Review* 2 December 1999; KKC (1999).

Figure 9.1 Year-on-year change in the value of retail sales in four Asian countries

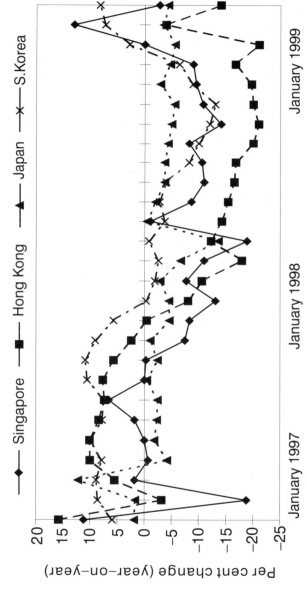

Source: Government Statistical Offices.

The effects have been very variable. As the table shows, most Asian economies shrank during 1998, although China and Vietnam did manage to retain some growth during this period. Whilst, the per capita GDP in Thailand in early 1999 was back where it had been in 1990, measured in US dollars, wiping out a decade of growth (Goad 1998), the reforms of the economic and financial sectors seem to be taking hold. Indeed, the Pacific Economic Cooperation Council expects all but three of the 19 Pacific Rim economies to return to moderate growth in 1999 (*Asian Wall Street Journal* 9 June 1999).

The economic crisis has hit marketers and retailers operating in the region very hard. The total loss of purchasing power in Asia between the middle of 1997 and the middle of 1998 was estimated at US$500 billion. As a result, consumer spending throughout Asia is estimated to have fallen over the same period by 10–15 per cent on consumer products and 40–70 per cent on luxury goods. (Taylor Nelson Sofres Ltd – quoted in *The Nation* (Thailand) 21 October 1998). Or, to put it another way, retail sales in Asia were believed to be down 30 per cent during the first eight months of 1998 (*Economist Intelligence Unit* 1 September 1998).

Unfortunately, most Southeast Asian countries still focus on the production side of their economies and the collection of retail sales figures can be mixed. Accordingly, Figure 9.1 shows the year-on-year change in the value of retail sales in four of the largest Asian economies, not necessarily those in Southeast Asia. Whilst the Japanese retail sector has been in decline for a number of years (although this may be exaggerated by the means of compiling the data), it can be seen that retail sales declined steeply across the board from late 1997 and throughout 1998. Equally, it can be seen that retail sales everywhere but Japan rebounded in early 1999. We can look at some more specific Southeast Asian examples in detail to show the problems with which marketers have been faced.

Indonesia

Retail price inflation in November 1998 stood at 78.2 per cent year-on-year, with the consumer price index up 75 per cent during the period January–November 1998 (*Asian Wall Street Journal* 30 November 1998). At the same time, unemployment rose to an estimated 15–20 million people by the end of 1998 (15 per cent of the workforce), with 80 million people (40 per cent of the population) below the poverty line (*Indonesian Observer* 22 January 1999).

The Indonesian Retailers Association estimates that total retail sales in 1998 were down 30 per cent on 1997, at Rp 170 trillion (US$ 20 billion), with the electronics sector hardest hit at an estimated 60 per cent (*Indonesian Observer* 12 February 1999). In addition, retail shopping patterns were badly affected by the increased levels of crime, sporadic rioting and continued street protests. During the second half of 1998 grocery shopping was typically undertaken in the morning and, with shoppers hurrying home, department stores were almost empty after 8.00 p.m. In the run-up to the Parliamentary Assembly in early November 1998 there was a sharp drop in the number of customers willing to travel to shopping centres because of the possibility of disturbances on the streets. The main retail companies reported sales down 70 per cent in that week (*Asian Wall Street Journal* 10 November 1998).

Malaysia

The owners of some 100 shopping centres scheduled to come on-stream in Malaysia by the year 2000 have canceled or deferred their plans. In 1998 new rentals in Malaysia fell 10–15 per cent on average and by up to 40 per cent at the top end of market. As a result, retailers have been lobbying for rental renegotiations and reductions

Singapore

Overall retail sales fell through 1998 as shown in Figure 9.1. However, this masks the differences between retail sectors: clothing sales fell heavily throughout 1998, whilst the sales of supermarkets and furniture stores were not hit as hard. Part of the difference came about because unemployment levels did not rise in the same way as in other countries; instead, these sectors were affected by the drop in tourists and other visitors. Many of the problems in Singapore came about because retail restructuring and the expansion of retail floorspace, both in the central area and the suburban centres, continued throughout 1998.

Thailand

Inflation rose 8 per cent in the first 11 months of 1998, whilst the pressure on the baht was felt most intensely on non-food items. In part, this was because of an increase in the value added tax on luxury items imposed in October 1997, and changes to import duties introduced in February 1998. These tax burdens were passed on to consumers resulting in a 20–25 per cent increase in the prices of imported goods.

The Thai Retailers Association has estimated that average retail sales revenue declined by between 20–30 per cent in 1998 and by a further 5–6 per cent in the first four months of 1999. Sales at department stores fell between 20–40 per cent, supermarkets were down between 10 and 15 per cent, discount stores in Bangkok were down 10 per cent and stores upcountry by 20 per cent. Convenience stores were the least affected but still saw a sales decline of between 5 and 10 per cent in 1998 (*Bangkok Post* 20 May 1999).

This is not the place to try to unravel the background to this crisis; there are already many books and articles which deal with the political, social and economic trends that led up to it and the varying effects which it has had on the region and its constituent parts (see, for example, Jomo (1998), Lingle (1998), Krugman (1999) and the material and internet links collated by Nouriel Roubini of the Stern School of Business, New York University, available at his website: *www.stern.nyu.edu/~nroubini/asia/AsiaHomepage.html*). Rather, we are concerned with the implications of the sudden changes that have occurred for the marketing activities of European companies and the manner in which they have speeded or hindered the trends already present in the region.

There are three basic ways of viewing the Asian economic crisis. First, it can be seen as a minor blip on the graph of economic growth; normal service will be resumed shortly. Secondly, and the obverse of the first, we are seeing the downfall of the 'Asian Economic Miracle' and the ridiculing of the calls for recognizing a distinctly Asian means of managing economic growth. Thirdly, we are seeing a necessary stage of retrenchment during which much unfinished business regarding the governance of business and the reform of financial, legal and political systems will need to be completed. This is necessary if a solid economic and social substructure is to be built under the superstructure of a modern manufacturing sector that has been erected over the past 30 years.

As will become clearer below, it is argued here that the first of these views is largely invalid. The economic downturn of the past two years has been a major economic event with severe implications for marketers and retailers (as well as offering a convenient cover to explain away previous bad decisions). Not only is there no way back for the sector itself, but marketers operating in Asia have begun to recognize the need for change and reorganization of the system if they are not to be caught in a destructive cycle of 'boom and bust'. The second and third views need not be seen as mutually incompatible. This certainly is the interpretation used here of the views expressed by Paul Krugman in his (in)famous article on 'The Myth of Asia's Economic Miracle' (Krugman 1994). One of the elements of that paper which is often overlooked (but very relevant here) was his description of the inefficiencies of the service sector in many Asian countries. Reform of this sector, including retailing, was seen by Krugman as vital if the changes in the manufacturing sector were to be consolidated. We shall come back to this point below.

THE SHORT-TERM REACTIONS OF EUROPEAN COMPANIES TO THE ASIAN ECONOMIC CRISIS

What follows from this brief analysis of the effects of the Asian economic crisis is that marketers and retailers in Southeast Asia have had to deal with some, if not all, of the following problems:

- Lower levels of disposable incomes, brought about by rising levels of unemployment; a lower propensity to spend amongst those still in work because of worries about losing their jobs; and, reduced demand for the products made in local factories.
- A reduction in the number of tourists and other visitors. Many visitors from Europe, the USA and Japan were deterred initially by worries over social and political unrest in Southeast Asian countries, whilst many of the potential visitors from within the region were unable to travel because of their changed economic circumstances. A wide number of European companies selling consumer goods, particularly luxury goods such as fashions, cosmetics and accessories, have been badly affected by these changes in the number and countries of origin of tourists.
- Changes in local purchasing patterns from luxuries to necessities but also changes within categories. For example, the evidence suggests that in Jakarta a typical couple with four children spend only about US$ 1 a day on food and daily necessities. Yet currency depreciation and price increases means that the family's purchasing power may be just half what it was before the crisis. The typical family can no longer afford to serve chicken or red meat at meals,

and fish can only be afforded occasionally (van Heemstra 1999). It is also likely that they will have given up saving altogether.

- Shopping habits and distribution patterns have also changed. In Jakarta, households have changed back from stocking up at the supermarket for household consumables, to day-by-day purchases at small local shops. Throughout Southeast Asia there has been an increase in the equivalents of the ¥100 stores, in one-person kiosks selling everything from soap to car lubricants, small rural delivery vans and even three-wheel bicycles designed to carry a wide range of consumer products (van Heemstra 1999).
- Major changes in the prices of raw materials and finished goods caused by fluctuations in exchange rates, the imposition of currency controls, and higher import duties or value added taxes on luxury items.

We have to be careful to remember, therefore, that European marketers have been faced with a wide range of problems and a mixture of situations between countries and between urban and rural areas within a country. Equally, we need to be clear that the term 'European marketers' covers a wide range of companies of different sizes, operating in different sectors and with widely different levels of experience and strategic objectives. Taking just consumer marketing (not business-to-business markets), they range from the makers of upmarket luxury brands to the distributors of mass-market consumer goods. As a result, there has been no single response to the economic conditions which can be said to have characterized European marketers. However, it is probably true to generalize that the Asian economic crisis did not cause most European firms to change their strategies; the change came instead in the form and usage of the various marketing tactics available. We can look at the main tactics in turn before looking at several examples of how companies have used such tactics to bolster their overall strategies.

Price

As we shall see in the illustrations below, changes in price have been a major tool for many European companies, particularly given their heavier reliance on imported goods compared to local companies. Many companies raised their prices in order to cover their overheads and other costs which could not be varied in the short term. As a result, looking at sales figures does not necessarily reflect what is happening in the marketplace. For example, Unilever reported that in the Asia-Pacific region during 1997–98, sales actually grew by 13 per cent, with volume up just 2 per cent but prices up by 12 per cent (Massot *et al.* 1998).

However, prices may have to be analysed on a regional basis, in that they may have been lowered in countries such as Indonesia where demand has fallen furthest, but raised in Singapore where demand has held up better. In many instances, however, manufacturers and importers looking to retain their markets have had to absorb some of the price increases because they have been just too large to pass on to the consumer as a whole.

Products

Companies such as Unilever have had to look to reformulate their products in order to get prices down or to develop affordable unit-package sizes that can still deliver value to the consumer. In some markets, there has been more development and use of refill packaging as a more economical way to purchase household necessities. In others, margarine, for example, has been supplied in large boxes from which it is then sold in scoops according to consumer needs (van Heemstra 1999). Even at the luxury end of the market, Dunhill has developed a new product range with the Asian market in mind. It has been designed to offer value for money through design, rather than as a means of cutting price which could end up damaging the brand (*Business Times* (Singapore) 20 October 1998).

There has also been pressure to look for new local sources of supply or to develop local manufacturing capacity. For example, Boots Retail, the local arm of the British pharmacy chain which operates 30 stores in Thailand, has plans to manufacture high-volume health and beauty products through local sub-contractors. Currently, Boots' private label comprises about 50 per cent of the products sold in the stores and all of these are imported from the United Kingdom. In some cases, these imported brands are cheaper than comparable ones that could be made locally, because of large bulk purchases and Boots' substantial bargaining power. However, manufacturing other private-label products locally could reduce manufacturing costs by up to 20 per cent and it would increase flexibility and management efficiency; it would be possible to get new products into the local market sooner (*Bangkok Post* 6 May 1999).

A change to local production can bring consumer and political benefits too. In January 1998, Courts Mammoth Bhd, the British furniture and electrical retailer based in Malaysia, joined the Malaysian government's call to buy local. The company already had a policy to import designs and styles but to have its furniture made locally, whilst many of their electrical items also came from the Malaysian plants of European, American and Japanese multinationals. In addition to promoting this activity to Malaysian consumers more positively (and so helping to reduce imports), local manufacturers were also now able to export their products through the company to the other 17 countries where they have other outlets (*The Star* (Malaysia) 4 May 1998).

Distribution

European marketers have had to come to terms with two major changes in their patterns of distribution. The first has been the increased number of large multiple retail chains in Southeast Asian countries, many of them also now owned by European companies (this point will be dealt with below). Second, they have had to face the challenge of the growth in the number of small shops and kiosks in order to develop 'capillary' networks that can reach far-flung points of sale in both urban and rural areas (van Heemstra 1999). This is a major problem in terms of maintaining or even increasing sales penetration, whilst retaining control over the supply and the image of the products involved.

ILLUSTRATIONS

We can see the manner in which these marketing issues have been expressed by looking at examples of the way European firms operating in Southeast Asia have responded to the changes over the past two years.

Nestlé Malaysia

Nestlé Malaysia is the largest food and beverage company listed on the Kuala Lumpur Stock Exchange (illustration based on Anon 1997; Shafee 1998; Sanda 1998; Chan 1999; Khoo 1999; Mehta 1999). Nestlé's products are basic, small-ticket items that people (especially those in the urban areas) buy irrespective of economic conditions. These

Table 9.2   Nestlé Malaysia's product portfolio

Market	Estimated sales contribution (%)	Estimated market share (%)	Main brands
Milk products	30	40–45	Milkmaid, Teapot, Nespray, Everyday
Milo	19	>80	
Instant coffee	20	>80	Nescafé
Food and sauces	15	50	Maggi, Nestum, Milo
Confectionery/others	14	n/a	Smartees, Milo

Source: Anon 1997; Shafee 1998; Sanda 1998; Chan 1999; Khoo 1999; Mehta 1999.

products include well-known brand names such as Nescafé instant coffee, Nespray powdered milk, Milo, and Maggi instant noodles (Table 9.2). As relatively mature brands, growth in demand at the start of 1997 was below 10 per cent per annum, in line with population and consumer spending growth. Any further earnings growth was expected to come from margin improvements from higher operating efficiencies. Raw material costs account for about 70 per cent of Nestlé's total costs. As consumer items, retail prices of the company's products are elastic, and hence Nestlé has to absorb any additional burden of raw material costs in the short term.

After the economic crisis hit, the following changes and adjustments were made by Nestlé:

- Before the economic crisis, Nestlé Malaysia was targeting 12 per cent volume growth but this was dropped to 5 per cent. Even so, this was still a very positive forecast, based on the company's belief that consumers were still purchasing food for home cooking.
- For FY98 and FY99, Nestlé was expected to give out 90–95 per cent of net profits for dividends.
- Turnover was boosted by price increases of 12–15 per cent across most of the product range in January and March 1998. The price increase was higher for beverage and milk-based products and less for the more income-elastic products such as sweets and confectionery. Volume dropped overall by about 13–14 per cent in response to the price increase amidst the lower consumer purchasing power. Second-half revenue was higher than that in the first half, reflecting the full impact of the price increase.

- However, the company allowed margins to be squeezed during FY98. The retail price increases for its products were not enough to cover the increase in raw materials and packaging, particularly as many of these are imported and contracted in US dollars. For example, the prices of skimmed-milk powder, local palm oil, cocoa, wheat flour, sugar and tin cans rose by between 23 per cent and 90 per cent from July 1997 and May 1998.

- There was no reduction in advertising expenditure as the company believed that it would be able to increase its market share at the expense of competitors who could not spend on brand-building. There was an increased emphasis on giving out product samples.

- Despite the increases, beverage products like Nescafé and Milo are thought to have gained some market share, but sales of milk-based products like full-cream milk and other dairy products suffered due to the intense price competition.

- Nestlé trimmed down the number of appointed dealers from 150 to 90 and this should be reduced further to 60 by early 2000. The company has not faced significant levels of bad debt but it has been keeping a close watch on its distributors.

- Nestlé Malaysia has been prompted to bring forward plans to use its expertise in producing halal culinary products (including chocolates) which can be exported to Nestlé companies overseas for sale to the Muslim community.

- Nestlé's strategy for increasing its ringgit 2 billion turnover calls for the introduction of new business lines such as chocolate and confectionery, chilled products (yogurts, fresh milk, fruit juices), ice-cream and canned/bottled drinks (for example mineral water, Nescafé, Milo and Nestea in cans).

The net result was that by mid-1998 Nestlé Malaysia was trading at a 10 per cent premium to the market compared to its historical 25 per cent premium. Between mid-1997 and mid-1998, the company outperformed the market by 88 per cent mainly due to the fact that the market perceived it to be a safe stock through its entrenched position in the food and beverage industry, attractive dividends, and its net cash position.

In early 1999, Nestlé Malaysia was a major beneficiary of falling raw materials costs, caused by slumping worldwide demand. At the same time the ringgit appreciated after capital controls were introduced in September 1998. To help recoup some of the cost increases felt in 1998, in January 1999 the company again raised prices. This time round, the price increases were more selective, ranging from about 10–12 per cent for Nescafé to 12–18 per cent for confectionery. For highly competitive and lower foreign-content products like Nespray milk powder, prices were effectively reduced via discounts for early payment and freebies such as a small pack of Milo for every purchase. Nestlé has also embarked on an aggressive promotional campaign for some of its food products: for example, six packets of Maggi instant noodles were offered at the price of five (a discount of about 15 per cent).

A European Retailer of Electrical Products in Singapore

In discussion with the management of a European retailer of electrical products, the following principal trends as responses to the Asian economic crisis were identified:

- *A stronger focus on the bottom line*: they clearly believed that the senior executives for European companies in Asia are far more accountable for expenditure than ever before. This major retailer has enjoyed substantial funding from such manufacturers in the past. It is clear that since the onset of the crisis this has been harder to negotiate and most suppliers have been pushing for a fixed percentage of turnover rather than various open-ended activities.
- *Transparency*: a move towards a more 'divisional approach' with the transparency of profit and loss moving to the top of the agenda. Philips, in particular, has split its consumer electronics division into small domestic appliances and audio/video for greater accountability.
- *Price deflation*: prices have come down substantially, particularly for more aspirational products. VCD players have halved, 29-inch TVs have fallen by some 30 per cent, but rice cookers, blenders and so on have been reasonably stable.
- *Price wars*: these seem most prevalent in new technology areas and this has had one major implication in that it shortens the lifecycle of valuable new products.
- *Staffing*: most manufacturers (and particularly the larger employers) have laid off staff. On the other hand, and like many of its competitors, this retailer has not laid off staff but has 'renegotiated terms with every man and his dog (ad agency, media owners, landlords, third-party distribution, cleaners…you name it).' It has also trebled its training budget as a means of improving service levels and cutting staff turnover.

- *Product ranges*: inventories have been sharply reduced by both manufacturers and retailers compared to the start of the crisis. Manufacturers have rationalized their ranges with fewer models and less-fragmented product offerings. Retailers have also taken the opportunity to get rid of problem stocks.
- *Fewer key retail partners*: since the start of the crisis this retailer has ceased trading with Ariston, Hitachi, Aiwa and Mitsubishi as both manufacturers and retailers seek fewer more meaningful partnerships. This was always talked about but hard times have triggered the action.
- *Marketing*: significant reductions have been seen in corporate hospitality, product launches, extravagant promotions and so on. This retailer, on the other hand, has maintained or even increased advertising in order to stimulate demand and to try to influence store choice.
- *Regional players*: more of a regional rather than a national outlook has been adopted as manufacturers have sought to maximize efficiencies. Singapore is fast becoming a regional marketing hub. This retailer is also seeking to 'go regional' in its business partnerships.

In summary, the management believes that,

> It is no coincidence that retailers and manufacturers alike have placed such a heavy emphasis on the financial control aspect as the regional recession has been a strong wake up call to those who felt the good times would go on forever. From the perspectives of control, loyalty, service and quality the recession has been overdue and we are already seeing a markedly better attitude from staff who now realize the importance of job security and of quality practices.

Adidas Thailand

Adidas claims 40 per cent of Thailand's 1.2 billion baht market in branded sports apparel and equipment. Yet, they found that sales in 1998 were static largely because of the fall in the number of tourists and of their spending money. Although the company has over 400 distributors throughout Thailand, it has had to terminate distribution contracts with only 40 local dealers who had failed to pay up.

Adidas's response to the economic crisis has been to try to stimulate demand from those tourists and other travelers who are still coming to Thailand. Its overall strategy has been to redesign its outlets to conform with the company's Asia-wide patterns, for example by bringing in a number of concept stores in high-traffic areas, as well as refitting its concessions in major department stores. Alongside these changes, the company planned to allocate 10–12 per cent of sales to marketing, with 60 per cent of this going to television and print media to inform the public and to stimulate demand.

Swatch AG Singapore

Swatch AG is the marketing/distribution arm of The Swatch Group, selling the range of Swatch watches and accessories in Singapore. The company buys its watches from ETA, the manufacturing arm of The Swatch Group at prices which are dependent on the volume of the order rather than Swatch AG's marketing strategy.

In addition to the drop in sales attributable to the economic recession, Swatch AG's margins in Singapore were also hit by the strengthening of the Swiss franc against the Singapore dollar. (At its peak in 1998, the Swiss franc rose by about 20 per cent against the Singapore dollar.) Since Swatch AG was unable to cut most of its fixed costs in the short term, the company saw the use of price increases as the only way to minimize its losses. Although a price cut might dampen sales, these had already dropped in the wake of the recession and a price increase would allow some losses to be recouped in margins. Accordingly, the retail prices of Swatch AG products in Singapore were raised by between 4 and 15 per cent during 1998.

As had been hoped, the price increases did not have much of a negative impact on sales volumes (aided no doubt by the fact that most other watch brands also increased their prices at this time). However, the increased average wholesale price helped to improve the bottom line and hence generated a bigger budget for advertising and promotions. This actually allowed Swatch AG to gain market share in Singapore where income levels were less affected than in neighbouring countries and so their marketing efforts were able to stimulate consumer spending. As a Swatch watch is seen as an impulse fashion buy, a constant strong share of voice in relevant media to maintain awareness was seen to be more important than using low price to maintain market penetration. Indeed, Swatch AG did not believe that they could have gained much more market share in Singapore by dropping their prices. Raising prices maintained the brand image and it also increased margins which could be used to continue investment in R&D and innovative products. As such, therefore, it is a clear example of the use of different tactics to maintain the company's strategic direction.

THE EXTENSION OF EUROPEAN RETAIL COMPANIES INTO SOUTHEAST ASIA

For at least the last 30 years, most Southeast Asian countries have erected incentives to encourage a manufacturing base and manufacturing exports, which have included barriers to the entry of foreign retailers into the domestic market (Davies 1993). In addition, the *keiretsu* and *chaebol* systems in Japan and South Korea, and also possibly the companies dominated by the Overseas Chinese, have encouraged sales in retail chains of products made by other firms within the grouping. And, finally, retailing (along with other service sectors) has been used as a social security net for those pushed out of manufacturing, with major economic and political implications.

One immediate issue of the Asian economic crisis has been the pressure on governments to liberalize their investment laws. This, in turn, has meant more competition from foreign retailers, where European retailers (amongst others) have been able to enter some countries in force for the first time in many years. In just two years we have seen European companies build store networks through acquisition, through joint ventures and through organic growth (Table 9.3). This in itself has raised worries about 'Fire-Sale' investment in which foreign firms are able to buy into a country just because of currency movements, not because they are actually any more efficient at operating the assets which they acquire (Krugman 1998).

Table 9.3 shows some large store networks and it is impressive to see just how quickly companies such as Ahold and Carrefour have expanded. What is more important, however, than just their size is the difference in operating practices. European manufacturers have, the author would argue, often tried to fit in to the local economy more than European retailers are likely to do. Some of their practices during the economic crisis were noted above but we can quote further examples here. European multinational retailers have considerable levels of potential power in the previously fragmented Asian markets. Backed up by their home and other overseas store networks they have had good reasons for expanding into Asia (saturation in their home markets), as well as experience in devolving management to the local

Table 9.3   Sample of European retailer store networks in Asia, 1998–99

Country of Origin	Retailer	Sector	Indonesia	Malaysia	Singapore	Thailand	Vietnam
Belgium	Delhaize	GMS	12		22	10	
Canada/Czech	Bata	Footwear	*	*	*	*	
France	Auchan	GMS				1	
France	Au Printemps	Department Store			W		
France	Carrefour	GMS		4	1	10	
France	Cora	GMS					
France	Galleries Lafayette	Department Store			W		1
Italy	Benetton	Clothing	*	3	3	*	
Netherlands	Ahold (TOPS)	GMS	7	47	13	47	
Netherlands	Makro	GMS	9			16	
Netherlands	Makro Office Centre	Furniture				7	
Sweden	IKEA	Furniture		1	1		
UK	Body Shop	Personal care	17	25	16	12	
UK	Booker	GMS		2			
UK	Boots	Pharmacy & personal care				30	
UK	British Home Stores	Clothing		1			
UK	Courts	Electrical & furniture		44	11		
UK	HMV	Audio			1		
UK	Inchcape	Clothing	3	7	20		
UK	Kingfisher	DIY & electrical			7		
UK/Japan	Laura Ashley Japan (L. Ashley & Aeon)	Clothing		1	3		
UK	Marks & Spencer	Clothing	6	3	8	6	
UK	W. H. Smith	Books and Audio		*	*		
UK	Tesco	GMS				14	

Notes: * = the retailer concerned has a presence in this country but no details are known, W = the retailer concerned has withdrawn from this location, GMS includes general merchandise stores, supermarkets, hypermarkets and warehouse clubs. All numbers should be treated as approximate, given the speed of change in the industry in this region.
Source: Author's calculations based on published sources, company accounts and webpages.

level. This is one reason why they have been more successful to date than either their American or Japanese counterparts. The introduction of multinational retailers has been based upon:

- The duplication of specific organizational forms, such as hypermarkets or warehouse clubs, which have already proved to be successful in other countries, along with the transfer of the relevant managerial skills. Carrefour, for example, reckoned that in its response to the Asian economic crisis it was able to draw on its managers' experience of the hyperinflation that had hit its Latin American markets in previous years.

- The use of the same sophisticated research and survey techniques used in their other markets to determine customer needs and wants. These have allowed them to tailor or remodel their stores faster and more efficiently than many of their Asian counterparts who have had to cut back their expenditure in such areas.

- The introduction of massive amounts of information technology and the same back-office systems that have been developed to keep tight controls over their other operations. In so doing, they have been forcing the pace of change in local economies. These retailers now have the clout to force through some of the necessary changes in industry-wide standards in areas from bar-coding, through pallet sizes to e-commerce. As such, they will also tend to push the industry in the direction they wish to go. For example, CRC Ahold, operator of the TOPS supermarket chain in Thailand, has set up its own wholly-owned logistics facilities for foods and non-foods. The aim is to reduce its inventory from 30 days to just 10 days, to improve product quality control and production forecasts, and to save time. Following the European pattern, the facility will be managed for Ahold by Exel Logistics, a UK-based professional logistics firm which already handles a distribution centre for Marks & Spencer in Thailand (*Bangkok Post* 16 March 1999).

- These sorts of deals have also increased the pressure on manufacturers and other suppliers. Many of the largest Southeast Asian retailers have still been too small in the past to enter the market for private-label products. This is no longer the case and so the balance of manufacturing practices is being disturbed. Retailers are also looking, on the one hand, to rationalize their product lines and the number of their suppliers, whilst increasing the integration and the interchange of information with those companies which they retain.

- Their power in this area can also be seen in their approach to price. For years the pricing policies of many of the European marketers operating in Southeast Asia have been at the top end of the quality scale and they have looked to maintain their brand image against price-cutting by their distributors. Even where Asian retailers have looked to introduce discount formats, they have been criticized for basing their operations on one-off price cuts rather than the more modern Everyday Low Pricing format (Goldman 1998).

- It came as a shock, therefore, to suppliers in Singapore when the newly-arrived Carrefour began to sell products below the recommended retail price. It subsequently won a court case brought by one supplier who had claimed that it was damaging the value of an established brand. Bernard Rolland, Carrefour's managing director, commented that: 'Carrefour will vigorously defend its right to sell goods to the public at the lowest possible prices and this has been vindicated at court. The point is, we choose to do it. If I want to, I could offer it for free. I pay for it. I am very disappointed that Lam Soon has gone to the court. Suppliers should come to the negotiating table' (*Business Times* (Singapore) 4 November 1997). This was a blatant use of market power as well as showing the potential introduction of Everyday Low Pricing into Southeast Asian economies as a means of gaining and maintaining market share during periods of recession.

- Companies have introduced or expanded the use of innovative means of gaining and rewarding customers. For example, in-store marketing in Thailand has typically accounted for just 2–3 per cent of the product marketing budget of manufacturers, compared with 35 per cent in parts of Europe and America. CRC Ahold, the operator of the TOPS chain in Thailand, has been experimenting with the use of special offers on the back of receipts. These are linked to in-store prizes offered by manufacturers, the number of which is limited to four per month. In addition to involving manufacturers, TOPS is increasing its marketing budget by 50 per cent over 1998 because of the increased level of competition in the market. Interestingly, if the programme works well, TOPS plan to apply it elsewhere in the Southeast Asian region (*Bangkok Post* 3 May 1999).

- Also, European retailers are talking of improving customer satisfaction through their retail practices, better staff training and so on. For example, after the British company Kingfisher bought the Electric City chain in Singapore, the new General Manager commented that, 'Singapore's retail sector, although mature, still has many opportunities for improvement, especially in areas such as customer services and logistics practices' (*Business Times* (Singapore) 24 March 1999).

- European retailers in Thailand, led by Carrefour, have even been successful in getting changes made to the government controls that were meant to prevent foreigners from gaining control of Thai retail companies. The need for capital amongst local companies, often because of their inability to service their debt, meant that they were unable to keep to their side of their joint-venture agreements. As the Europeans have been keen to expand during the economic crisis to gain market share and to take advantage of the reduced costs of land and property, they have been allowed to take control of some companies. These sorts of moves have, however, sparked major complaints from local retail associations which see the foreign companies taking market share from local retailers, particularly the smaller shops.

In one sense, these issues were not dependent upon the Asian economic crisis. They are driven by the internal logic of the particular system of retailing and of its relationships with consumers and with manufacturers and other suppliers. The role of the economic crisis has been to trigger their introduction now, rather than at some unspecified point in the future, and to change their form. Without the economic crisis there is little doubt that not as many European retailers would have come into Southeast Asia, or at least not so close together. They are driven by the currently relatively low costs of local companies and of land and property. The economic problems have also left governments with fewer reasons for resisting their arrival. They have been covered in depth here, however, because whilst many of the marketing practices adopted by manufacturers and importers over the past two years may prove to be ephemeral, the retail changes look likely to have longer-term implications. Even if political pressures later force ownership back to local shareholders, the influx of European retailers seems likely to change not just the complexion of the retail sector but also of the manufacturing sector.

One way to think about the process might be to see the Japanese retailers who expanded throughout Southeast Asia during the three decades up to 1995 as (by and large) *strategy-takers*. As such, they have operated marketing practices and policies such as consignment buying and the use of staff linked to manufacturers and wholesalers which have tied them very tightly to the strategies of their main suppliers (and these practices have been taken on board by a wide range of other retailers from other Asian countries over the same period). For good or bad, those practices seem likely to be broken down in the very near future. The European retailers who have taken a keen interest in Asia over the past decade might be seen more as *strategy-makers*. They are quite willing to work with or against manufacturers and distributors depending upon whether or not such actions further their own plans. On the one hand, this might mean that consumers will benefit from better stores, better service and lower prices. On the other hand, it may also bring the retailers into conflict with governments which have, at least until recently, taken a wide range of measures to protect their domestic retail sectors in order to underpin national industrial and manufacturing policies.

CONCLUSION

The Asian economic crisis has had a major effect on the practices of European marketers and retailers in the Southeast Asian region, but this effect has hit harder because of the way in which the sector has developed over recent years. For many, and particularly in the hardest-hit economies such as Indonesia, there have been few signs of subtlety in their responses but rather a desperate need to survive or to retreat. In countries such as Thailand where demand has been weak but has not died altogether, marketers have reformulated their products, changed their prices to reflect their new cost structures and found new ways to distribute those products. Finally, in areas such as Singapore where the economy has remained relatively healthy but consumers have been wary of spending because of worries about the future, marketing has concentrated on stimulating demand for existing products. This may have been done through price cuts, but also through finance deals, multi-packs or the provision of more information and more opportunities to buy.

What this view should not do, however, is blind us to the fact that there are now several large, well-run European retail chains in Asia which have, almost unnoticed, expanded throughout the region. What seems certain is that the economic crisis is speeding up the rate of change and producing a number of alliances and opportunities which would have seemed impossible only a couple of years ago. What is less obvious is which firms will prosper in this changed environment and what the reaction will be from governments which have been reluctant until now to pass over the power to control their domestic service sectors.

References

Anon (1997) 'Nestlé Malaysia', *New Straits Times*, 1 May.

Chan, P. (1999) *Nestlé Malaysia*, Arab–Malaysian Securities (from Investext), 24 March.

Davies, K. (1993) 'Trade Barriers in East and South-East Asia: The Implications for Retailers', *International Review of Retail, Distribution and Consumer Research*, vol. 3(4), pp. 345–65.

Goad, P. (1998) 'Asia's Puzzle. The Region's Brutal Economic Contraction Looks Set to Continue, But a Distant Hope Still Beckons', *Wall Street Journal*, 26 October.

Goldman, A. (1998) 'Discount Retailing in Japan: A Revolution in the Japanese Distribution System?' Paper presented to the American Marketing Association and Japan Marketing Association Conference on Japanese Distribution Strategy, Honolulu, Hawaii, 22–24 November.

Jomo, K. S. (ed.) (1998) *Tigers in Trouble. Financial Governance, Liberalisation and Crises in East Asia*, London: Zed Books.

Khoo, V. (1999) *Nestlé Malaysia*, SG Securities (Singapore) (from Investext), 24 March.

KKC Keizai Kikakuchō (1999) *Ajia Keizai 1999* (Asian Economy 1999), Tōkyō: Ōkurashō Insatsukyoku.

Krugman, P. (1994) 'The Myth of Asia's Miracle', *Foreign Affairs*, vol. 73(6), pp. 62–78.

Krugman, P. (1998) 'Fire-Sale FDI?', downloaded from: *web.mit.edu/krugman/www/whatsnew.html*.

Krugman, P. (1999) *The Return of Depression Economics*, London: Allan Lane.

Linebaugh, K. (1998) 'Indonesian Unrest to Further Hit Retail Sales – Hero Execs', *Wall Street Journal*, 30 November.

Lingle, C. (1998) *The Rise and Decline of the Asian Century*, Hong Kong: Asia 2000.

Massot, S. *et al.* (1998) *Unilever*, Morgan Stanley, Dean Witter (from Investext), 9 November.

Mehta, A. (1999) *Nestlé Malaysia*, Ing Barings (from Investext), 24 March.

Sanda, C. (1998) *Nestlé Malaysia*, Credit Suisse First Boston Corporation (from Investext) 9 December.

Shafee, S. (1998) *Nestlé Malaysia*, ABN Amro Hoare Govett (from Investext), 12 May.

van Heemstra, A. R. (1999) 'Marketing in a Recession', *Far Eastern Economic Review*, 13 May, p. 34.

Part IV
Corporate Finance

10 Options for Strategic Change: The Importance of Internal, Debt and Equity Financing for Multinational Corporations

Dennis S. Tachiki

INTRODUCTION

Although the Asian crisis has brought an abrupt halt to the investment euphoria of the multinational corporations (MNCs) in Southeast Asia, they are cautiously increasing their presence in this region. Among the various flows of international capital, foreign direct investment (FDI) is one of the few categories showing a marginal net increase (IMF 1999). Japanese companies have been primarily taking a larger equity stake in their local joint ventures to consolidate their production networks, whereas European companies are more likely to pursue the merger and acquisition of local companies, particularly in the services sector (UNCTAD 1998). Consequently, the MNCs are continuing to favourably bet on the future of this region.

In allocating part of their global assets to Southeast Asia, MNCs are pursuing distinct short-term and medium-term strategies. In the short-term, all MNCs operating in Southeast Asia are simply trying to cut overhead costs and operational capacity to maintain domestic and overseas sales. In the medium-term, some MNCs are expanding and acquiring local assets that would strategically position them for the anticipated economic recovery in the region. How well the MNCs can simultaneously pursue these two strategies depends on their access to the local, regional and international financial and capital markets. The collapse of the local financial markets after 1997 is forcing MNCs to depend on their internal sources and international financial markets for working capital. They anticipate that the reforms underway in Southeast Asian countries will pave the way for local corporate finance options in the future to leverage their business objectives. Should this transition unfold smoothly, they stand to realize significant returns on their direct investments in the region (Hamlin 1999).

The road from strategy to execution, however, is not smooth. In one stroke, the Asian crisis exposed not only the weaknesses in the Asian financial and capital markets, but also the over-optimism in the business plans of the MNCs for this region. Chastened MNCs are now getting back to business fundamentals in order to create value for their stakeholders that compares favourably with other regions of the world. In this connection, Southeast Asia is becoming more than a good production base for MNCs. The changing industrial structure and demographics in the region requires MNCs to develop a flexible direct investment strategy to tap the emerging technological capabilities and consumer markets. Examining the interaction between FDI strategies and financial and capital markets, then, provides a good framework for illuminating the corporate finance options for MNCs to execute their business plans. Within this framework, this chapter provides an overview of (1) how MNCs finance their FDI, (2) the structure of the Southeast Asian financial and capital markets, and (3) the emerging corporate finance options available to MNCs operating in Southeast Asia.

FINANCING FDI STRATEGIES

A multinational corporation can invest in Southeast Asian countries through various means. On one side of the investment spectrum, it can enter arms-length business relations – for example, licensing, technological agreements, original equipment manufacturing (OEM), and other contractual arrangements. On the other side of the investment spectrum, it can make direct investments – for example, joint ventures and wholly-owned subsidiaries. These are the basic options a MNC weighs in deciding to operate outside its home country, with each option having different implications for corporate finance. Since historical data show that MNCs have been leaning towards direct investment as their mode of entry into Southeast Asian countries, we will focus mainly on their financing of FDI (IMF 1999).

Japanese FDI dramatically increased in Southeast Asia from the mid-1980s, accounting for nearly half of this region's inward direct investment before peaking in the early 1990s. European FDI began in earnest in the early 1990s, and up to the Asian crisis it accounted for 12 to 32 per cent of the FDI flows into Southeast Asian countries. The aggregate flow of FDI from the world into Southeast Asia over the past two decades has pushed Singapore, Indonesia and Malaysia into the ranks of the top ten recipient developing countries, followed closely by Thailand, Vietnam and the Philippines (UNCTAD 1998).

Multinational corporations are attracted to this region partially because the Association of Southeast Asian Nations (ASEAN) has been relatively successful in promoting economic cooperation among its ten member countries, easing the cross-border flow of goods, people, money and information. Japanese MNCs have responded by strategically segmenting product lines and production processes and locating them across the ASEAN region, particularly in Indonesia, Malaysia, the Philippines, Singapore, Thailand and Vietnam. Their cross-border production networks are noticeably evident in the textile, electrical machinery and transport equipment industries (Tachiki 1998). In contrast, European FDI in Southeast Asia tends to be country-specific in industries such as chemicals (Indonesia); petroleum refinement (Singapore, Malaysia, Thailand and the Philippines); financial and retail services; and in large infrastructure projects in the telecommunications and heavy machinery industries (Masaki and Kawate 1998). In the horizontal division of labour among the Asia-Pacific countries, then, Southeast Asia has attracted a wide range of FDI from the primary sector to resource-based and low value-added manufacturing to the service sector (Dobson and Chia 1997).

Wide variations in the investment strategies, target countries and industries of the MNCs would suggest the need for a variety of financial sources: short- and long-term capital, local and international debt, and equity markets, and so on. Instead, we find that the MNCs primarily fund their FDI through internal sources. An internal source is a broad category that typically includes retained earnings, depreciation and intersubsidiary fund transfers (loans). Between 1970 and 1994, North American (96.1 per cent) and British (93.3 per cent) MNCs mainly resorted to internal sources in capitalizing their overseas operations, closely followed by German (78.9 per cent) and Japanese (69.9 per cent) MNCs (Grünbichler 1999). A more nuanced reading of the data reveals that much of the MNCs' equity contribution in Southeast Asia takes the form of personnel, machinery and technological assistance. This is particularly the case in joint ventures with local partners, where the local partner (for example a joint venture or strategic alliance) contributes a percentage of the equity for the overseas subsidiary, much of which is procured from local financial and capital sources.

The second largest funding source for the MNC is debt financing. Commercial bank loans constitute the most common corporate finance option, with local commercial banks being the main source of funds. A commercial bank will extend a loan to a MNC's subsidiary based on one of three guarantees: first, the overseas subsidiary can borrow directly from a local commercial bank based on the strength of its credit rating; second, the local commercial bank may request the guarantee of a third party institutional lender – in the case of the Japanese MNCs, usually the overseas branch of a Japanese bank in Hong Kong or Singapore will guarantee the local commercial bank loan to the overseas subsidiary; and, in the third case, the parent company and/or the local partner guarantees the loan to the overseas subsidiary.

Placing a distant third as a funding source for the MNCs, we could group together the remaining options for corporate finance, including equity, capital transfers, trade credits, investment incentives, and other sources. Although these sources are small, they can tip the direct investment decision towards the benefit side of the cost–benefit equation. Public agencies in Thailand, Malaysia and Indonesia, for example, have provided generous incentives to MNCs to locate in certain regions of their countries and/or produce goods for the export market. Moreover, in the Philippines, short- and long-term commercial paper plays an important role in the cash flow of MNCs.

If we step back to examine the different weighting of these options for financing FDI, it is clear that MNCs either act conservatively or aggressively. When they are conservative, they execute their business plans based on the financial strength of the parent company and internal cash flow of the overseas subsidiary. When they are aggressive, they leverage the debt–equity ratio of their overseas operations. During the rapid growth of the early 1990s, the MNCs that followed the leveraged path achieved extraordinary profits. Consequently, they made more conservatively managed MNCs look stodgy. In the aftermath of the Asian crisis, however, the MNCs following a conservative path have emerged in better shape than those that followed a leveraged path. This reveals the relative absence of competitively priced medium- and long-term financial instruments in the Southeast Asian financial and capital markets that can spread risk in both good and bad times.

FINANCIAL AND CAPITAL MARKETS IN SOUTHEAST ASIA

Ideally, many MNCs would prefer to fund their FDI from local sources. This militates against foreign exchange risks and provides access to local information. Yet Southeast Asian countries are still at various stages in the development of their financial and capital markets (Cole, Scott and Wellons 1995; Zahid 1995). On the one hand, the Indochinese countries (Vietnam, Cambodia and Laos) have very few market-driven financial institutions and products. On the other hand, Singapore is evolving into a regional financial centre. Among the Southeast Asian countries falling in between, there is wide variation in the breadth and depth of their financial and capital markets (BIS 1997). Consequently, the MNCs have been piecing together the available country, regional, and international corporate finance options to fund their overseas operations.

Country Financial Options

Southeast Asian governments have had a dominant role in their financial and capital markets through central banks, development banks, and specialized bank and non-bank institutions. Since the 1980s, however, they have been gradually liberalizing their monetary policies leading to the establishment of financial and investment institutions in the private sector (Masuyama, Vandenbrink and Chia 1998). Outlining the variations in the types and roles of these institutions is a simple way to illustrate the depth of the financial systems in Southeast Asian countries.

• *Financial institutions*. Commercial banks are the cornerstone of the financial institutions in all Southeast Asian countries. They account for 40 to 60 per cent of the private assets in the ASEAN 6 (Brunei, Indonesia, Malaysia, the Philippines, Singapore and Thailand). A commercial bank is the primary channel for short- and medium-term debt financing; however, it normally 'rolls-over' a loan for creditworthy customers, partially filling the need for a long-term debt instrument. Moreover, commercial banks offer the MNCs a standard set of services, such as overdrafts, discounted bills and leasing. An overdraft permits a company to write checks exceeding deposits up to its maximum line of credit. A discounted bill – such as a post-dated check, a promissory note, or a bill-of-exchange – is a financial instrument sold at a discount of its face value. In recent years, commercial banks have also added leasing to their repertoire of services. All of these services add flexibility and liquidity to the working capital of the MNCs.

- *Investment institutions*. A variety of investment institutions have emerged in Southeast Asia with the growth of the equity markets, accounting for 20 to 30 per cent of the private assets in the ASEAN 6. Most prominent are finance companies, which have expanded the market for installment-plan finance and leasing finance. Merchant banks play an equally prominent role but they have developed their business niche as intermediaries in the money and capital markets. Some typical services include: the underwriting of securities; acting as a broker; lending money and issuing certificates of deposit in the market; and servicing the institutional marketplace for equity issues. Securities firms are also major players. They underwrite new issues and trade shares that provide companies with the equity to finance their operations. Insurance companies, mutual funds and pension funds are other investment institutions establishing a role in local financial systems.

Clearly the institutional depth of the financial systems in the ASEAN 6 is skewed towards financial institutions. In this connection, local commercial banks provide much of the depth to the financial systems. As we move towards the corporate finance options among investment institutions, the ASEAN 6 financial systems become much shallower, especially when we exclude the state financial institutions. On both of these dimensions of the financial system – financial and investment institutions – the other member countries of ASEAN – Cambodia, Laos, Myanmar and Vietnam – are still at an early stage. As these financial systems mature, it has become easier for the MNCs to procure local capital and use retained earnings to expand their presence in a host country.

Regional Financial Options

Singapore is an emerging financial centre in Southeast Asia, acting as an intermediary in the flow of finance and capital from the international financial centres of the world – Japan, the United States and Europe – to Southeast Asia. A comparative focus on the strengths and weaknesses of the Singapore financial market, then, provides a good benchmark of the breadth of the financial and capital markets in this region.

- *Stockmarket.* The Stock Exchange of Singapore (SES) handles trading on the main, domestic over-the-counter, and foreign over-the-counter boards. In addition, corporate bonds, loan stock and warrants are listed and traded on the SES. The volume of stocks listed and traded on the SES is not as large as on the Tōkyō Stock Exchange or the Hang Seng Stock Exchange (Hong Kong). Yet the SES has one of the most efficient settlement systems in the region with room to expand. In this connection, the Central Limit Order System of the Securities Clearing and Computer Service is generally acknowledged as a world-class fully-automated trading system.
- *Bond market.* The bond market in Singapore is relatively smaller than the ones in Tōkyō and Hong Kong for several reasons. First, the Singapore government has been reluctant to internationalize the Singapore dollar, and, second, the Central Providence Fund provides the government and companies with sufficient low-cost funds. Singapore does trade in Dragon bonds, bonds that are offered, priced and listed on at least two Asian markets; however, it has not been active in the larger yen-denominated Samurai Bond market nor the Hong Kong bond market.
- *Derivatives market.* Singapore established the SIMEX (Singapore International Monetary Exchange) in 1984, the first Asian futures market. From a small beginning, it has expanded to include the listing of the Nikkei 225 stock index futures and the MSCI Hong Kong index. The SIMEX now extends beyond the region with links to the Chicago Mercantile Exchange through a mutual settlement system. It is now considering a link with the London International Financial Futures Exchange. All of these developments are integrating Singapore into the global derivatives market and are giving it a distinct competitive edge over its regional competitors.
- *Offshore market.* The Singapore Asian Dollar Market handles offshore currency transactions. This market dates back to 1968 when the Bank of America opened the Asian Currency Unit account, marking the separation of domestic and international banking in Singapore. Its offshore market has been relatively successful, but the international banking facilities in Thailand (Bangkok International Banking Facilities), Malaysia (Labuan Island), and to a lesser extent Indonesia are now providing a new challenge.
- *Foreign exchange market.* Singapore has established a niche in currency swaps and other foreign exchange instruments, particularly in the US dollar, Japanese yen and German mark. A good example is Singapore's handling of Arbi loans that are secured in

one country and converted to the desired local currency, usually at a specific future date under a forward exchange contract. Today, Singapore is one of the largest foreign exchange markets in the world.

The breadth of the Singapore financial and capital markets are generally wider than the markets of its ASEAN neighbours. It has noticeable strengths in the foreign exchange and derivative markets both in Southeast Asia and the world. Singapore has been able to establish itself in these financial market segments by liberalizing its monetary policies, cultivating market confidence, and building a world-class financial infrastructure in such areas as personnel, technology and facilities for transactions. Where it falls short on these benchmarks in the region, Malaysia and Thailand have been able to establish innovative schemes in the offshore market niche, and Tōkyō and Hong Kong have developed attractive securities and bond markets. Consequently, the MNCs consider the strengths of the financial and capital markets in Tōkyō, Hong Kong, Singapore and Sydney in locating their regional headquarters.

International Financial Options

Advances in telecommunications, cross-border financial products and public–private institutional arrangements are bringing about some convergence in the financial and capital markets of the world. Multinational corporations, international financial centres, and bilateral and multilateral assistance organizations are some of the major drivers facilitating this process. Examining the reach of these organizations provides some idea of the extent to which the Southeast Asian countries are integrated into the global financial and capital markets.

- *Multinational corporations*. MNCs act as financial intermediaries when they tap the international banking centres to finance their operations in Southeast Asia. The transfer of funds are increasingly moving over the dedicated satellite and cable communications of the MNCs, allowing the 'netting' of financial transactions among the overseas subsidiaries and only transferring the net proceeds. This creates a virtual global financial centre within the MNC, reducing the need for the services of financial intermediaries. Although Southeast Asia is one of the top FDI recipient regions of the world, it is not clear how many of the MNCs active in

Southeast Asia use this technology. The mass media has reported a few cases of 'netting' by Japanese MNCs, and it is most likely that the number of MNCs using this method is limited to those that have regional headquarters and/or operational headquarters in Southeast Asia.

- *International financial centres.* Southeast Asian countries have been linking their financial and capital markets to the international financial centres during the 1990s. The Asian crisis dramatically revealed the large flow of portfolio investments and hedge funds into Southeast Asian countries, and, in turn, Asian MNCs are listing on overseas stock exchanges, issuing convertible bonds, bonds, derivatives, swaps, and using American Depository Receipts and Global Depository Receipts. A further development is the mutual linkage of equity markets. For example, in addition to the case of the Singapore SIMEX, the Hong Kong Hang Seng will list and trade shares in conjunction with NASDAQ. These shares will trade in the local currency, but the trading rules will be based on those governing the NASDAQ in the United States. These lessons and trends suggest that where regulations and investor safeguards are in place, large financial transactions will resume between the international financial centres and Southeast Asia.

- *Bilateral and multilateral assistance organizations.* The World Bank group and the Asian Development Bank are developing and supporting institutional arrangements to fill gaps in local financial and capital markets. Take the case of project finance, which involves a private sponsor that finances and takes responsibility for a long-term capital project. This requires the sponsor to draw on the international financial centres to underwrite a project in another part of the world. In principle, this financial bridging activity spreads risk and rewards across national borders. In practice, the public and private sectors still need to mutually agree on architecture for defining the role of stakeholders, minimizing risk, and securing long-term finance. New infrastructure projects are at a virtual standstill; however, given the fiscal constraints on Southeast Asian governments and the need for infrastructure to stimulate further economic growth, the use of project finance should increase in the future.

The integration of the Southeast Asian countries into the international financial and capital markets is spotty. The telecommunications infrastructure is still not adequate for MNCs to completely bypass financial intermediaries, and the variety of international financial instruments available to the MNCs operating in Southeast Asia is still limited. The liberalization of monetary policy and implementation of investor safeguards has not always achieved global standards and norms. These are some of the hurdles Southeast Asian countries must remove in order to attract international investors and larger direct investments from abroad.

OPTIONS FOR STRATEGIC CHANGE

In the aftermath of the Asian crisis, the MNCs have three basic options for strategic change in their Southeast Asian operations. First, they could exit the host country; second, they could stay in the host country and pursue a more modest business plan; and third, they could strategically reposition their assets in Southeast Asia.

The hardest hit MNCs are those producing goods with a high percentage of imported inputs for the domestic market. According to the local press, these companies are usually small- and medium-sized enterprises (SME). The depreciation of local currencies and the collapse of many consumer markets are squeezing the SMEs' cash flows from both sides. Those unable to gain access to working capital and reposition their businesses have exited from Southeast Asia.

International Monetary Fund (1999) data show that most of the MNCs are remaining in Southeast Asia. They have had to cut their overheads by reducing working hours or employees, cutting operational capacity, changing the product mix, and securing working capital from their parent companies. Although local commercial bank lending has virtually dried up across the region, some progress in disposing of non-performing loans should open the way for debt financing to resume in the medium term. The financial and investment institutions are also becoming more active in the financial markets. In Thailand, for example, the government has injected capital into the secondary market reviving the local bond market. MNCs procuring raw materials, intermediary parts and components from local sources and then exporting their products are able to finance operations from their internal cash flow. These MNCs are now pursuing a more modest business plan consistent with current conditions and the positive medium-term prospects for the regional economy.

The MNCs able to reposition their assets in Southeast Asia may benefit the most from the process of liberalization and economic cooperation unfolding in this region. The Asian crisis has forced the Southeast Asian countries to accelerate the liberalization of their financial and capital markets. Structural adjustments in improving foreign debt management, restructuring the financial sector, reducing the role of the state sector, establishing a strong macroeconomic framework, and further trade liberalization are slowly coming into place. Adding another dimension to this liberalization process is the merger and acquisition of local banks by foreign financial service institutions. This may diversify the types of financial products available for corporate finance, especially in the stock and bond markets. Further progress in this area, however, will depend on the establishment of financial benchmarks, rating agencies, liquidity in the secondary market, efficient settlement systems and tax reform.

Another secular trend emerging in the ASEAN region before the Asian crisis had been the gradual liberalization of trade and investment policies. These experiments have taken the form of economic zones, growth triangles and free trade areas. Under the banner of economic cooperation, this has led to a greater flow of goods, people, money and information across national borders. Most of the discussion in the ASEAN forum has been about trade (goods) but very little has been about the flow of people, money and information. Recently, the ASEAN ministers ratified the ASEAN Investment Area (AIA), addressing some of these latter issues and providing the MNCs with greater access to the member countries. Moreover, many of the Southeast Asian governments are allowing higher foreign equity ownership, opening 'protected industries' especially in infrastructure and service sectors, and providing incentives for investments in underdeveloped regions of the country and fostering supporting industries.

Internal, debt, and equity financing have been important for MNCs developing a presence in Southeast Asia. With the advent of financial reforms and economic cooperation in this region, new options for strategic changes in corporate finance should emerge for MNCs in the new millennium.

References

BIS (Bank for International Settlements) (1997) *The Maturity, Sectoral and Nationality Distribution of International Bank Lending*, first half, Basel: BIS.

Cole, D. C., H. S. Scott and P. A. Wellons (eds) (1995) *Asian Money Markets*, Oxford: Oxford University Press.

Dobson, W. and S. Y. Chia (eds) (1997) *Multinational Corporations and East Asian Integration*, Toronto and Singapore: International Development Research Institute and Institute for Southeast Asian Studies.

Grünbichler, A. (1999) *Options for Strategic Change: Multinational Corporations and Corporate Finance*, Paper presented at the DIJ Conference 'Economic Crisis and Transformation in Southeast Asia: Strategic Responses by Japanese and European Firms' in Tōkyō, 17–18 June, 1999.

Hamlin, M. A. (1999) *The New Asian Corporation: Managing for the Future in Post-Crisis Asia*, San Francisco: Jossey-Bass.

IMF (International Monetary Fund) (1999) *International Financial Statistics*, Washington DC: IMF.

Masaki, O. and K. Kawate (1998) 'Business Development of European Companies in Asia', *RIM*, vol. 39, pp. 37–49.

Masuyama, S., D. Vandenbrink and S. Y. Chia (eds) (1998) *East Asia's Financial Systems: Evolution & Crisis*, Tōkyō and Singapore: Nomura Research Institute and Institute of Southeast Asian Studies.

Tachiki, D. S. (1998) 'Modes of Corporate Institutionalization: Japanese FDI Strategies in the Asia-Pacific', in D. Dirks, J.-F. Huchet and T. Riebault (eds), *Japanese Management in the Low Growth Era: Between External Shocks and Internal Evolution*, Berlin: Springer, pp. 73–89.

UNCTAD (United Nations Conference on Trade and Development) (1998) *World Investment Report 1998: Trends and Determinants*, New York: United Nations.

Zahid, S. N. (ed.) (1995) *Financial Sector Development in Asia: Country Studies*, Manila: Asian Development Bank.

11 Corporate Finance Strategies of Japanese Firms: Sophistication of Local Financing

Etsuko Katsu

INTRODUCTION

With the beginning of the Asian crisis, Japanese foreign direct investment (FDI) into Asian countries (here, 'Asian countries' includes NIEs, ASEAN countries, and China) fell drastically. According to data provided by the Japanese Ministry of Finance (MOF), after a stable net flow of around more than 10 billion dollars from 1995 to 1997, Japanese FDI into Asian countries decreased 44 per cent in FY 1998 (Foreign Direct Investment Statistics at www.mof.go.jp). Among Asian countries, net FDI flow into ASEAN countries fell most drastically, especially net FDI flow into Indonesia and the Philippines which fell by 59 per cent and 49 per cent respectively in 1998 (*Nihon Keizai Shinbun* 6 April 1999).

The decrease of Japanese FDI into Asia was a result of both the drastic shrinking of domestic demand after the financial crisis, and the difficult financial situation of parent companies in Japan. However, the impact on affiliates of Japanese corporations operating in this region differed according to their export ratios and their local content ratios (Figure 11.1). Companies focusing on domestic markets suffered from the drastic contraction in domestic demand, whilst, in contrast, corporations that mainly exported products to third countries profited by a devaluation of local currencies against the dollar. However, the ratio of local content also affected the profitability of these companies. Corporations that had low local content experienced increasing costs of imports, parts and raw materials, thus reducing profits.

With a change to floating exchange rates and wide fluctuations of interest rates characterizing Asian currencies after the crisis, subsidiaries of Japanese corporations had to manage interest rate risks

199

Figure 11.1   Influence of the crisis by structure of manufacturing

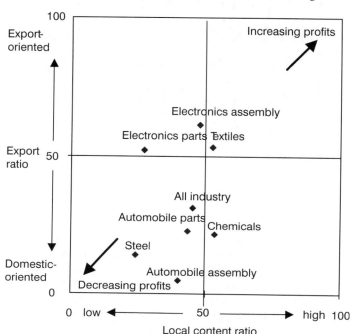

Notes: Export ratio (%) = export to non-ASEAN countries/total sales of ASEAN subsidiaries. Local content ratio (%) = supply from ASEAN countries/total sourcing supply of raw materials and parts of ASEAN subsidiaries.
Source: Export–Import Bank of Japan (1999, p. 56).

and foreign exchange risks more precisely. In order to improve the management of these risks, they had to strengthen regional head-quarters functions, especially in the areas of marrying and netting foreign exchanges, the management of global financing, and the gathering of information.

This chapter examines the behaviour of subsidiaries of Japanese corporations in Asia after the Asian crisis, from the point of view of corporate finance. Finance shaped how multinational companies (MNCs) responded to the crisis, and we shall point out the need for regional financial headquarters while also identifying a need for Japanese banks to take a more active role in providing MNCs with more sophisticated financial services and ways to raise funds. Thereby, the role of Japanese banks is also important for the further internationalization of the yen. For the sake of their economies, countries in the region must establish more sophisticated financial systems, especially an enhanced, long-term bond market. In these respects, the New Miyazawa Initiative will play a crucial role in raising funds to stabilize the Asian economy and to support structural change including the restructuring of financial systems.

FDI AND THE LINKS BETWEEN FDI AND TRADE

FDI capital flows from developed economies to the Pacific Basin have increased in importance over the past few years. Private flows in particular were more significant than official flows in regard to economic development, and in this process direct investments of Japanese companies played the leading role (Kosaka 1996, p. 109).

In the second half of the 1980s, Japanese direct investment accelerated as the appreciation of the yen, together with rapidly rising wages at home, provided Japanese firms with an incentive to move manufacturing operations abroad. Protectionist trade polices in the USA and in European countries also drove the rush of Japanese FDI into Asia. To avoid the pressures of protectionism, Japanese firms transferred manufacturing to Asian countries to then export products to third countries.

At the same time, FDI has contributed to the economic growth of developing countries. According to traditional theories, FDI is determined by differences in factor proportions among countries. Differences stimulate the adjustment of real exchange rates thus encouraging countries with abundant capital and labour shortages to direct FDI into countries with little capital and abundant labour (Nakamura and Oyama 1998, p. 3). FDI, in effect, transfers superior technology, managerial know-how, brand recognition and efficient channels for the distribution of products. This pushes the recipient country's production frontier upwards, while it also increases employment and fixed investments in the recipient country. When accompanied by trade between home and host countries, FDI naturally leads to the expansion of MNC networks. This deepens the integration of the host countries' economies into the home countries' economies (*ibid.*, p. 4). In terms of horizontal integration, FDI is likely to increase exports from home to host countries as well as imports from host to home countries. This is true because integrated assembly

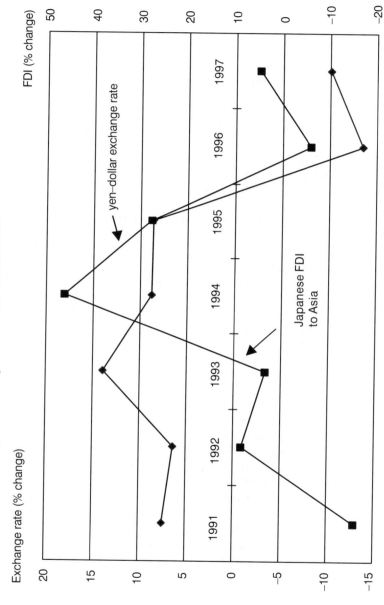

Figure 11.2 Yen–dollar exchange rates and Japanese FDI to Asian countries

Source: MOF (Japan) and IMF, various years.

lines in host countries require the import of intermediate goods for their production. Also, FDI may shift the export base for third markets from home to host countries, leading to a decrease of exports from the home country and an increase of exports from the host country. FDI by MNCs has thus substantially supported the Asian countries' development, making Asia one of the highest economic growth regions in the world in the first half of the 1990s.

FDI from Japan into Asian countries was very sensitive to changes in factor prices, and in turn to changes in yen–dollar exchange rates. Because the Asian currencies were virtually linked to the US dollar, the dollar became the dominant international currency in East Asian exchange rate policies. Most Asian countries assigned a heavy weight to the US dollar, and many of them virtually tied their currency to it alone (Frankel and Wei 1993, p. 325). As Figure 11.2 indicates, there is a correlation between the yen–dollar exchange rate and FDI from Japan into Asia; when the exchange rate appreciated, the growth of FDI from Japan to Asia accelerated. As a result, labour-intensive industries shifted production to countries with low labour costs. When looking at the linkage between the horizontal type of FDI and trade, one can conclude that stabilizing Asian foreign exchange rates against the yen leads to an expansion of FDI and trade in the Asian region, since integrated assembly lines in host countries still require imported intermediate goods.

FINANCING THE SUBSIDIARIES OF JAPANESE CORPORATIONS IN ASIA

Financial Structure

Generally, Japanese corporations depend heavily on borrowing from banks, though this differs according to the size of the corporation and the condition of capital markets. Large corporations tend to finance themselves from capital markets directly, in contrast to small and medium-sized corporations that rely on banks. As for subsidiaries of Japanese corporations, several options exist such as remittances from parent companies, financing from their own cash flow, finance from banks including overseas offices of Japanese banks, or tapping into the capital markets of host countries.

According to data of the Export–Import Bank of Japan (now Japan Bank for International Cooperation), subsidiaries of Japanese

Table 11.1   Finance structure of subsidiaries of Japanese corporations (%)

Region	Remittances from head-office			Reinvestment			Local borrowing		
	1995	*1996*	*1997*	*1995*	*1996*	*1997*	*1995*	*1996*	*1997*
NIES	53.3	32.1	47.1	13.7	41.1	13.7	33.0	26.9	39.3
ASEAN	43.3	43.0	43.2	27.2	26.1	19.6	29.5	30.9	37.2
China	83.9	67.6	56.4	6.1	7.6	6.4	10.0	24.8	37.2
USA, Canada	46.7	48.2	34.7	35.9	32.2	37.0	17.4	19.5	28.2
EU	59.5	63.6	56.9	25.7	21.9	31.2	14.9	14.6	11.9
All regions	59.5	51.1	47.1	25.9	27.5	26.0	19.9	21.5	26.8

Source: Export–Import Bank of Japan (1999, p. 16).

corporations demonstrated a trend towards localization of the main part of their fund-raising. Table 11.1 shows the finance structure of subsidiaries of Japanese corporations in three categories, namely local borrowing, reinvestment, and remittance from the head office. In comparison to other areas like North America and the EU, Asian subsidiaries of Japanese manufacturers have, to quite a large extent, reinvested profits based on internal reserves. This trend must be seen in the context of the stability and the high level profits in Southeast Asia during the 1990s. Especially for the newly-industrializing economics (NIEs) in the area, the share of reinvestment was quite high because of the high profitability of the region's subsidiaries.

Also high in comparison to other regions was the share of local financing, and subsidiaries have even increased this share in the last few years. This expansion was made possible by measures of financial liberalization from the middle of the 1980s that eased restrictions on the entry of foreign-owned financial institutions into host countries. In general, Asian countries in the 1980s moved in the direction of less government intervention in financial services, which echoed broader trends towards deregulation and the privatization of markets.

Asian countries progressively opened their banking sector to entry and expansion by privately-owned and foreign-owned banks. Governments also reformed their policies towards securities markets, encouraging expansion. They began deregulating bank deposits and lending rates, encouraging the expansion of private-sector non-bank financial intermediaries, such as finance companies, leasing companies and investment trusts. In addition, governments established offshore dollar-denominated money markets, such as Thailand's Bangkok International Banking Facilities (BIBF) in 1993 and Malaysia's Labuan offshore centre in 1990 (Zahid 1996).

As financial liberalization proceeded, it became easy for the subsidiaries of Japanese corporations to raise funds in the region. However, the lack of prudent regulation, an absence of risk-management know-how in the banks, and improper corporate governance all made financial problems worse after the currency crisis. Actually, most Asian countries saw the need to strengthen their regulatory and supervisory frameworks for financial markets after the crisis.

Restrictions on Long-term Funding

One of the reasons Asian subsidiaries of Japanese corporations depended on reinvestment and local finance (mainly from banks that readily provided short-term finance), was that raising long-term funds in local markets was heavily restricted; local corporate debt markets were especially rare. Long-term funds are crucial for corporations to make asset investments. According to MITI data on the long-term debt structure of subsidiaries in North America, the EU and Asia, we

Figure 11.3 Long-term debt structure of Japanese subsidiaries, 1992 (%)

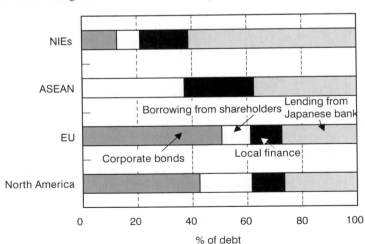

Source: MITI (1994).

can see that in Asia the share of corporate bonds is extremely low (Figure 11.3). Especially in ASEAN countries, the share of bonds for financing is near zero, pointing to the almost non-existence of sophisticated corporate bond markets.

A second characteristic of the structure of long-term debt is that subsidiaries in Southeast Asia are heavily dependent on financing from Japanese banks. The tight relationship between corporations and banks that is prevalent in Japan has been transferred to Asia. In Japan, banks and lending corporations have traditionally had very close relationships (Aoki and Patrick 1994, pp. 5–8), where Japanese banks hold shares in lending companies enabling them to influence the management of related firms. Often, banks were not only the largest creditor but also the largest shareholder. Relationships of this sort include reciprocal shareholding, the supply of management resources, and the provision of various financial services. These services include loans and other credits; trustee administration; the guarantee and underwriting of bond issues; the operation of payment settlement accounts; foreign exchange dealings; and investment banking services relating to securities or corporate acquisitions. Japanese banks also provide services to their customers through overseas networks. These close relationships with their Japanese customers secured them an important role in Southeast Asia. However, after the implementation of deregulation measures, the so-called Japanese version of the Big Bang, many characteristics which made the Japanese system different from the Anglo-Saxon model, such as the mutual holding of shares, *keiretsu* (interrelated business groups), or the main-bank system, are slated to disappear (Katsu 1998, 123–4). (The Japanese Big Bang initiative aims to revitalize Japanese financial markets so that they become the equal of the international markets in New York and London by the year 2001.) Japanese banks will have to shift from their traditional role of holding deposits and lending, to their new role of supplying various advanced financial services.

A third characteristic shows the limits of close cooperation between Japanese banks and Japanese MNCs overseas. This is because their close cooperation yields a share of 'other long term debt' that is relatively high. When Japanese banks provided funds, they avoided local currencies and instead supplied Japanese affiliates with dollar-denominated funds booked in the main Asian offshore centres of Hong Kong and Singapore. (However, it has to be assumed that after the establishment of offshore markets such as the BIBF (Bangkok International Banking Facilities) in 1993, or the Malaysian Labuan market in 1990, some funds were shifted from Hong Kong and Singapore's offshore markets to those offshore markets.) In this sense, Japanese banks have been reluctant to hold market risks. When funding in local currencies by Japanese banks was provided, it tended to be short-term and in the form of revolving loans. Interest rates for funds in local currencies have generally been very high and have tended to fluctuate drastically. For foreign subsidiaries operating in these markets, the improvement of local money market efficiency by the introduction of new institutions and instruments in Asia will contribute to the stabilization of future financing.

Managing Foreign Exchange Risk and Other Market Risks

The crisis has revealed the vulnerability of many Japanese corporations active in Asia to foreign exchange risks. As yen–dollar exchange rates began fluctuating drastically, especially after the middle of the 1980s, export-oriented Japanese MNCs became very sensitive to changes in foreign exchange rates, and these changes directly influenced their profit structure. In order to limit these influences, they tried to marry their exchange positions, in order to strive for an equilibrium of their dollar-denominated flows and stocks. Japanese MNCs tended to choose dollar-denominated transactions because Asian currencies were virtually linked to the dollar and the costs of trading in the dollar were relatively cheap. Infrequent use of the yen in trading reflected the absence of a foreign exchange market where the yen and Asian currencies were traded directly, and the absence of a futures market where companies could hedge exchange risks (MOFCFE 1999).

Sophisticated financial management means managing market risks promptly and efficiently. For large MNCs based in Japan, concentrating business functions in regional headquarters has been one response to the Asian crisis. In addition, the companies have adjusted labour, changed management of prices, increased the local content ratio, and negotiated lower prices for imported materials. For Southeast Asia, regional headquarters are usually established in Singapore. The government of Singapore uses tax incentives to encourage the establishment of so-called Operational Headquarters (OHQ) or Business Headquarters (BHQ) that coordinate activities in third countries. The functions of OHQ or BHQ include financial management, procurement of goods, marketing, research and development. Companies concentrate the handling of various risks in these regional headquarters.

The establishment of operational headquarters that include financial functions has several merits. First, such a move can decrease market risks for MNCs by matching or netting foreign exchange positions worldwide. Second, companies can manage global asset liabilities and cash-flow more efficiently by using advanced financial technology and manipulating foreign exchanges. Finally, companies can achieve economies of scale. Here, MNCs have the advantage of being able to concentrate foreign exchange transactions and other financial transactions, thereby saving on transaction costs with financial institutions. To achieve these advantages, offshore financial subsidiaries must be strongly integrated in the overall company organization through close communication between overseas and head-office staff. In upgrading their financing practices, MNCs were supported by the revision of Japan's foreign exchange law in April of 1998 (Kojima 1997); the change relieves companies of the need to conduct exchanges through authorized foreign exchange banks. MNCs can now engage in the multi-netting of their global position by themselves, and can shift their trade settlement from exchange-bill settlement to remittance settlement. This will probably contribute to the efficiency of cash management and to the strengthening of a company's profit structure.

After the Asian economic crisis, many Japanese MNCs actively sought a more efficient way of managing their cash positions. Japanese MNCs increasingly integrate the activities of financial subsidiaries and at the same time establish strong relationships with international banks. For example, Matsushita decided to trade with only one money centre bank to manage their global cash positions. The company has three financial subsidiaries, one in each region: a New York subsidiary for the North American region, a Dutch subsidiary for the EU region, and a Singapore subsidiary for Asia. Global settlements are concentrated with one bank (in this case, Citibank) which saves on commissions and other costs (*Nihon Keizai Shinbun* 27 October 1999).

Changes in Corporate Financing After the Crisis

According to the results of a recent survey by the Export–Import Bank of Japan, corporate finance changed after the crisis. First, in the NIEs, the share of remittance from home offices increased dramatically; the financial situation of subsidiaries, especially in Korea, deteriorated so suddenly that the main offices injected capital as an emergency response. Second, in China, the share of remittances from home offices has fallen as new foreign direct investment uses a higher share of local finance, such as loans from local banks or Japanese banks. Third, in ASEAN countries also, the share of local finance increased. This reflects a policy enforced by the New Miyazawa Initiative, known officially as 'A New Initiative to Overcome the Asian Currency Crisis', which includes a public finance guarantee programme to support Japanese corporations which suffer from funding problems because of the shortage of credit in Asia. According to a September 1998 MITI publication, around 40 per cent of the Asian subsidiaries of Japanese corporations suffered heavily from stricter conditions for credit from private financial institutions (MITIBK 1998).

The New Miyazawa Initiative includes support measures totalling US\$ 30 billion, of which US\$ 15 billion are available for medium-term to long-term financial needs of economic recovery in Asian countries. Another US\$ 15 billion has been set aside for implementing short-term economic reforms. Long- and medium-term support will be given through funding for trade finance, and assistance to small- and medium-sized enterprises; for supporting corporate debt restructuring; for strengthening the social safety net; and for stimulating the economy. The plan also aims to extend Export–Import Bank of Japan (JEXIM) loans to Asian countries and to guarantee bank loans to Asian countries.

Overall, the Asian crisis has highlighted the urgent problems of the subsidiaries of Japanese corporations in obtaining necessary funds. On the one hand, companies had to revise their own cash-flow situation by restructuring and compressing dividends. On the other hand, the need remains for Japanese banks to promptly provide the appropriate funds in times of need. Overall, subsidiaries will need to increase their efforts to 'localize' funding.

For financially troubled subsidiaries operating in Southeast Asia, the overall economic outlook brings some relief. In 1999, the Japanese economy showed signs of recovery and stock prices stabilized. Asian economies also began to bottom out and the worst appeared to be over. This development will lead to the expansion of demand for plant equipment in Asia and will also make it easier for headquarters to inject funds into subsidiaries outside Japan.

The Role of Japanese Banks

As described above, FDI from Japan to Asian countries increased after the appreciation of the yen after the 1985 Plaza Accord. Keeping pace with this, Japanese banks have intensified their overseas activities in Asia; the number of representative offices and subsidiaries numbered 421 at the end of 1995 (MOF 1996, p. 140). In this sense, Asia became the most important region for Japanese banks, surpassing North America; financial institutions were lured to the region by potentially huge profits and high growth prospects. (The relaxation of barriers to entry for foreign banks by Asian authorities, thus allowing full-branch status, has led to severe competition among some Japanese money centre banks. For example, there was a drastic expansion of outstanding BIBF loans that brought the symptoms of a bubble economy into Asian economies.)

Japanese banks offered affiliates of Japanese companies a variety of services and in the process established close relationships. However, after the Asian crisis, in the process of restructuring, many Japanese banks withdrew their offices to reduce their exposure in the region. Bad loans were making it difficult to stay within the BIS capital requirements ratio, and as a result they had to reduce their overseas assets. Second, fearing insolvency, their costs of dollar fund-raising became very high as international lenders in the inter-bank market charged a 'Japan Premium'. Third, in the recovery programmes as agreed with the Financial Recovery Committee (FRC), they promised to reduce their assets in Asia and to integrate their overseas offices. According to Sakura Bank data, money-centre banks in Japan made a schedule to reduce the number of their offices in Asia from 173 offices and 157 subsidiaries in 1997, to 92 offices and 99 subsidiaries in 2003 (Takayasu 1999). The recent wave of mega-mergers of banks in Japan will further accelerate these trends. (In August 1999, the Industrial Bank of Japan, Fuji Bank and Daiichi-Kangyo Bank prepared to merge in FY 2001. In September 1999, Sumitomo Bank and Sakura Bank announced a merger.)

BIS data show that banks in Asia reduced their outstanding claims on Indonesia, Korea, Malaysia and Thailand after the crisis (Figure 11.4) (BIS 1999). Japanese banks continued to withdraw from the emerging economies of Asia in the second half of 1998, with their share reaching a 14-year low of 29 per cent of total foreign finance. They are continuing to reduce their presence in the international inter-bank market.

In contrast, continental European banking groups are progressing in the globalization of their activities, most notably German, Swiss, French and Dutch institutions. They now challenge the predominance of Japanese banks in this market, with shares in Asia of close to 50 per cent at the end of 1998 (Figure 11.5).

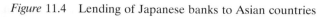

Figure 11.4   Lending of Japanese banks to Asian countries

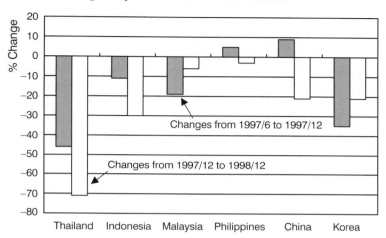

Source: BIS (1994).

Figure 11.5   Distribution of bank lending to Asia by country of origin of banks

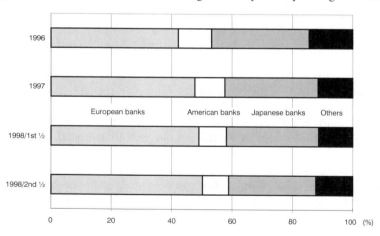

Source: BIS (1999).

Efforts by European banks to establish a foothold in Asia reflect the
strong pace of economic reexpansion in the region combined with the
heavy reliance of Asian countries on banking intermediation. (This is
in contrast to the preference shown by Latin America for capital

market financing (BIS, 1997).) The relatively high margins paid on project-related structures may also have added to the incentive for European banks to develop business in the region. More recently, falling interest rates, currency stability and the revival of stockmarkets suggest a renewal of large capital flows into the region. In these circumstances, Japanese banks must improve their financial services in order to increase their competitiveness with US competitors or European megabanks. Types of service will include cash management, risk management and trade financing. Also, Japanese banks have to prepare for the next stage of expansion of their assets in Southeast Asia.

CONCLUDING REMARKS

Though the economic impact of the Asian crisis grew deeper in 1998, evidence suggests that the crisis has bottomed out and that recovery began in 1999. Asia is a region where we can expect a high rate of economic growth in the next century. Also Asia will still be the world's growth centre because foreign capital and technology will push the production frontier upwards. To maintain a high rate of economic growth in the region, trade and investment must become more active. To activate trade and investment, Southeast Asian countries must first liberalize their economies; framework-type cooperation such as the ASEAN Free Trade Area (AFTA) or the AESEAN Industrial Corporation (AICO) is already in effect. However, further development of this framework policy is still essential if horizontal trade integration is to tie Southeast Asian economies to developed countries.

Second, the countries in the region should strengthen the infrastructure that underlies the provision of financial services. Accounting frameworks, disclosure standards and the implementation of training programmes to develop skilled professionals are one kind of prerequisite for the development of such an infrastructure. Financial markets constitute another kind of requirement. The bond market remains underdeveloped and the markets for corporate bonds conspicuously lag behind. To facilitate efficient corporate fund-raising and to develop securities markets to supplement the banking systems, these markets must be put in order. Ongoing changes in financial technology such as computerized trading and the computer-based pricing of derivative financial instruments will supplement the development of the bond market. In time, these measures will create well-functioning securities markets that are easier to use and attractive to investors.

Third, Japanese banks in Asian countries need to supply Japanese companies in the region with more sophisticated financial services and ways to raise funds. With the Asian and Japanese economy becoming more integrated, subsidiaries of Japanese banks will influence both Asian economies and the internationalization of the yen. In order to take a more dynamic role in Asia, Japanese banks should solve their bad-loan problems in Japan as soon as possible, and once again expand their businesses in Asia. Such enlargement will enable them to provide yen-denominated credit to the subsidiaries of Japanese multinationals. The internationalization of the yen will draw Japanese and Asian economies closer, which will contribute not only to the prosperity of the Asian economy, but also to the prosperity of the global economy.

According to the Export–Import-Bank of Japan (1999), many subsidiaries required support from their parent companies to survive the crisis. Around 40 per cent of subsidiaries anticipate that their operations in Asia will be restructured, and for the prosperity of the Asian economy, continued net FDI flow is of crucial importance. To realize these inflows of FDI it is essential to establish the necessary environment to provide needed funds to MNCs promptly, and MNCs must establish regional headquarters to manage their corporate finances more efficiently. European subsidiaries of MNCs are now very active in the takeover of Asian corporations, whilst, in contrast, subsidiaries of Japanese corporations have adopted a wait-and-see attitude.

References

Aoki, M. and H. Patrick (1994) *The Japanese Main Bank System*, Oxford: Oxford University Press.

BIS (Bank for International Settlements) (various issues) *The Maturity, Sectoral and Nationality Distribution of International Bank Lending*, Basle: BIS.

BIS (Bank for International Settlements) (various issues) *International Banking and Financial Market Developments*, Basle: BIS.

Export–Import Bank of Japan (1999) *Report on Outward FDI in 1998*, Tōkyō: Export–Import Bank of Japan.

Frankel, J. A. (1993) 'Is Japan Creating a Yen Bloc in East Asia and the Pacific?', NBER Working Paper no. 4050, Cambridge, Mass.: NBER.

Frankel, J. A. and S.-J. Wei (1993) 'Yen Bloc or Dollar Bloc? Exchange Rate Policies of the East Asian Economy', in I. Takatoshi and A. Krueger (eds),

Macroeconomic Linkage: Savings, Exchange Rates, and Capital Flows, Chicago: University of Chicago Press, pp. 294–334.

Goldberg, L. and M. Klein (1998) 'Foreign Direct Investment, Trade and Real Exchange Rate Linkages in Developing Countries', in R. Glick (ed.), *Managing Capital Flows and Exchange Rates: Perspectives from the Pacific Basin*, Cambridge: Cambridge University Press.

IMF (International Monetary Fund) (various years) *International Capital Markets*, Washington DC: IMF.

Ito, T. and A. Krueger (eds) (1996) *Financial Deregulation and Integration in East Asia*, Chicago: University of Chicago Press.

Katsu, E. (1998) *Gurōbaru kyapitaru kakumei: kokusai shihon idō to kinyūgyō* [Global Capital Revolution – International Financial Flows and the Financial System], Tōyō Keizai Shinpōsha.

Khan, M. S. and C. M. Reinhart (eds) (1995) 'Capital Flows in the APEC Region', Occasional Paper no. 122, Washington DC: IMF.

Kojima, Tomotaka (ed.) (1997) *Kaisei gaikoku kawase-hō Q&A* [Revised Foreign Exchange Law Q&A], Tōkyō: Zaikei Shōhōsha.

Kosaka, A. (1996) 'Interdependence Through Capital Flows', in T. Ito and A. Krueger (eds), *Financial Deregulation and Integration in East Asia*, Chicago: University of Chicago Press, pp. 107–46.

MITI (Ministry of International Trade and Industry) (1994) *Kaigai tōshi tōkei sōran* [Foreign Investment Statistics], Tōkyō: Ōkurasho Insatsukyoku.

MITIBK (Ministry of International Trade and Industry Bōeki Kyoku Kawase Kinyūka) (1998) *Ajia no genchi hōjin ni taisuru kashi shiburi no jōkyō ni tsuite* [About the Credit Crunch Confronting Japanese Subsidiaries in Asia], Tōkyō: MITI Bōeki Kyoku Kawase Kinyūka.

MOF (Ministry of Finance) (Japan) (various years) *Annual Report of the International Finance Bureau*, Tōkyō: MOF.

MOFCFE (Ministry of Finance Council on Foreign Exchange and Other Transactions) (1999) *Internationalization of the Yen for the 21st Century – Japan's Response to Changes in Global Economic and Financial Environments*, Tōkyō: MOF.

Murakami, M. (1998) 'Higashi Ajia ni okeru shinshutsu Nikkei kigyō no shikin chōtatsu' [Raising Funds for the Subsidiaries of Japanese companies in East Asia], *FRI Review*, vol. 2(1), pp. 94–107.

Nakamura, S. and T. Oyama (1998) 'The Determinants of Foreign Direct Investment from Japan and United States to East Asian Countries, and the Linkage Between FDI and Trade', Working Paper Series 98–11, Tōkyō: Bank of Japan – Research Department.

Saito, J. (1996) *Deepening of Economic Interdependence in the Asia-Pacific Region: Its Structure and the Driving Forces*, Paper Delivered at the International Symposium 'Deepening of Economic Interdependence in the Asia-Pacific Region', Economic Planning Agency, Tōkyō, 22 October 1996.

Takayasu, K. (1999) 'Hōgin no Ajia senryaku sai kōchiku ni mukete' [Restructuring of Asian Strategies by Japanese Financial Institutions], *RIM* (Sakura Institute of Research), vol. 45, pp. 42–55.

Zahid, S. N. (ed.) (1996) *Financial Sector Development in Asia*, Oxford: Oxford University Press.

12 Corporate Finance Strategies of European Firms: Between Opportunities and Continuation

Steen Hemmingsen

INTRODUCTION

The purpose of this chapter is to describe the corporate finance strategies of European firms in Southeast Asia after the currency crisis that started with the devaluation of the Thai baht in July 1997, and which soon spread to neighbouring countries becoming a full-fledged financial and economic crisis encompassing the whole region. Although currencies in Southeast Asian countries were to some extent linked to the US dollar, the financial markets in the region were not as integrated as in Europe. At the outbreak of the crisis in the summer of 1997, there were also differences between the macroeconomic positions of the different countries in the region. The most vulnerable countries were those with substantial short-term foreign debt compared to their foreign exchange reserves. Indonesia and Thailand were hit much harder than Singapore and the Philippines. Malaysia decided, as the only country in the region – albeit at a later stage – to impose capital controls and fixed the ringgit at 3.80 to the US dollar in September 1998. Despite important differences between single countries, this chapter will only refer to individual countries when considered relevant.

Figures 12.1 and 12.2 illustrate the currency and interest rate developments in Southeast Asia from May 1997 to May 1999, offering probably the best indicators to describe the far-reaching changes of the financial environment in the Asian region since the summer of 1997. As can be seen from Figure 12.1, the exchange rates stabilized in the second half of 1998 and have since been relatively stable at a

215

Figure 12.1 Currency developments against the US dollar (indexed)

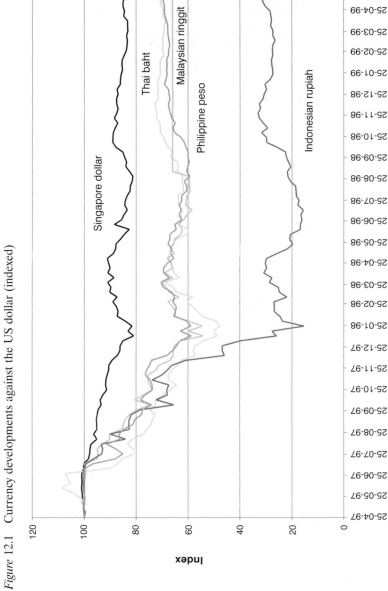

Source: Datastream.

Figure 12.2   Short-term interest rate developments (indexed)

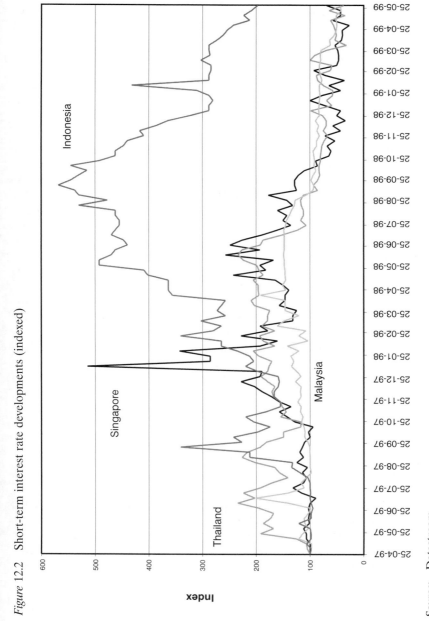

Source: Datastream.

level 20–30 per cent below the pre-crisis level. With the exception of Indonesia, interest rates in 1999 returned to a level lower than before the crisis. This development was caused by liquidity returning to the region, partly because of improved trade balances and partly from a gradual return of international portfolio investors who pulled out during the crisis. The returns of funds have contributed to a rebound of the local stockmarkets. Also, the real economy is picking up, although at a slower pace and with differences from country to country.

While the improvements in local financial markets are clearly registered by the developments in market prices, relevant data is missing regarding the financial reactions of European multinational companies (MNCs) during and after the crisis. Thus this chapter aims at giving such an overview of the perspectives of European MNCs and their strategic adaptations in their corporate finance behaviour in Southeast Asia. The methodology used in preparing this chapter has been to conduct interviews with financial managers from a limited number of European MNCs in addition to the writer's own experience as senior financial advisor to a larger European trading company based in Singapore. In addition, interviews and discussions have been carried out with representatives of three major global banks as well as with personnel of an international export credit organization. Furthermore, information has been collected from the international financial press. While this methodology does not claim to provide a representative coverage of the subject matter, it will hopefully help to give relevant indications as to how European MNCs have perceived the crisis and what actions have been taken.

EUROPEAN CORPORATE PERSPECTIVE: THE PRE-CRISIS SITUATION

Most European multinational firms have perceived their presence in Southeast Asia as a must at least since the early 1990s. The background for this is the well-known impressive economic and social developments up to 1997 with an average growth of 6 to 8 per cent compared to a 2 to 3 per cent growth rate in Western Europe and the USA at the same time. Also the substantial liberalization of trade and financial markets in recent years has enhanced the region's attractiveness for Western firms. In the financial area, a substantial

Table 12.1 Sovereign ratings and outlook in Southeast Asia, July 1996

| | *Moody's* | | *Standard & Poor's* | | |
	Short-term	*Long-term*	*Short-term*	*Long-term*	*Outlook*
Indonesia	–	Baa3	–	BBB	Stable
Malaysia	P – 1	A1	A – 1	A+	Stable
Philippines	–	Ba2	–	BB-	Positive
Singapore	P – 1	Aa2	A – 1+	AAA	Stable
Thailand	P – 1*	A2	A – 1	A	Stable

* Currently under review for potential downgrade.
Source: Euromoney (1996), p. 6.

liberalization of financial markets took place up to 1997. In addition to the development of Singapore as a regional financial centre, this included abandoning capital controls and the development of off-shore currency and derivative markets in Thailand, Malaysia and Indonesia.

Concerning currency and interest rate risks, these were perceived as relatively low as reflected in the macroeconomic developments and the ratings outlooks of international rating agencies. Table 12.1 illustrates the stable to positive outlook for all countries in the region as seen by Standard & Poor's by July 1996. Moody's had put Thailand on review for a potential downgrade, but only regarding its short-term rating. With the exception of the Philippines, the major countries in Southeast Asia maintained an investment grade rating of the sovereign risk.

In the 1996 publication of Euromoney's *Asian Exotics: A Guide to the Currencies of Asia*, the following was written with regard to the financial outlook for the Southeast Asian region:

The fundamentals of a growing and robust capital foreign exchange market in non-Japan Asia are clearly in place – high economic growth, manageable inflation, prudent fiscal management, superior domestic savings and a high capacity to service debt. All the factors mitigate transfer risk with which the foreign markets are primarily occupied. Over the next ten years the World Bank estimates the economic growth in non-Japan Asia will average at 7.5 to 8 per cent annually. (Euromoney 1996, p. 7)

Because of the exchange rate regime in most of the Southeast Asian countries, the currency volatility in the period 1990–96 was actually lower than for the German mark or the Japanese yen (Euromoney 1996, p. 14). As a consequence of the liberalization of the financial markets in the region, subsidiaries of European companies had no major problem in securing finance. In many cases it was also possible to hedge financial risks although most markets were not sufficiently large and liquid to enable the hedging of longer maturities. Despite the potential gains from not hedging the currency exposure and financing in US dollars or German marks at lower interest rates, most MNCs tended to hedge their cash flows when possible. Although difficult to document, it is nonetheless the author's impression that most European MNCs did not hold speculative positions exploiting the imperfect markets in the region.

Despite the attractiveness of the region, the combined size of the economies of Southeast Asia implied that for most European companies the overall exposure – that is measured by capital employed – to the region was a rather small proportion of its total investments. In that respect the situation for European firms differed from that of Japanese firms which had a much larger exposure to the region.

From a financial point of view, most European MNCs did not consider Southeast Asia as a region separated from the rest of Asia. The finance and treasury functions were typically rather centralized and funds were managed with a global perspective. In recent years capital markets in Europe and the USA have been very liquid and have offered very competitive opportunities for raising capital; opportunities more flexible than in Southeast Asia where the corporate bond markets have not been as well-developed. In addition, the profit situation for European firms has been positive providing also internally-generated funds for investments around the world. Also in this respect the European situation differs from that of the Japanese.

In sum, for the parent companies of European companies the financing of activities in Southeast Asia was not seen as a major problem during the pre-crisis period. In most cases, local subsidiaries could raise the necessary funds without local banks requiring parent-company support, and in addition funds could be raised from international banks or supplied from the parent company as intercompany lending. The stable exchange rates and the existence of a number of financial instruments facilitating hedging in Southeast Asia meant that the financial risks were not perceived as substantial by European firms. The commercial opportunities were thus not seen as restricted by any financial risks in the region.

FINANCIAL IMPACT OF THE CRISIS: IMMEDIATE EFFECTS ON EUROPEAN FIRMS

The effects of the crisis were naturally felt hardest by the corporate subsidiaries operating in the region (as opposed to their headquarters in Europe). Most subsidiaries were faced with the same problems and challenges as local companies. Thus from a financial point of view many subsidiaries of European firms – like their Japanese or US counterparts – experienced cash-flow problems as a result of the abrupt decline of demand and the sudden need to support key suppliers and local joint-venture partners. In addition, soaring costs of the interest on loans and problems in securing trade finance including letters of credit from local banks became evident. The financial results of many European subsidiaries in 1997 and 1998 reflected deterioration even in local currency. Transaction and translation losses in 1997 amplified this effect to the profit and loss as well as the balance sheets of parent-group accounts. In 1998, however, part of the translation losses were reversed as currencies strengthened.

In this situation it was necessary in many instances for parent companies to directly support the financing of their subsidiaries. Local as well as international banks started to request support from parent companies in the form of loan guaranties or capital increases. For European exporters into the region, their experience was that many local banks were no longer able to provide letter-of-credit facilities. On the commercial front, special issues arose regarding local joint-venture partners and key suppliers. These firms were in many instances experiencing serious cash-flow problems due to a lack of demand and the fall-out of the local financial system. In this situation, the European MNCs together with their subsidiaries had to decide whether to support their partners and under what conditions.

Despite the lessons drawn from the Mexican crisis in 1994 and the presence of some warning signs regarding the macroeconomic position of various countries in Southeast Asia, at least in Thailand, the scope and intensity of the financial problems in Asia took most corporate executives by surprise. The crisis, however, not only created problems but also opened up a number of opportunities.

POST-CRISIS PERSPECTIVE AND POSSIBLE STRATEGIC CHANGES

By the end of 1999, many observers seemed to feel that the crisis was over. Looking at the stabilization of exchange rates, the reduction in interest rates and the increase in stockmarket values in the region, this view seemed to be well-supported. However, the question still remains whether the previous growth rates in Southeast Asia will return. From a theoretical perspective there seem to be varying opinions with regard to this question. Paul Krugman, in his famous article, already warned in 1994 that the rapid growth in Southeast Asia was mainly based upon the increased use of factor inputs as opposed to increased productivity, thus predicting a future slowdown in growth (Krugman 1994). However, other economists seem to maintain that there should be no reason why the region should not return to the growth levels previously realized. The crisis in their opinion was thus more due to a panic spreading across the region rather than to a change in economic fundamentals (Montes 1998; Moreno, Pasadilla and Remolona 1998).

For financial managers of European companies the developments over the past two years seem to have led to a downward revision of the growth prospects for the region and an increase in the perception of the financial risk associated with doing business in the region. In discussions with European managers, reference is especially made to the continued uncertainties regarding the financial position of the two major economic powers in the region, Japan and China. Developments in the currencies and financial markets of these two countries are perceived to be a very substantial factor of influence for the future economic (and political) situation in Southeast Asia.

A consequence of the crisis has been that the perception of stable exchange rates more or less pegged to the US dollar has disappeared, or at least been substantially revised. Although most Western MNCs had also, before 1997, hedged their operating currency exposure, the demand for financial products hedging currency and interest rate exposure has increased whereas the supply of these products in the region has been reduced. There are of course regional differences; whereas hedging is still almost impossible in Indonesia, markets have returned to normal in Singapore with Thailand somewhere in between. The hedging of exposure in Thai baht in May 1999 still appeared to be possible only for smaller amounts and shorter maturities than in the pre-crisis period.

It should be emphasized, however, that European MNCs do not see the increased financial risk from operating in Southeast Asia as an obstacle to their strategic expansion plans in the region. This also appears to be the case for American MNCs. The Asia-Pacific president of GE-Capital – one of the first movers in terms of M&A in Thailand after the outbreak of the crisis – for example stated:

> Our strategy is very opportunistic ... we don't have specific pools of capital set aside for specific countries and specific reasons. Thailand went into crisis first. Thailand had the IMF in early. Thailand got its auction process together early so we've participated more.
>
> *(Financial Times* 21 October 1998)

In terms of sensitivity towards national feelings when pursuing take-overs, European firms appear to be among those acting most carefully. When ABN Amro, for example, bought into the Thai Bank of Asia in 1998, among other statements it agreed to preserve the local management and the bank's name. This deal is still considered to have been one of the region's most successful takeovers in the post-crisis period (Vatikiotis 1999, p. 21).

Other companies have postponed expansion programmes due to the reduced demand, but most companies still consider the region as an essential part of their international strategies. The depreciation of exchange rates also makes local production more competitive as compared to exporting into the region. In fact some European MNCs claim that they see the crisis more as an opportunity than as a threat (also see Legewie and Davies in this volume). As the balance sheet of local companies deteriorated in 1997 and 1998, it was widely expected that a lot of bargain opportunities for acquisitions would present themselves for MNCs, including European firms. This actually seems to have been the case for some fast movers. The number of trans-actions, however, appears to have been substantially less than most observers had expected (*Financial Times* 30 April 1999). Goad (1999, 38) offers an overview of acquisitions by foreign Investors in Asia finalized in the period between January 1998 and April 1999: Among the ASEAN countries, Thailand topped the list with 81 transactions involving foreign investment of US$ 10.6 billion. In second place were the Philippines with Malaysia, Singapore and Indonesia showing lower levels of transactions. Regarding industries, financial services headed the list in terms of number of deals as well as amounts involved. In the non-financial sector telecommunications, electronics and cement were high on the list.

With regard to the cement sector, a clear regional acquisition strategy by major European players was employed during the financial crisis in Southeast Asia. This reflects the strategies also followed in Latin America after the Mexican crisis earlier in the decade. As the economic growth in Southeast Asia up to 1997 involved a strong construction boom, the region's production capacity for cement was substantially increased. Although total M&A activity in the region did not increase rapidly in 1998, there were at least 14 transactions involving Western firms investing in the cement industry; the total amount was more than US$ 1 billion (*The Economist* 19 June 1999, p. 82). The major European players involved were Blue Circle from the United Kingdom and Switzerland's Holderbank. Holderbank obviously saw the economic crisis as an opportunity to expand quickly in the region by buying up assets at reasonable prices and by urging more deregulation by local governments during this process.

By mid-1999, the ownership of the region's various cement industries has been transformed compared to the pre-crisis period. Foreign companies are now estimated to own about 60 per cent of the companies in this industry compared to less than 20 per cent before 1997 (*ibid.*). Several purchases were made of small and financially-precarious companies where local producers were struggling to reduce foreign currency debt, but such bargain opportunities within the industry are now no longer available, illustrated by the change in the price per ton of cement capacity which increased from US$ 70 in some deals immediately following the outbreak of the crisis to US$ 150 by mid-1999 (*ibid.*).

The maximum ownership permitted by foreign investors has also been increased in a number of countries as a response to the crisis. Malaysia, for example, increased its foreign equity cap in the telecommunications industry from 30 per cent to 61 per cent, which in turn might have influenced British Telecom to acquire part of the shares in a financially distressed local company. Also, in Thailand, the limit on foreign ownership has been lifted and several European MNCs have indicated that they are now seeking a larger ownership share of existing joint ventures.

Despite these stated changes in policies regarding foreign ownership and bankruptcy legislation, the actual implementation of these changes seems to have been slow. Companies which by Western standards would be considered bankrupt, have been able to continue trading in order to wait for the upturn. Also many local owners have not unexpectedly declined to sell at prices which they considered unrealistically low. It does appear that the window of opportunity for the acquisition of companies in the region by European firms is becoming more and more narrow as the region's economic and financial climate stabilizes.

An indication that the risk in the region is still higher than pre-crisis levels is the margin on corporate credits. European companies indicate that the margin on Asian credits has almost doubled compared to pre-crisis levels, one consequence of which has been that many European companies have tended to fund their activities in the region out of their parent company's balance sheets and through financial markets in Europe and/or the USA where cheaper financing with longer maturities can be raised. In order to hedge the currency risk these funds might then – depending on the markets – be swapped into local currencies .

Another lesson European MNCs have drawn from the crisis relates to local joint-venture partners. During the financial turmoil many such partners were not able to participate in the necessary strengthening of their joint-venture's balance sheet, and some partners even experienced serious financial distress. This gave rise to problems in cases where the European partner only had a minority stake in the joint venture. Several MNCs seem to have changed their policy towards joint-venture partners and will in future pursue joint ventures only where they can achieve a controlling share. It is also to be expected that more care will be exercised before entering into partnerships where there is a politically-related dimension. In this respect, some unpleasant lessons for European companies were learned in Indonesia. Generally speaking, it can be expected that in the post-crisis period there will be an increased tendency to involve parent companies in the financing of activities in the region where this was not already the case in the past. Reasons for this are banks requiring parent-company support as well as the increased perception of financial risk in the region.

Only the very largest MNCs seem to have a regional treasury centre, and when such a centre is established it usually covers the whole of the Asia-Pacific region and not only Southeast Asia. The preferred location for such centres would correspond to the preferred locations for regional headquarters which seem to be divided between Hong Kong and Singapore (*The Economist* 3 April 1999, p. 59; Kölling 1999, pp. 20–1).

CONCLUDING REMARKS

The financial crisis in Southeast Asia in 1997–98 confronted the subsidiaries of European multinational corporations with many of the same problems to which local companies were exposed. This necessitated backing from parent companies in order to weather the storm financially. The crisis does not seem to have led European companies to withdraw from this region as Southeast Asia continues to be an area of high priority within the international strategies of European multinational firms. Financially, the risks are perceived larger and the growth prospects probably smaller than during the pre-crisis period. The region, however, remains attractive with commercial opportunities still outweighing increased financial risks.

Despite the 'normalization' of financial markets, which – with the exception of Malaysia – have remained open, European companies are tending, at least in the medium term, to pay more attention to international financial markets in funding their activities in the region than they did during the pre-crisis time.

A contributing factor to the crisis seems to have been the lack of synchronization between financial liberalization and the development of a financial infrastructure including prudent supervision in the region. The strengthening of such an infrastructure would benefit the local financial markets. Some countries like Singapore seem to have adjusted their infrastructure during the crisis, that is making it more attractive to local as well as international companies. Other countries still have an agenda of substantial restructuring projects to implement. The initiatives taken or not taken by individual countries will most likely influence the decisions of MNCs as to where in the region to place future priorities. Another consequence of the crisis is likely to be a stronger emphasis from European and other MNCs upon securing a controlling stake in joint ventures, as well as a stronger capitalization of new ventures and an increase in the profitability requirements regarding these.

References

Abonyi, G. (1999) 'Thailand: From Financial Crisis to Economic Renewal', ISEAS Working Paper, Singapore: Institute of Southeast Asian Studies.

Arndt, H. W. and H. Hill (eds) (1999) *Southeast Asia's Economic Crisis: Origins, Lessons, and the Way Forward*, Singapore: Institute of Southeast Asian Studies.

Buckley, A. (1998) *International Investment-value Creation and Appraisal*, Copenhagen: Business School Press.

Euromoney (1996) *Asian Exotics: A Guide to the Currencies of Asia*, Hong Kong: Euromoney Publications.

Goad, G. P. (1999) 'Optimism vs Medicine', *Far Eastern Economic Review*, 17 June, pp. 38–9.

International Monetary Fund (1999) *World Economic Outlook*, Washington DC: IMF Publications.

Kölling, M. (1999) 'Headquarter – Harter Wettbewerb', *Asia Bridge*, vol. 4(8), pp. 20–1.

Krugmann, P. (1994) 'The Myth of Asia's Miracle', *Foreign Affairs*, vol. 73(6), pp. 62–78.

Montes, M. F. (1998) *The Currrency Crisis in Southeast Asia*, Singapore: Institute of Southeast Asian Studies.

Moreno, R., G. Pasadilla and E. Remolona (1998) 'Asia's Financial Crisis: Lessons and Policy Responses', in Asian Development Bank (ed.), *Asia: Responding to the Crisis*, Tōkyō: Asian Development Bank Institute.

Radelet, S. and J. Sachs (1998) *The East Asian Financial Crisis: Diagnosis, Remedies, Prospects*, Cambridge, Mass.: Harvard Institute for International Development.

Vatikiotis, M. (1999) 'Pride and Prejudice', *Far Eastern Economic Review*, 5 August, pp. 20–1.

Part V
Conclusions

13 Economic Crisis and Transformation in Southeast Asia: The Role of Multinational Companies

Jochen Legewie and Hendrik Meyer-Ohle

THE ENGAGEMENT OF MULTINATIONAL COMPANIES IN SOUTHEAST ASIA BEFORE THE CRISIS

The collapse of the Thai baht in July 1997 marked the beginning of the Asian currency and financial crisis that evolved within months into a major economic crisis encompassing the entire region. This development drew into question the validity of the so-called economic success model of Southeast Asian countries. It also confronted multinational companies doing business in this region with a suddenly changed environment raising the question of what would be their short- and long-term strategic reactions. The companies' responses are in particular important as these firms, their investments and technology transfer have been a major driving force behind the economic growth of Southeast Asia so far. Thus, our analysis aims at an understanding of the general behaviour and nature of MNCs in times of crisis while simultaneously assessing the character and extent of any remaining national differences that may impact on these firms' behaviour in such times. From the point of view of developing countries, here Southeast Asia, analyses such as these are important in order to better forecast the effects of sudden growth declines on the investment and employment situation and hence on the general economic development.

The first engagement of Western and Japanese MNCs in Southeast Asia dates back to the last century. Besides resource exploitation, the first companies began with marketing activities and the establishment of their own sales subsidiaries as early as the 1920s as in the cases of Unilever, Philips and Ajinomoto in the Philippines, Thailand and

Malaysia. The real take-off of MNCs' engagement in the region, however, started in the 1960s when foreign companies began to increase their exports to this region, soon to be followed by the establishment of their first production facilities. The next 30 years were characterized by the well-known influx of foreign capital that aimed not only at securing local markets, but that also turned Southeast Asian countries into export platforms for the world market in a number of industries. Table 13.1 illustrates that FDI inflows rose especially quickly after 1988. Since then, manufacturers that so far had dominated foreign engagement in these countries were increasingly joined by foreign firms of the service sector including financial institutions, retailers and transport companies (World Bank 1992; Chen and Drysdale 1996).

Until 1996–97, this complementary relationship between single Southeast Asian countries on the one hand and multinational companies on the other continued to develop and flourish nearly uninterruptedly. It constituted an 'economic miracle' (World Bank 1993) with an average annual growth of 7 per cent over three decades (Keizai Kikakuchō 1999, pp. 310–11). (For a critical discussion of this 'miracle' see among others Krugman, 1994.) On the production side, this process resulted in a continuous increase of the output of local production. Simultaneously, on the sales side, interest in these rapidly growing markets rose so strongly that finally by the mid-1990s nearly every MNC had established itself firmly in Southeast Asia, either by own production and/or by sales subsidiaries.

However, it has to be noted that even by the mid-1990s Southeast Asian countries were still far from constituting a region with integrated industries. Instead, the single economies were characterized by industries well-protected and competing against each other resulting in an intra-ASEAN trade ratio of no higher than 15 per cent in real terms (Legewie 1998). The main reason behind this low level of integration in Southeast Asia, despite the strong economic and export growth, was the simultaneous implementation of two different economic policy strategies. Starting in the 1970s, all governments began to follow an export-promotion strategy with a liberal trade and investment policy for selected industries, especially in labour-intensive sectors of the textile industry and in consumer electronics. On the other hand, they continued with the exception of Singapore to pursue the policy of import-substitution in other areas to protect domestic industries by high tariff barriers and other import impediments (Masuyama, Vandenbrink and Chia 1997; Radelet and Sachs 1997). This two-fold

Table 13.1   Foreign direct investment in Southeast Asian countries, 1985–98 (US$ millions, approval basis)

	Singapore	Malaysia	Thailand	Indonesia	Philippines	Vietnam	ASEAN 6
1985	404	386	870	853	132	n.a.	2 645
1986	546	654	953	848	78	n.a.	3 079
1987	686	818	1 947	1 520	167	n.a.	5 138
1988	830	1 863	6 250	4 411	473	147	13 974
1989	833	3 194	7 995	4 714	804	364	17 904
1990	1 224	6 517	8 029	8 751	961	512	25 994
1991	1 425	6 202	4 988	8 778	778	1 147	23 318
1992	1 678	6 975	10 022	10 323	284	1 926	31 208
1993	1 966	2 443	4 285	8 144	520	2 615	19 973
1994	2 833	4 321	5 875	23 724	2 374	3 722	42 849
1995	3 424	3 652	16 492	39 915	1 871	6 524	71 878
1996	4 108	5 812	13 124	29 931	967	8 497	62 439
1997	4 016	4 078	10 616	33 833	1 993	4 463	58 999
1998	3 120	3 321	6 565	13 563	912	4 059	31 540
Total	29 995	50 236	98 011	197 074	12 314	33 976	421 606

Note: Figures for Singapore and Malaysia only show the manufacturing sector. A direct comparison of investment figures between single countries can be misleading as each country applies different statistical methods in registering foreign direct investment.

Source: Keizai Kikakuchō (1999), pp. 352–3.

strategy was made possible in all countries by the same measure, namely the creation of export platforms in enclave economies. By introducing export-processing zones the Southeast Asian governments offered the opportunity to export-oriented companies to circumvent existing tariffs for the import of capital goods while enabling them to produce cost-efficiently for the world market, exploiting location advantages such as cheap labour. This kind of export promotion stands behind a remarkable, sometimes even dominant share of FDI inflows to Southeast Asia since the 1970s.

This special kind of export promotion by export enclaves did not only appeal to the ASEAN governments because it helped to attract foreign capital and technology and to spur exports, but also because its special character allowed the single countries to keep tariff and non-tariff import barriers high for a long time and thus helped to protect domestic markets and industries. But this import-substitution policy also hindered stronger industrial integration within the region. In most cases it led to a sub-optimal allocation of resources by multinational companies that were forced to build up multiple production, sales and other facilities in single countries when they tried to penetrate local markets. But it did not prevent Japanese and Western firms from stepping up their local engagement, especially since the late 1980s when gradual liberalization started to take place in more and more sectors, though only slowly and to different degrees varying by country and industry.

Within this widespread 'international' interest in Southeast Asia, Japanese firms have so far been the leading force within MNCs' engagement in this region. While this fact does not come as a surprise with Japan being an Asian nation itself, the dominance of Japanese companies still remains noteworthy, especially in the manufacturing sector (see Table 13.2). In terms of sectors, the main focus of Japanese firms has been on industries like textiles, automobiles and electronics, especially consumer electronics. European MNCs by contrast have shown a wider industrial spread with some concentration in the chemical sector and industrial electronics.

Which are the factors that have shaped corporate strategies under-lying the MNCs' engagement in Southeast Asia up to the crisis? Were differences in corporate nationality more important than industry or location effects? Corporate nationality effects describe the transfer of national characteristics of ownership advantages abroad to rebuild them there as sources of competitive advantage. Analysing different patterns of internationalization strategies, location effects focus on the

Table 13.2   Composition of foreign direct investment in the manufacturing sector of Southeast Asian countries by nationality of origin between 1987 and 1996

	Composition (%)					
	Total (US$ billions)	*Japan*	*Europe*	*USA*	*NIEs*	*Others*
Singapore	20.1	29	25	44	n.a.	2
Malaysia	43.3	22	15	12	36	15
Thailand	65.5	43	13	17	26	1
Indonesia	86.9	17	17	4	24	38
Philippines	5.9	14	12	22	24	28
ASEAN 5	221.7	27	18	14	25	16

Note: NIEs = Taiwan, South Korea, Hong Kong, Singapore; figures for NIEs include round-trip investment by overseas Chinese and investment by Japanese subsidiaries operating in NIEs. Others include joint investment from two or more countries.
Source: Legewie (1998), p. 220.

impact of a special country/region and its specific business conditions on a corporate strategy. Industry effects likewise describe the influence of industry-specific characteristics on the formulation of corporate strategies. Obviously the MNCs' strategies and behaviour have, to a certain extent, been influenced by a wide variety of factors. Japanese firms, particularly in automobiles and electronics, for example, have transferred their well-known system of vertical *keiretsu* relations from Japan to Southeast Asia. This transfer of ownership advantages is one of the major explanatory factors for the large number of Japanese small and medium-sized enterprises that rebuilt a part of the Japanese industrial organization in Southeast Asia. The transfer of a system based on a long-term established industrial organization also helps us to understand the relative low level of autonomy usually found among Japanese affiliates operating in Southeast Asian countries.

Overall, however, the interplay of location and industry effects has clearly dominated corporate nationality as the important determinants of MNCs' behaviour in Southeast Asia in the past. The most obvious difference between Japanese and Western firms lies in the strong orientation of Japanese MNCs towards domestic and regional markets as opposed to the much stronger export orientation towards the overseas markets of European and US companies as illustrated by

Dobson and Chia (1998). Ramstetter has shown for Thailand that remarkably higher export-sales ratios of European and US firms are not confined only to electronics, but that they can be found in a wide range of different machinery industries (1998, pp. 118–23). The stronger orientation of Japanese MNCs towards national and regional markets is partially a result of location and geography, with Japan being itself an Asian nation. Hence, it is not surprising that Japanese firms have always attributed a special importance to Asian markets that are located in their own backyard.

Industry effects and thus the particular industries that Japanese and European MNCs have focused on have been of similar significance. The different emphasis placed on domestic and overseas markets is best illustrated by the contrast in Japanese-dominated consumer electronics (partly aiming at highly protected domestic markets) and industrial electronics with the strong participation of US and European firms (aiming nearly exclusively at overseas markets). The same holds true for textiles or automobiles where Southeast Asian markets have been highly protected by trade barriers and investment restrictions. These industry conditions forced Japanese companies, that were eager to sell to these markets, to engage more in joint ventures with local partners than their European competitors had to do. Thus, the chosen mode of ownership (preference given to joint ventures by Japanese firms versus preference for wholly-owned subsidiaries by Western firms) is more the result of industry and location effects than the outcome of corporate nationality.

Despite these general differences between Japanese and European firms in terms of market orientation, mode of ownership or industrial organization, most MNCs were hit in a similar, namely negative way by the Asian crisis after July 1997. The major short-term impact of the devaluation of local currencies was the increase in foreign-currency debts and subsequently a sharp drop in regional demand. Falling sales volumes and deteriorating prices both strongly affected the profitability of most firms. Simultaneously, rising prices for raw materials and components, sometimes even coupled with problems in securing these imports, further complicated the local operations of manufacturers. These and financial problems were limited not only to the affiliates of MNCs, but were also found among their local joint-venture partners, suppliers and distributors adding to the direct negative effects of the crisis.

However, at the same time, positive effects for MNCs also surfaced, though not always with a similar immediate impact and only rarely offsetting the negative effects described above. Among these positive effects are an increased export competitiveness as the result of the devaluation of local currencies, declining costs for input factors such as land, office space and in particular labour, an easing of restrictions on FDI and new incentives by national governments, and weakened local competitors offering opportunities for new acquisitions.

DIRECT REACTIONS TO THE CRISIS

In terms of their response to the crisis, companies active in the region faced several options. Due to the difference in the levels of involvement in the areas of marketing and production, not all options were feasible to all companies. The main areas of decision included the following: the closing or cutting down of operations; rationalizing internal operations; changing supplier and distributor relationships; adapting marketing strategies; and taking the crisis as a chance to expand operations. Apart from the first option, the nature of the other options allowed for them to be combined as suited the companies, and indeed most companies did so. However, there were differences in the selections made. This can be attributed to various factors such as the overall strength and support of parent companies, the experience of companies with previous situations of crisis, organizational restrictions, the belief in the validity of past decisions combined with expectations for the future development of the markets.

Following the first dramatic developments and the very pessimistic prediction of most onlookers concerning the prospects of recovery, it would have been no major surprise had more companies opted for the first choice of leaving the markets altogether. Yet, this has only been the case for some Japanese retailers and financial institutions who reduced their engagement following the crisis in Southeast Asia. In both areas Japanese companies had previously stepped up their engagement considerably in the late 1980s and early 1990s. Many of these investments failed to be profitable in the first place and the crisis just seemed to have provided the final impetus to reduce engagement. At the same time, companies in these sectors not only faced a serious environment in Southeast Asia, but also in Japan. Japanese banks are still weathering the aftershocks of the burst of the 'bubble economy' while retailers have been facing stagnant consumer markets all through the 1990s. Especially as companies from Europe and Asia make fast inroads into these markets at the moment, it will be difficult for companies now retreating to make a comeback later. It also has to be asked whether the retreat of Japanese companies is affecting the ability of other Japanese companies in a negative way as these companies might lose important partners supporting their business in the region (Katsu in this volume).

The majority of companies decided to sustain their engagement in the market. At the same time they embarked on sharp internal restructuring programmes with the aim of quickly adapting their operations to a situation which was no longer characterized by strong growth but called for the need to maintain their market position, regain profitability and increase competitiveness.

Immediate reactions to the crisis by Western as well as Japanese companies in the area of production included reductions in working time, cuts in salary, forced vacations, the laying-off of personnel and the temporary or permanent closure of plants. Companies also tried to increase exports to make up for drops in local demand. However, it has to be pointed out that increasing exports from Southeast Asia was not an easy task. As these affiliates are often in direct export competition with production facilities of the same MNCs located in other regions, expanding exports beyond the Asian region was seldom achieved in the short run. Japanese subsidiaries were strongly supported by their headquarters by increasing the sourcing of products.

Meanwhile, however, a rise in export competitiveness based on both the devaluation of currencies and serious restructuring efforts of companies has become apparent. Many MNCs have started to report rising exports to overseas markets from their affiliates since 1999, indicating that the region has regained its export strength. Another option was the increase in local content on the supply side. To become independent from currency fluctuations was considered an important means to regain cost competitiveness. However, it has to be pointed out that in many cases strong local suppliers were not available. At the same time such measures only progressed to a certain extent as they conflicted with the coordinated and concentrated purchasing of inputs, which is said to be a major advantage of multinational companies. As companies are adjusting procurement patterns, however, these changes have to be seen more from the perspective of long-term and regional strategies than from a short-term and local perspective.

In marketing their goods for local markets, companies faced a much stiffer environment. They were caught in a situation where the sourcing of goods became more expensive through currency devaluation while consumers struggling with reduced incomes demanded even lower prices. Companies thereby had to shoulder part of the cost increases themselves leading to drops in profitability. In this situation, most Japanese companies kept up or even intensified their long-term market-oriented strategies (such as introducing new global or regional brands) and focused their attention on restructuring internal operations and external relations with suppliers and distributors. Heavy localized European multinationals, however, did not limit their actions to internal activities but used past experiences from crisis situations in other parts of the world to quickly introduce new products, change packaging sizes and develop new distribution channels and even increase budgets for promotion.

The crisis also challenged companies in the area of corporate finance. Following a long period of stable exchange rates and based on continuous high evaluations by rating agencies and international institutions (Hemmingsen in this volume), companies had concentrated on production and marketing. Japanese companies, especially, reported heavy exchange rate losses pointing to the need to upgrade their regional corporate financial activities and risk management.

Another anticipated development at the beginning of the crisis was an increase in M&A activity (Table 13.3). These activities can be best understood by viewing the crisis not as a threat but a chance. Mainly Western firms became active and took over companies in all industries from manufacturing to financial services and retailing. Some companies, like European retailers, had for some time targeted these markets for potential expansion, but had been reluctant to do so due to strict investment rules and the rapidly rising costs of land and construction. The crisis not only lowered these costs but also gave companies an opportunity to successfully lobby local governments for changes in regulations. The clear shift away from minority investments with the purpose of setting up a presence and establishing a relationship with a local company, to majority acquisitions with control over companies, would not have been possible without changes in government regulations (Davies in this volume).

In contrast, Japanese companies limited their engagement to raising capital stakes in existing joint ventures often acquiring a majority stake. This can either be explained by the already high presence of Japanese companies in the region, a current lack of financial resources, or a general preference for greenfield investments over acquisitions (Tejima 2000) when entering new markets. At least the fact that many companies had to rely on a programme by the Japanese

Table 13.3 Cross-border M&A activity in Southeast Asia, 1991–98 (US$ millions)

	1991	1992	1993	1994	1995	1996	1997	1998
Total acquisition	1 781	7 066	5 042	10 474	11 472	13 614	12 121	8 004
Majority interest	129	294	878	1 333	813	1 778	4 997	4 859
Majority interest/Total acquisition	7.2%	4.2%	17.4%	12.7%	7.1%	13.1%	41.2%	60.7%

Note: Singapore, Malaysia, Thailand, Indonesia, Philippines; 'majority interest' refers to cases in which the investor acquires more than 50 per cent voting securities of the resulting business.
Source: UNCTAD (1999).

government for financing changes in the capital structure of their joint ventures points to a lack of liquidity on their side (Legewie and Katsu in this volume).

In the long run, the crisis might be mainly remembered by companies as a window of opportunity for quickly reducing internal costs and a chance to transform relationships with suppliers, distributors and joint-venture partners, a process which under less severe circumstances might have been more complicated and time-consuming. For many companies the need for reforms had been apparent well before the crisis but companies were reluctant to take any measures which had the potential to interrupt operations during times of fast growth. The crisis also highlighted the need to formulate original long-term strategies for the development of activities in the region. Here also companies had been in the process of doing so before the crisis, however, the crisis stressed the need for the rapid implementation of these changes.

LONG-TERM STRATEGIC ORIENTATION

The background for future corporate strategies in Southeast Asia is characterized by the rapid environmental changes that have taken place in this region since the early 1990s. The three most important factors are the regional market growth, the regional trade liberalization and the gradual lift of investment restrictions that started well before the crisis and that are all expected to prevail in the long run. These three factors create an environment suited to the enforced implementation of regional production and sales strategies by multinational companies regardless of their nationality.

Undoubtedly most MNCs are currently shifting the strategic focus of their activities in Southeast Asia to exactly such a regional view. Within production, the main emphasis is on achieving economies of scale and scope by utilizing production and procurement (and even R&D) networks on a regional basis. Companies increasingly aim at creating efficient production capacities that serve regional markets but that can also be integrated into their global production networks to a much higher degree than until now. Within sales a similar reorganization of marketing activities can be observed in Southeast Asia. At the core lies the rapid introduction and strengthening of regional brands which is supported by corresponding marketing measures to expand sales from the domestic to the regional level.

As a result of this new regional focus, the number of companies setting up regional headquarters is steadily rising with their functions meanwhile stretching from logistics and financial support to the regional coordination of procurement and sales. Besides this shift towards the regionalization of company activities we also note an increasing integration of products, processes and functions into the global networks of MNCs, a trend UNCTAD refers to as 'complex integration' strategy (1999). This trend does not only come with a higher degree of regional and global integration of company activities, but also with the reduction of some business functions in the MNCs' home countries.

While the trend towards regional strategies can be observed for both Japanese and European MNCs, their starting positions differ to some extent. Japanese firms that have so far focused strongly on domestic markets are expanding their regional scope by gradually integrating neighbouring countries into their respective production and marketing strategies. So far this geographical enlargement rarely extends beyond the level of ASEAN countries plus Taiwan, as in the case the automobile industry. China or Japan are never included but continue to be both treated as separate markets and thus separate organizational units.

Those European firms that used to concentrate on exports from Southeast Asia to overseas markets, by contrast, now turn their interest increasingly to the regional market itself. However, they tend to see Asia more as an entire region in itself and not as separated into Southeast Asia, China, Japan and other sub-regions. Accordingly, they are inclined to operate on a larger regional scale sometimes even including China or Japan into their regional strategies.

In addition, Asian operations of European MNCs are much more integrated into the global market than those of their Japanese competitors with the notable exception of the electronics industry. In general, European firms only turned to Asia after having made inroads into the European and North American markets. In the case of Japanese firms, activities in Asia are by contrast often their main and sometimes even their sole international engagement. Even most of the well-known multinational players of the automobile and electronics industry are less internationalized than their European counterparts both in terms of production and sales (Meyer-Ohle and Hirasawa in this volume; TSS 1999). This low degree of internationalization is also shown by the transnationality index produced by UNCTAD which captures the importance of foreign assets, sales and employment in a firm's overall activities. The transnationality index of the world's top 100 MNCs gives an average value for Japanese firms of 39.5 as opposed to 47.9 for North American companies and 62.5 for those of the European Union (UNCTAD 1999, p. 82). This implies that European firms fit much more within the concept of Ohmae (1985) and his postulation for a strong market presence in each of the triad powers of North America, Europe and Asia. Despite their strong presence in Southeast Asia, the regional operations of Japanese firms in this region are still more limited to a dependent though complementary relationship to the core operations at home in Japan than being an integral part of a strategy encompassing the whole Asian region.

The different starting positions of Japanese and Western MNCs in Southeast Asia make it highly probable that we will continue to notice some variations in their corporate behaviour from an organizational point of view. Any discussion of these differences must go beyond the rather general distinction between long-term sales-oriented strategies followed by Japanese firms, and short-term profit-oriented strategies of Western MNCs or the specific distinction whether or not a MNC chooses mergers and acquisitions as a market entry and expansion strategy. The analysis rather leads us back to the general discussion of MNC strategy (Young in this volume) and the various concepts proposed by Perlmutter (1969), Porter (1986), Prahalad and Doz (1987), or Bartlett and Ghoshal (1989).

The most obvious questions are: Will Japanese firms continue to run their operations in Southeast Asia mainly as a mere geographical extension of their industrial system in Japan as suggested by Hatch and Yamamura (1996)? Or will Japanese headquarters allow their local affiliates a higher level of autonomy in decision-making and thus transform them into more equal partners in global network operations? Will there be differences in the areas of R&D, production, sales and finance? Finally, will operations in Southeast Asia be increasingly integrated into a global network of firms' activities and at which speed? And by contrast, what will be the responses of European MNCs to this set of questions?

Here we cannot answer each question in detail so we will rather concentrate on selected aspects that might help to foresee future corporate behaviour in the region. In general, there is an undeniable trend of convergence in the strategies of Western and Japanese MNCs both stressing the regional aspect of their activities as outlined above. This fact must be stressed and be kept clearly in mind when discussing the remaining differences.

One such difference lies in the Japanese firms' continuing preference for a more centralized approach to their activities in Southeast Asia than their Western competitors. Most of them will obviously persist in restricting the autonomy of their local affiliates. Hence, they strongly resemble the 'global' company type in the meaning of Bartlett and Ghoshal (1989) as opposed to the 'multinational' and 'international' type to be found more among European MNCs. Such Japanese behaviour is understandable with regard to their strong focus on production activities in Southeast Asia that still serve as the main geographical extension of their production and R&D systems at home. Thus, a close interplay between operations in Japan and Southeast Asia will remain important to further build cost advantages through centralized global-scale operations (Yoshihara in this volume).

On the other hand, the growing importance of Southeast Asia as a market will undoubtedly raise the importance of sales subsidiaries and thus require an increased level of autonomous decision-making by them in the future. European (and US) firms that are already ahead in this regard will continue to set the pace here as they will probably serve as a model for their Japanese competitors of how to build up regional and global brands and thus to integrate operations on a regional and global scale. In addition, the combination of a growing presence of Western firms in Southeast Asia and the ongoing liberalization of regional markets will lead to the further introduction of global standards in conducting business there. These changes will affect, in particular, Japanese MNCs that might not be willing to easily dissolve long-term established business practices and contacts with suppliers and distributors as they present one of their most valuable assets in the region.

While corporate nationality had some influence in the past, findings presented in this volume have shown that the nationality of single firms will decrease in importance in the future for several reasons. First, there are no longer (and one might doubt whether there have been before) only 'typical' Japanese or European firms. This is best illustrated by a company like Sony which is often referred to as an American company in Japan. Second, the increasing number of cross-border mergers like Nissan and Renault or DaimlerChrysler and Mitsubishi Motors no longer permits us to classify corporate strategies as either Japanese or European. Third, the same applies to the rapidly rising number of strategic international alliances that are either restricted in time or scope with respect to the business segment involved. Fourth and finally, we notice the rising importance of business networks that not only include various manufacturers, but also financial institutions, trading houses and retailers, transport companies and others. This trend automatically comes with a mixture of different nationalities involved, especially in a region like Southeast Asia where the business environment is increasingly characterized by both liberalization and internationalization.

However, the distinction between multinational companies from abroad and local firms will remain significant. The importance of such a distinction has even risen in Southeast Asia where the crisis clearly strengthened the position of foreign MNCs compared to the position of their local competitors.

THE ROLE OF MULTINATIONAL COMPANIES IN THE FUTURE ECONOMIC DEVELOPMENT OF SOUTHEAST ASIA

Multinational companies have over the years built up a formidable presence in Southeast Asia and in this process also contributed to the overall economic development of their host countries. This is most distinct for the smaller countries of Southeast Asia. In Singapore, affiliates of foreign companies account for over 60 per cent of exports today, and in Malaysia the share of foreign companies in exports has risen from only 17 per cent in 1985 to over 50 per cent in 1996. Concerning employment, foreign companies account for 52 per cent of employment in the manufacturing sector of Singapore (1996) and for 43 per cent in Malaysia (1994) (UNCTAD 1999, pp. 408–11).

The effects of foreign direct investment in respect to economic development of host countries are diverse. In a positive sense multinational companies can contribute to economic development by providing not only capital and employment but also technology, skills, brands, organizational and managerial practices, access to markets and competitive pressures. While the first points are generally accepted and only the degree to which MNCs contribute in reality is discussed, the last point, competitive pressures, is more controversial. Competitive pressures can on the one hand lead to efforts of local companies to increase the efficiency of their operations and thereby may not only lead to lower prices but also to better products. On the other hand, competitive pressures by MNCs may be too strong for local companies to cope with, leading to the crowding out of local companies and initiatives, thereby conflicting with the aims of local governments to nurture local entrepreneurship. Studies for Southeast Asia, however,

Table 13.4   Private and official capital flows to Asia, 1996–2000 (US$ billions)

	1996	1997	1998	1999	2000
Private capital flows	*174.3*	*71.0*	*8.6*	*39.3*	*26.8*
Direct investment	45.4	51.1	53.4	49.6	45.9
Portfolio equity	19.1	6.0	5.0	15.2	9.1
Commercial banks	75.6	−8.3	−52.2	−21.9	−24.5
Nonbank creditors	34.2	22.2	2.4	−3.7	−3.8
Official capital flows	*3.6*	*35.5*	*28.7*	*8.5*	*12.4*
International agencies	0.2	24.7	21.4	−1.5	5.1
Bilateral creditors	3.4	10.8	7.3	10.0	7.3

Note: Figures for 1999 and 2000 are forecasts.
Source: Institute of International Finance.

show that FDI in these countries so far has led to an increase in domestic investment (crowding in), while for other regions such as South America neutral or even crowding out effects were calculated (UNCTAD 1999, pp. 171–3). Considering these various effects of FDI it now seems to be necessary to discuss what role multinational companies played during the crisis and how long-term strategies outlined in this book may affect future economic development in Southeast Asia.

Considering the role of multinational companies during the crisis, reactions by MNCs overall seemed to have stabilized the economic situation of host countries. Foreign direct investment has proved to be a quite reliable form of capital inflow during times of crisis compared to portfolio investments and international bank loans (see Table 13.4). This has certainly been true for the manufacturing sector, where companies did not pull out of the markets and have sustained their engagement although they at first expected periods of up to five years before returning to pre-crisis levels. For the financial and real estate sector, by way of contrast, this statement has to be questioned. Although globally-acting financial players stood behind the fast liberalization of financial markets in the Asian countries, the same financial companies played an important part in triggering the crisis when moving out of Asia in 1997 in the first place.

The prudent reactions shown by manufacturers and marketers throughout the crisis draws into question whether there really existed a special need to restore investor confidence as a basis for the economic recovery of the region as postulated by most observers. A loss of confidence was obviously shown only by financial investors and portfolio managers but not by real investors who displayed a quite different attitude towards the crisis (Yanagihara in this volume).

The stabilizing role of multinational companies was especially important in employment where European and Japanese companies alike tried to maintain their core workforce. Before the crisis, securing a qualified workforce had become a main bottleneck for the further expansion of companies in the region. Partly due to a higher level of exports, but also based on an overall long-term orientation, multinational companies retrenched the workforce to a lesser degree than local companies. MNCs also contributed to keeping up employment in local companies through their financial support to suppliers and distributors.

Companies have not only sustained their operations but also engaged in activities to upgrade them. Cost-saving, raises in productivity and increases in research and development became important to better adapt affiliates to a situation where they can no longer expect automatically growing consumer markets and at the same time face increased competition on world markets by other low-cost producers. As an interesting measure, Japanese auto-makers like Toyota and Honda even delegated otherwise unoccupied workers to home countries for additional training. In this respect, the interests of multinational companies and host countries went hand in hand, not only in keeping up employment but also in qualifying workers for performing more complicated tasks in the future. As with employment, MNCs again not only limited their restructuring and support activities to their own affiliates, but also integrated local suppliers and distributors in their efforts to increase efficiency.

Through these measures, multinational companies increased their pressure on local competitors. In stagnating consumer markets, where it is no longer possible to increase sales without at the same time increasing market share, affiliates of multinational companies started to look at expanding their market share at the cost of local firms. While local companies might try to counter these measures with activities of their own to raise efficiency, it must be doubted if all local companies have got the necessary resources to survive this increased pressure in the long run. This kind of crowding out of some local companies might be the necessary side effect of measures that have brought about considerable efficiency increases in the overall system.

While adaptive measures of foreign MNCs during the crisis helped to stabilize host economies in the short run, how will new long-term strategies affect the future economic development of the region? The inflow of new FDI into the region has slowed down after the crisis. At the same time, there has been a clear shift away from so-called greenfield investments to M&A activity and capital injections into existing joint ventures. While capital injections supported local joint-venture partners and thereby contributed to overall stabilization, M&A activity is often seen quite critically in the literature concerning the activities of multinationals in regard to host-country development (Dunning 1998). In contrast to greenfield investment, takeovers *per se* do not lead to an expansion or upgrading of economic activity. Foreign companies that have taken advantage of changes in exchange rates, and through takeovers have profited from the financial difficulties of owners, do not necessarily possess better capabilities to operate the company in the market afterwards (Krugman 1998).

It is still too early to evaluate the overall outcome of the high number of merger activities following the crisis in Southeast Asia. Some of the acquisitions might have saved companies from bankruptcy; some companies indeed only took over competitors, while other companies used M&A to quickly establish a position in the market and then started to transfer know-how to the acquired companies. This has been the case with European retailers and banks that are consequently building up advanced operations following the example of their home markets (Davies in this volume). Overall, the crisis led to an increased presence of foreign companies in all areas. One interesting point in this regard is the potential emergence of networks made up exclusively of foreign affiliates of multinational companies. In this regard it will be very important for host countries to find an answer to the question of what effects the emergence of such networks will have for economic development. If foreign affiliates can increasingly use the services of other foreign affiliates and reduce transactions with local companies, how will this affect spillovers to the economy of the host country in the long run?

Following the crisis in Southeast Asia, all countries have eased regulations to attract foreign investors, indicating a continued positive view towards FDI. Worldwide, the number of favourable changes for investment increased from about a 100 per year before the crisis to a level of 135 in 1998, Asia accounting for 51 changes alone (UNCTAD 1999, p. 115). However, these changes were not only made in regard to the crisis, but also with the coming integration of Asian markets in mind.

For companies, too, this will provide the chance to integrate functions in a regional context. This reduces the need to replicate corporate functions in each single country in the region. In the short run this integration may lead to a considerable reduction of employment, but in the long run it might be compensated by the increased attractiveness of larger markets that will also increase the feasibility for companies to increase their research and development functions in the region. So far only Singapore and to a certain extent Malaysia have succeeded in attracting corporate R&D facilities (Wong and Singh in this volume). The overall lack of such activities by foreign companies operating in the region is still seen as a major obstacle to future development; sustainable growth being dependent not only on the growth of input factors, but in the long run on increases in productivity and advancement of knowledge (Krugman 1994).

With increased regionalization and an increased number of countries competing for FDI, not only in Southeast Asia but also in China, South America or Eastern Europe, it will become even more important for countries to understand the strategic assumptions underlying the transnational activities of multinational companies (Dunning 1998, p. 60). Multinational companies are continuously upgrading their organizations. The use of more and more advanced information technology in this process erases many previously existing barriers to relocating corporate functions. In the search for locations, companies are not seeking to contribute to country development but are seeking their own profitability.

This is true for Japanese and European companies alike. This volume has shown that, up to now, major differences exist between these companies in reaching their goals in Southeast Asia. These differences can be mainly attributed to geographical and historical factors as well as industrial characteristics that have influenced the strategies of Japanese and European MNCs in the past. At the same time, however, corporate nationality did matter to some extent. The future role of national identity has to be questioned as differences in this regard are increasingly done away with and replaced by cultures of really transnational and globally competing companies.

References

Bartlett, C. A. and S. Ghoshal (1989) *Managing Across Borders: The Transnational Solution*, Boston, Mass.: Harvard Business School Press.
Chen, E. K. Y. and P. Drysdale (1996) *Corporate Links and Foreign Direct Investment in Asia and the Pacific*, Pymble, Australia: Harper Educational.

Dobson, W. and S. Y. Chia (eds) (1998) *Multinationals and East Asian Integration*, Ottawa: International Development Research Centre.

Dunning, J. H. (1998) 'Location and the Multinational Enterprise: A Neglected Factor?' *Journal of International Business Studies*, vol. 29(1), pp. 25–66.

Hatch, W. and K. Yamamura (1996) *Asia in Japan's Embrace: Building a Regional Production Alliance*, Cambridge: Cambridge University Press.

Keizai Kikakuchō (1999) *Ajia keizai 1999* [The Asian Economy 1999], Tōkyō: Ōkurashō Insatsukyoku.

Krugman, P. (1994) 'The Myth of Asia's Miracle', *Foreign Affairs*, vol. 73(6), pp. 62–78.

Krugman, P. (1998) *Fire-Sale FDI?*, downloaded from web.mit.edu/krugman/www/whatsnew.html.

Legewie, J. (1998) 'Wirtschaftliche Integration der ASEAN: Zur Rolle japanischer Unternehmen bei Entstehung und Umsetzung industrieller Kooperationskonzepte', *Japanstudien*, vol. 10, pp. 215–47.

Masuyama, S., D. Vandenbrink and S. Y. Chia (eds) (1997) *Industrial Policies in East Asia*, Tōkyō: Tōkyō Club Foundation for Global Studies.

Ohmae, K. (1985) *Triad Power: The Coming Shape of Global Corporations*, New York: The Free Press.

Perlmutter, H. (1969) 'The Tortuous Evolution of the Multinational Corporation', *Columbia Journal of World Business*, vol. 4, pp. 9–18.

Porter, M. (1986) 'Changing Patterns of International Competition', *California Management Review*, vol. 2, pp. 9–40.

Prahalad, C. K. and Y. Doz (1987) *The Multinational Mission: Balancing Local Demands and Global Vision*, New York: The Free Press.

Radelet, S. and J. Sachs (1997) 'Asia's Reemergence', *Foreign Affairs*, vol. 76(6), pp. 44–59.

Ramstetter, E. (1998) 'Thailand: International Trade, Multinational Firms, and Regional Integration', in W. Dobson and S. Y. Chia (eds) *Multinationals and East Asian Integration*, Ottawa: International Development Research Centre, pp. 107–30.

Tejima, Shigeki (2000) 'The Effects of the Asian Crisis on Japan's Manufacturing Foreign Direct Investment in Asia', in V. Blechinger and J. Legewie (eds), *Facing Asia – Japan's Role in the Political and Economic Dynamism of Regional Cooperation*, München: Iudicium, pp. 199–216.

TSS Tsūshō Sangyōshō (1999) *Kaigai jigyō katsudō dōkō chōsa gaiyō, dai 28-kai* [Outline of the Basic Survey on the Trend of Overseas Business Activities, no. 28], Tōkyō: Sangyō Seisakukyoku Kokusai Kigyōka.

UNCTAD United Nations Conference on Trade and Development (1999) *World Investment Report 1999 – Foreign Direct Investment and the Challenge of Development*, New York and Geneva: United Nations.

World Bank (1992) *World Development Report 1992*, New York: Oxford University Press.

World Bank (1993) *The East Asian Miracle – Economic Growth and Public Policy*, New York: Oxford University Press.

Index